Photography & Culture

Volume 5 Issue 1 March 2012

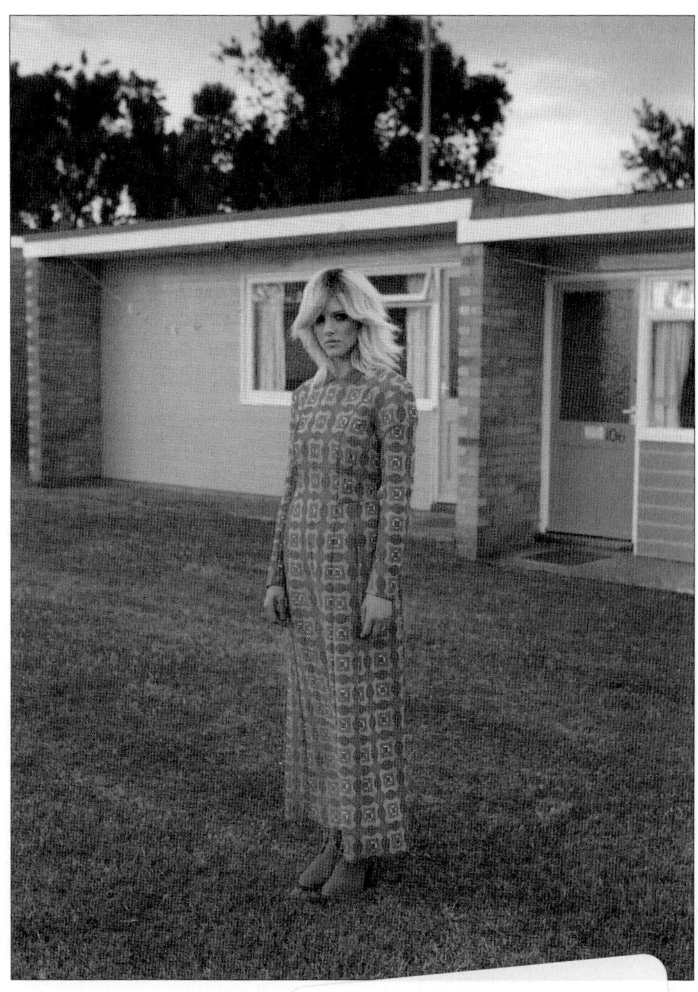

Editors
Kathy Kubicki
Thy Phu
Val Williams

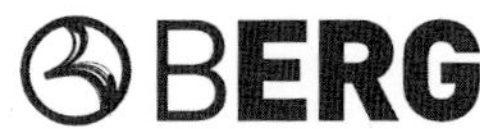

Aims and Scope

Photography & Culture is a new refereed journal that will be international in its scope and inter-disciplinary in its contributions. It aims to interrogate the contextual and historic breadth of photographic practice from a range of informed perspectives and to encourage new insights into the media through original and incisive writing.

Photography & Culture publishes research papers, discursive critiques and reviews. It appears at a key moment as photography evolves, for once again, to embrace a technological change that is shifting both contemporary usage and historic understanding.

Photography & Culture will quickly establish itself as a leading platform for critical thinking on photography and as essential reading the world over for academics, curators and practitioners with a central and indeed tangential interest in the media.

Submissions

To submit an article for consideration please contact Monica Takvam at photographyandculture@bergpublishers.com

Subscription Information

Three issues per volume (only two issues in 2008). One volume per annum. 2012: volume 5

Online

www.bergpublishers.com

By Mail

Berg Publishers
C/o Customer Services
Turpin Distribution
Pegasus Drive
Stratton Business Park
Biggleswade
Bedfordshire SG18 8TQ
UK

By Fax

+44 (0)1767 601640

By Telephone

+44 (0)1767 604951

Subscription Rates

Institutional
Print and Online: 1 year: £175/US$341; 2 year: £280/US$546
Online only: 1 year: £149/US$290; 2 year £238/US$464 (VAT charged as applicable)

Individual
Print: 1 year: £40/US$73; 2 year: £64/US$117

Full color images available online
Access your electronic subscription through **www.ingentaconnect.com**

Reprints for Mailing

Copies of individual articles may be obtained from the publishers at the appropriate fees. For information, write to

Berg Publishers
50 Bedford Square
London
WC1B 3DP
UK

Inquiries

Editorial:
Julia Hall, email: julia.hall@bloomsbury.com

Production:

Ian Buck, email: ian.buck@bloomsbury.com

Advertising:

Ellie Graves, email: eleanor.graves@bloomsbury.com

Berg Publishers is a member of CrossRef

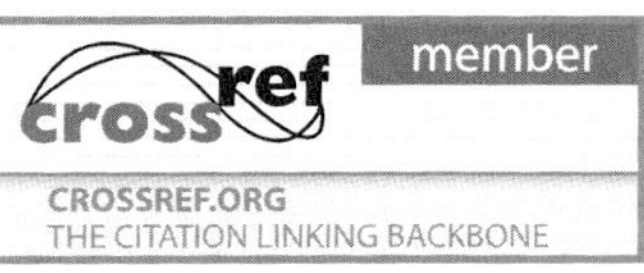

Photography & Culture

Volume 5   Issue 1   March 2012

Contents

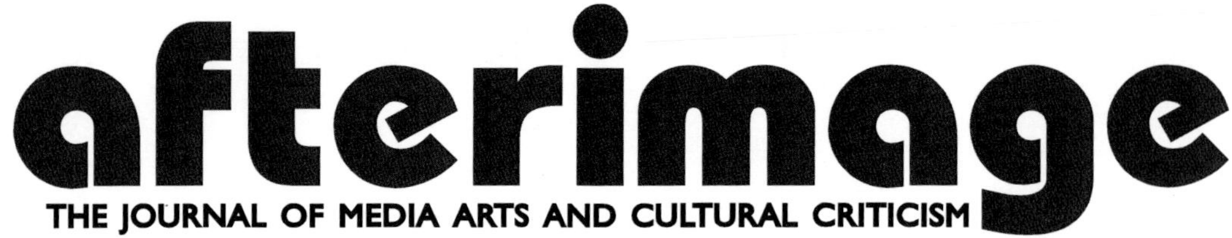

THE JOURNAL OF MEDIA ARTS AND CULTURAL CRITICISM

Afterimage is a bi-monthly journal of photography, independent film, video, new media, and artists' books, published by Visual Studies Workshop.

Since its inception in 1972, *Afterimage* has addressed these media through thought-provoking criticism, seminal theoretical analysis, and timely news coverage.

Afterimage provides a forum for a unified discussion of disciplines generally treated separately in other publications and locates common ground among media arts while recognizing the characteristics unique to each.

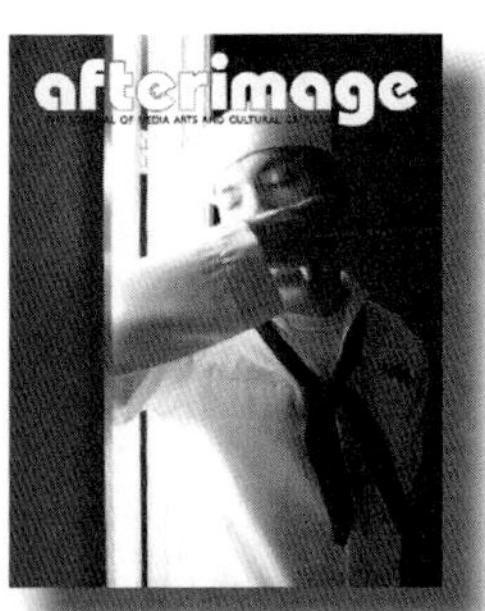

Subscribe to *Afterimage*

__ $20   Student, US only

(include copy of valid student ID)

__ $33   Individual, US

__ $100   Institution, US

__ $90   Individual, Foreign

__ $165   Institution, Foreign

Contact Information

NAME: ________________________________

ADDRESS: ___________________________

____

____

(STREET, APT/SUITE, CITY, STATE, ZIP, COUNTRY)

EMAIL: ______________________________

Payment Information

__ CHECK/MONEY ORDER*   __ VISA   __ MASTERCARD

CARD NUMBER: _________________________

*Please make check payable to Visual Studies Workshop (in U.S. funds payable to U.S. bank)

SIGNATURE: ____________________________

www.vsw.org/ai

@afterimage_mag

Please send payment to:
afterimage subscriptions
Visual Studies Workshop
31 Prince Street
Rochester, NY 14607
ph: (585) 442-8676 x 26
fax: (585) 442-1992

Photography & Culture

Volume 5—Issue 1
March 2012
pp. 5–8
DOI:
10.2752/175145212X13233396185396

Reprints available directly from
the publishers

Photocopying permitted by
licence only

From the Editors

There is always something new to say about photography, and *Photography & Culture* aims to be at the forefront of those discussions.

In December 2011 we completed a year-long series of talks at The Photographer's Gallery in London entitled "Writing Photography." During these talks and discussions we were lucky enough to have some of our authors on hand to expand upon their research and on the process of writing itself in relation to photography. This has been an amazing experience for everyone involved, as it became clear that there are endless possibilities, individual approaches, and important topics and subject matter that can continually be called into question under the auspices of photography itself, and in the writing on photography.

In his article in this issue, "A Curious Revolution Has Been Taking Place in the Dress of What Used To Be Called 'The Workman'," Alistair O'Neill examines a series of men's fashion photos shot by Walker Evans in 1963, intended for publication in *Fortune*, Time Incorporated's business magazine, where Evans was employed as special photographic editor from 1945–65. The 36 studies on 2¼ inch negative, 405 studies on 35 mm negative, and accompanying written correspondence are now part of the Walker Evans Archive, held at the Photography Department of the Metropolitan Museum of Art, New York. The marginal subject of men's fashion in Evans's work has previously received little investigation, but O'Neill discusses how this is at odds with the photographer's own view of the project, revealed in an animated letter by Evans in 1963 to the editor of *Fortune*, asking him to look at the pictures he had just taken: "I believe this thing has never been done before in pure form on this scale" (Evans 1963). O'Neill discusses how Evans's photos explore American men at work and their clothing choices, which were influenced by leisure, and how these images represented very new territory for Evans, as he also experimented with a Nikon F 35 mm camera, and these images pinpoint the first and only time that Evans wished to reclassify his work as a form of fashion photography.

"Battlefield Souvenirs and the Affective Politics of Recoil," by Wendy Kozol, continues the narrative of investigating previously hidden photographs, as she explores the ways in which archives that "bear the traces of military violence" are used by those who wish to look at photographic archives for evidence, using a personal and intimate encounter with a relative's archive of Second World War battlefield souvenirs alongside the United States' national encounter with the torture pictures from Abu Ghraib. Kozol discovers that battlefield archives render elicit and multifaceted negotiations in relation to "subjectivity, citizenship and witnessing." Instead of relying on a "moral" judgment of her own relative's war photographs, Kozol explores the notion of disavowal, choosing to look at these pertinent issues by using a removed and reflexive commentary on "spectatorship and historical accountability" in her fascinating article.

Visa Immonen's article, "Photographic Bodies and Biographical Narratives," examines new approaches of biographical writing and current theories on photography, and the resulting disputes between them. She looks at the life of State Archaeologist Juhani Rinne (1872–1950), whose photographs focus on the tensions between biography, narrative, and photographic bodies as the concept *image-body* maps out the territory between lived and represented bodies, knowledge and truth. Rinne's image-body draws attention to work and academic masculinity, alongside discourses on nationalism and civilized men. The article is a sensitive exploration of subjectivity, narrative structures, and truth through representations.

Mark Gisbourne's groundbreaking article, "Fields of Consciousness: The Ghost in the Machine," examines how everyday reality is seen via images of representation of the world through sign and symbols. Gisbourne asks a number of questions about consciousness and its physiological component being altered by the sensory experiences of the world through the changing conditions of cultural representation: for example, how do representations through perceived experiences interact between the body and the mind, and what is the effect of the "eternal recurrence" of images and ideas that daily saturate our lived experience? Gisbourne relates his philosophical discourse to the work of the photographer Warren Neidich, who has incorporated these controversial issues in his art work and writing for some time, with particular scrutiny by Gisbourne on Niedich's photographic and film/video-based work, incorporating aspects of his

performance-experience-experimental contents that constantly emerge from Niedich's thought-provoking art works.

In her contribution to the One Photograph section, exploring *Life on the Floor*, Marjolaine Ryley also uses her autobiography as she explores issues surrounding squatting in 1970s' London, asking, "What did a childhood spent 'on the floor' mean to me?" Ryley compares home life to that at *Villa Mona*—a "proper" family holiday home in Belgium—and discusses her current work *Growing Up in the New Age*, conceived during a residency at Braziers' International Artists' Workshop in Oxford, where "long buried memories from my childhood emerged," as Ryley discovers the important influence her parents' choice of lifestyle has had on her as an adult.

Anna Fox's photographs in the Portfolio section, "Resort 1," are the result of two years' practical exploration and research on photographing Butlin's at Bognor Regis, a seaside resort on the south-east coast of the United Kingdom. Fox, in her usual documentary-influenced practice, explores the new ways that Butlin's resort provides a leisure environment for public consumption. Fox studied the photographic work by the John Hinde studio in the late 1970s as a starting point; created as a result of a commercial commission from Butlin's, these were "highly staged and colorful photographs" shot on a large format camera by a team of photographers and assistants and with total collaboration from the company.

In Fox's beautiful shots of contemporary Butlin's she chooses to work in a similar way to her earlier portrait work such as *Zwarte Piet* (1994–99) and *Back to the Village* (1999–2006), a manner that helped to emphasize the performative aspect of the subject. Fox explains the difficulties of making documentary photographs in the context of a lived environment for holidaymakers and party revelers, and sensitively discusses her methodology and the collaborative aspect of her own project.

Photography & Culture   Volume 5   Issue 1   March 2012, pp. 5–8

The Archive in this issue contains a very powerful and difficult to contemplate set of images from an album in the archive of Brad Feuerhelm of *Ordinary Light*. Located in England, Feuerhelm oversees collaborations with individual collectors, artists, scholars, and institutions throughout the world.

German fencing or *Fechten* is a sport of dueling that was very popular in the years 1870–1945. Of primarily Germanic origin, though practiced also in Poland and Latvia, the men involved underwent tribe-like practices and emerged with highly visible wounds and scars, which they wore with pride within their collegiate communities. These dubiously constructed duels were often held outside of the sporting arena, as a way of communal male bonding through a rite of passage into German manhood through the act of drawing blood. The album holds an intriguing set of photographs that illustrate important hidden male behavior, made at a time when manhood, conflict, and nationhood were at the forefront of the German psyche. We feel privileged at *Photography & Culture* to be the first to publish this interesting set of important and fascinating images.

Photography & Culture   Volume 5   Issue 1   March 2012, pp. 5–8

**Photography &
Culture**

Volume 5—Issue 1
March 2012
pp. 9–20
DOI:
10.2752/175145212X13233396184955

Reprints available directly from
the publishers

Photocopying permitted by
licence only

"A Curious Revolution Has Been Taking Place in the Dress of What Used To Be Called 'The Workman'": Walker Evans's Unpublished Article on Men's Fashion

Alistair O'Neill

Abstract

This article considers an unpublished photo story by Walker Evans, shot in 1963 and intended for publication in *Fortune*, Time Incorporated's business magazine, where Evans was employed as special photographic editor from 1945–65. Titled "The Clothes: A Note on Sartorial Actuality," the assignment concerns the working dress of American men, and is shot on the streets of New York and the campus of Yale University, New Haven. Evans's intention was to reveal how the postwar concept of men's fashion was starting to infiltrate the representation of American men at work; attempting to capture a shift in the kinds of clothes worn by men for the purpose of work, noticeably influenced by the sphere of leisure. In correspondence with the editor of the magazine, Evans termed his work "documentary fashion photography" as an attempt to capture the readable quality of clothing in pictorial form. This article examines this body of work, paying particular attention to the hat as an item of apparel, once described by Evans as "a sort of defiant signature."

Keywords: Walker Evans, documentary fashion photography, clothes, hats

This article considers an unpublished photo story by Walker Evans, shot in 1963 and intended for publication in *Fortune*, Time Incorporated's business magazine, where Evans was employed as special photographic editor from 1945–65. The thirty-six studies on

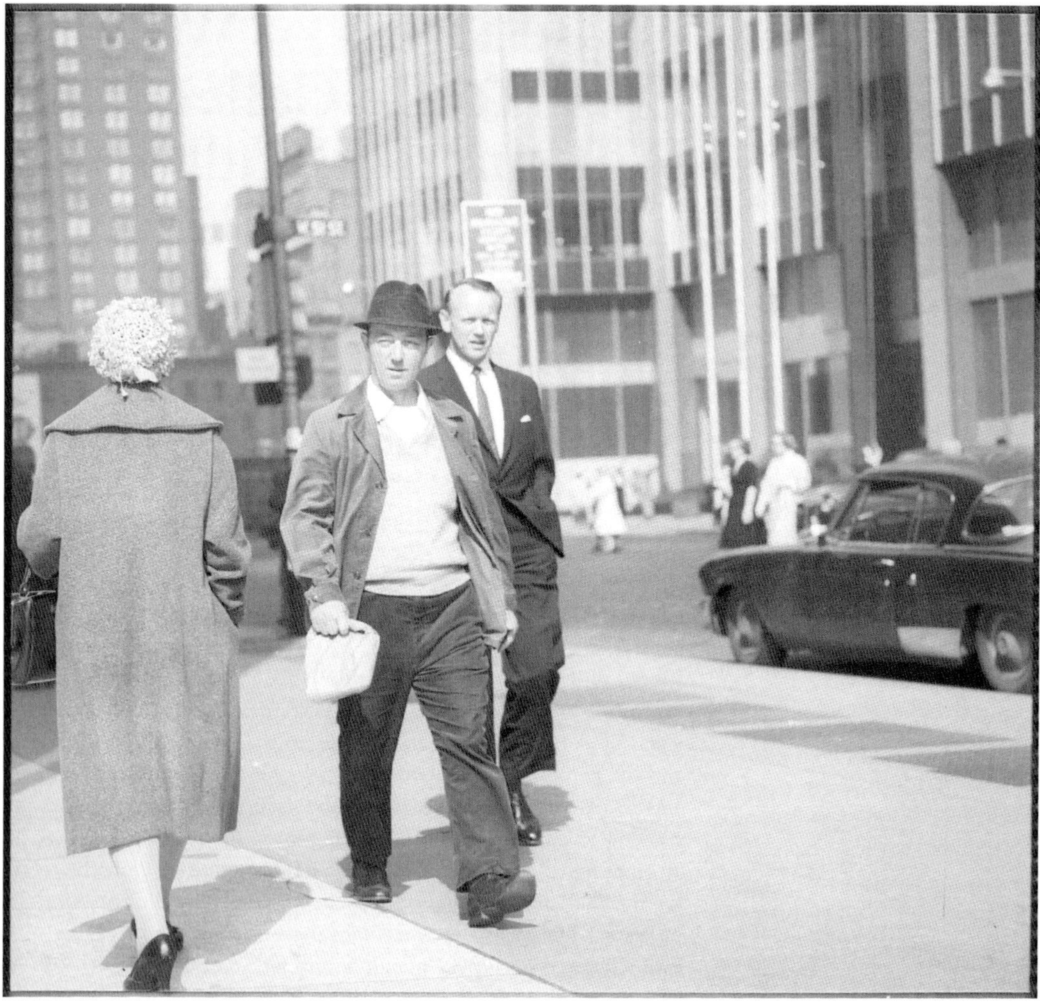

Fig 1 Walker Evans, thirty-six studies of men's fashion on New York City's streets. Made for unpublished *Fortune* portfolio, "The Clothes," 1963. Film negatives 2¼ × 2¼ in. The Metropolitan Museum of Art, Walker Evans Archive, 1994 (1994.252.24.1–36). © Walker Evans Archive, Metropolitan Museum of Art.

2¼ inch negative, 405 studies on 35 mm negative, and written correspondence are now part of the Walker Evans Archive, held at the Photography Department of the Metropolitan Museum of Art, New York.

Although elements of this body of work have been mounted in exhibitions and published in surveys of Evans's work, its semblance as a project from the photographer's late period, perhaps considered unsuccessful because it was unpublished, and dealing with the marginal subject of men's fashion, has left it the subject of little investigation. Yet this is at odds with the photographer's own view of the project, revealed in an enthusiastic letter typed by Evans in 1963 to the editor of *Fortune*, requesting a meeting to look at the pictures he had just taken:

> Natasha says you're available Friday for a look at my Great American Costume 1963 collection. Good; this is what I have: a rather wide spot-check of US everyday male raiment. The pictures are in effect documentary fashion photography and I believe this thing has never been done before in pure form on this scale.

Titled "The Clothes: A Note on Sartorial Actuality," the assignment concerns the working dress of American men, shot on the streets of New York and the campus of Yale University, New Haven. Evans's intention was to reveal how the postwar concept of men's fashion was starting to infiltrate the representation of American men at work; attempting to capture a shift in the kinds of clothes worn by men for the purpose of work, noticeably influenced by the sphere of leisure. The project marked new territory for Evans: not only was he experimenting with a Nikon F 35 mm camera, but it was the first and only time that he was explicit in wishing to reclassify his work as a form of fashion photography, even though he was on the whole dealing with occupational dress.

By 1963, Evans was familiar with the interest fashion magazines had shown in his work. In that year, *Mademoiselle* had published an article on collecting photographs using Evans's work as a central example, and *Harper's Bazaar* (US) had published a text by Evans accompanying the reproduction of works by Lee Friedlander. A year earlier, he had portraits of businessmen published in *Vogue* (US) and *Harper's Bazaar* (US) was the first to publish his portfolio of illicit subway portraits from the late 1930s in March 1962, largely due to the interest of Marvin Israel, *Harper's Bazaar*'s art director. They would later be published as a monograph in 1966 under the title "Many Are Called."

Evans was already a formidable figure for a younger generation of photographers finding commercial work in fashion magazines, such as Robert Frank, Diane Arbus, Louis Faurer, and Paul Himmel. Alexander Liberman, art director at *Vogue* (US), used the example of a photograph by Evans taken in Havana in 1932 when commissioning photographers such as Irving Penn or Louise Dahl-Wolfe to take fashion photographs for the title in the 1940s. According to Liberman, "While not a fashion photograph, I believe this is a statement essentially about style" (Harrison 1991: 46). But this is not to claim Evans as a photographer concerned with fashionability—as he always remained suspicious of "fashions" in the widest sense of the term and retained a strident disregard for design-conscious consumer goods.

And yet in spite of this distrust, "The Clothes" assignment for *Fortune* magazine offered Evans the chance to signal an engagement with this newly opened arena for photographers, and offered the possibility of bringing his work to a wider audience. However, *Fortune*'s decision not to publish "The Clothes," and Evans's departure from the magazine fairly soon after, should suggest that this optimism was short-lived. While articles about the American fashion industry, both in New York and in California, did feature in *Fortune*, the preoccupations of fashionability were beyond its remit, so Evans's wish to use the editorial pages to broker a different market for his work was unfulfilled.

Walker Evans is now widely recognized as one of the leading American photographers of the twentieth century. And although this reputation is arguably established by the work he produced for the Farm Security Administration of tenant farmers in Alabama in the 1930s, and the publication *Let Us Now Praise Famous Men* (1941) with James Agee, it is his capturing of the ubiquitous visual ephemera of metropolitan life that now seems most valued by contemporary visual culture. Evans's obituary in *The Times*

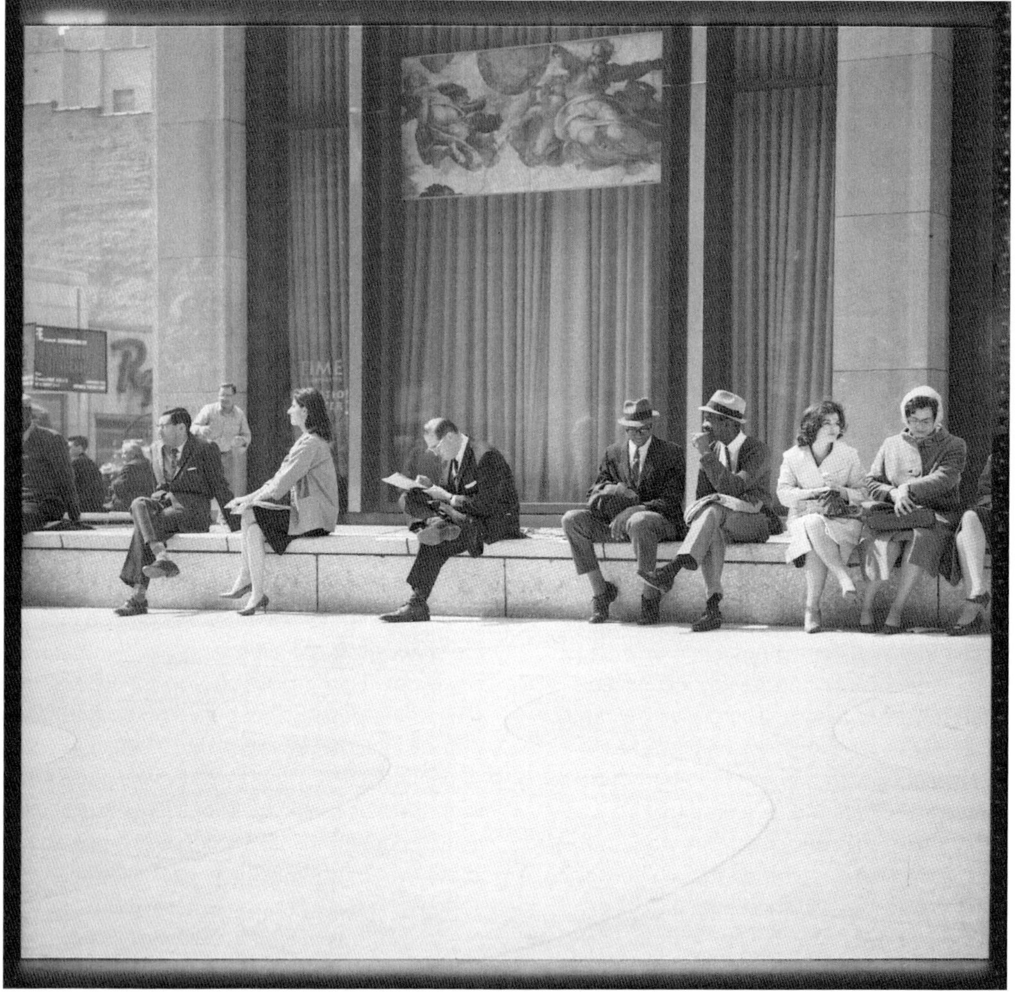

Fig 2 Walker Evans, thirty-six studies of men's fashion on New York City's streets. Made for unpublished *Fortune* portfolio, "The Clothes," 1963. Film negatives 2¼ × 2¼ in. The Metropolitan Museum of Art, Walker Evans Archive, 1994 (1994.252.24.1–36). © Walker Evans Archive, Metropolitan Museum of Art.

newspaper in 1975 described this subject matter as "the vocabulary of the invisible" (*The Times* 1975: 14), while Evans indebted his objectivity of treatment to the French nineteenth-century writer Gustav Flaubert—based on the author's principles of nonsubjectivity and the nonappearance of the author (Mellow 1999: 118).

In *American Photographs*, Evans's monograph published to accompany his one-man show at the Museum of Modern Art in 1938, Lincoln Kirstein asked that the photographs

demand and should receive the slight flattery of your closest attention. They are not entirely easy to look at. They repel an easy

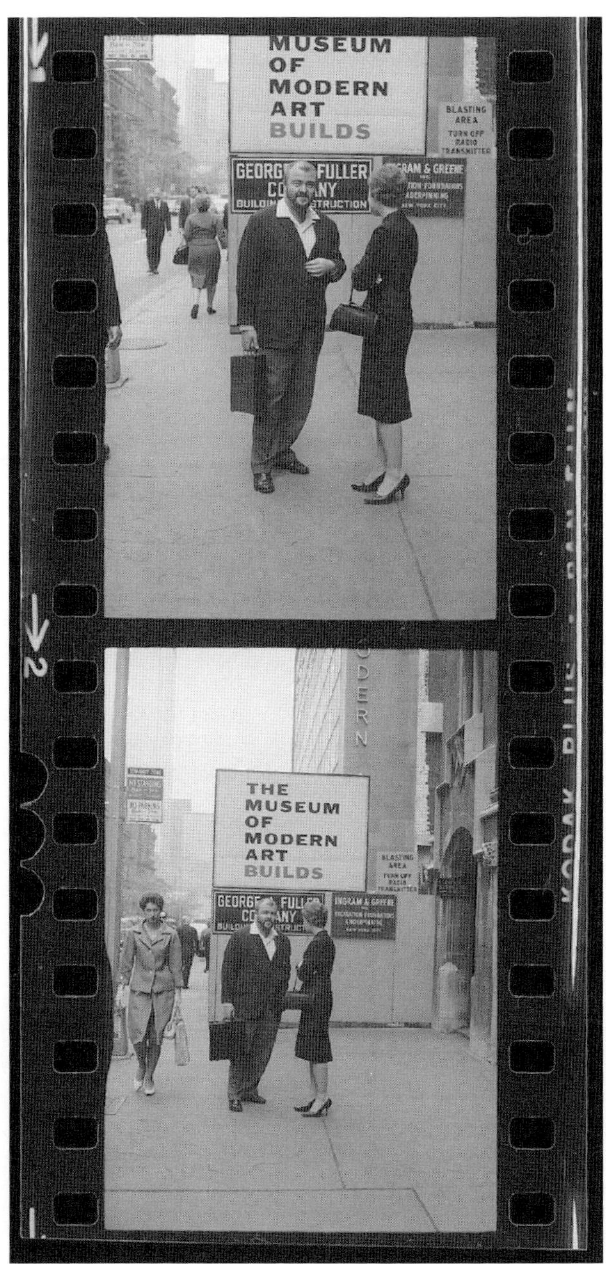

Fig 3 Walker Evans, 405 studies of men's fashion on New York City's streets and Yale University's campus, New Haven, Connecticut. Made for unpublished *Fortune* portfolio, "The Clothes," 1963. Film negatives 35 mm. The Metropolitan Museum of Art, Walker Evans Archive, 1994 (1994.253.645.1–405). © Walker Evans Archive, Metropolitan Museum of Art.

glance. They are so full of facts they have to be inspected with more care than quickness. The physiognomy of a nation is laid on your table. (Kirstein in Evans 1938: 195)

For Evans, the discredited science of physiognomy (the judgment of character by facial characteristics) was aided and abetted by another: the readable quality of clothing in pictorial form. In 1946, soon after his appointment at *Fortune*, Evans published "Labor Anonymous," a two-page photo story that presented a range of American workers resistant to the categorization of labor by the conviction of their sartorial individuality. The accompanying copy, likely to have been written by the photographer, states:

> The American worker, as he passes here, [usually] unaware of Walker Evans' camera, is a decidedly various fellow. His blood flows from many sources. His features tend now toward the peasant and now toward the patrician. His hat is sometimes a hat and sometimes he has molded it into a sort of defiant signature. (Evans 1946)

Clothing, according to the photographer's intent, was a readable language with a vocabulary, syntax, and grammar. So, just as there were ranges of apparel, so there were rules governing how they could be worn, just as there were a variety of ways of wearing them. Beyond the obvious indicators of class, rank, and status, the language could be expressive of disclosures and dispositions, aspirations and flaws.

Writing about "James Agee in 1936" in 1960, Evans described the writer so: "His clothes were deliberately cheap, not only because he was poor but because he wanted to forget them" (Evans and Agee [1941] 2001: V).

This concentration on the communicative potential of everyday dress would reach its apotheosis in the text that Evans would write for "The Clothes." As an aspiring writer and translator of French poetry before becoming a

photographer, Evans was unusual in writing his own copy for his photo stories, and his prose was often heavily worked on, with numerous revisions. The Walker Evans Archive contains eight versions of this unpublished text, the first written on July 15, 1963:

> A little detailed observation of the clothes people wear in the street can result in a lot of wonder, much amusement, some shock, and a touch of honor. It also causes furtive self-examination of one's own attire. For just how much personal fear or indolence, or even intelligence does one inadvertently reveal by the way one chooses one's clothes and by the manner with which one wears them?
>
> Alas, your daily costume quite distinctly speaks many languages as you might wish whispered or slurred. Indeed, how much cowardice is hidden by a bold neck tie sharply knotted? How much wisdom and assurance lies behind a way of wearing a muted spot on a coat or a discreet fray on a cuff? Verily, somewhere in every man is an unconscious clothes snob. (Evans 1963)

It is fair to say that in Evans's case, this discernment was not unconscious, but verily labored. In the letter sent to the editor of *Fortune* he revealed:

> You'll see that one fact emerges from the survey: there has been a definite revolution in "workman's" clothes—he has switched to PLAY clothes to work in. Even the rough worker, the day laborer as he used to be called, is a sporting lord attired in gay-colored, if creased and soiled, golf and beach wear—or anyway what he wears to work has its origins actually and ironically in the "leisurewear" category. I also reflect lesser revolutions like the prevalence of the black hues Italian touch [*sic*] on young white-collar men, who seem to be mourning for

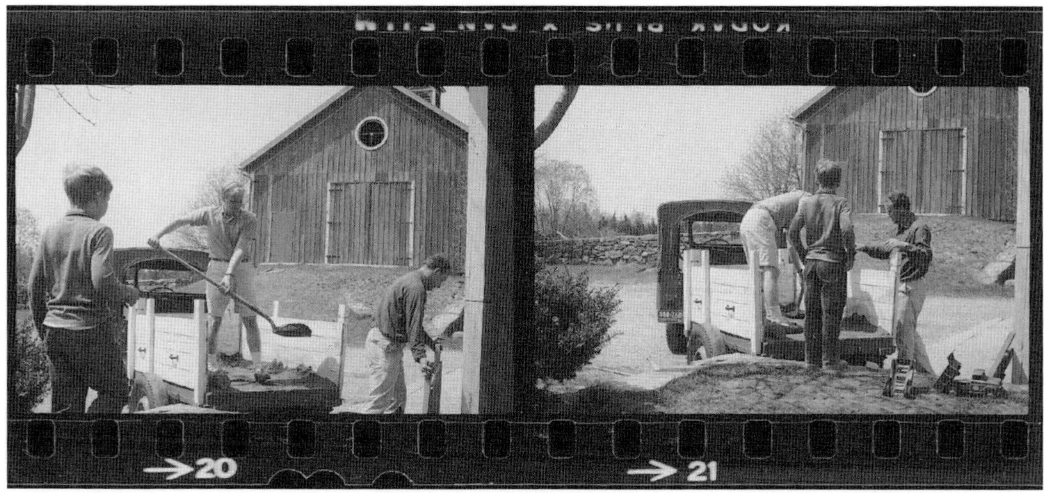

Fig 4 Walker Evans, 405 studies of men's fashion on New York City's streets and Yale University's campus, New Haven, Connecticut. Made for unpublished *Fortune* portfolio, "The Clothes," 1963. Film negatives 35 mm. The Metropolitan Museum of Art, Walker Evans Archive, 1994 (1994.253.645.1–405). © Walker Evans Archive, Metropolitan Museum of Art.

something, and to suffer from a compulsion to carry imitation attaché cases. (Evans 1963)

In this statement we find a neat encapsulation of what dress historians would later categorize as "the cultural shift toward informality" in men's dress that marked the early 1960s. As William R. Scott rightly observes in his study of the influence of West Coast clothing for men, typified by the open-necked shirt, "Men's penchant for fashionable clothing, long 'hidden,' was made visible through the simple act of dressing down" (Scott 2007: 154).

Most surprising of all is Evans's identification of the transference of workwear as a category of clothing, no longer just worn by blue-collar workers but also by educated youth, reflecting, according to dress historian Farid Chenoune, "an abrupt new crystallization of the slow and powerful subversion of dress codes by work clothes" (Chenoune 1993: 235), worn by young men keen to use the unfinished, unfitting, and

seemingly unfashionable nature of workwear to express their dissatisfactions and desires about the modern world they found themselves in. And again, to quote from Evans:

A curious revolution has been taking place in the dress of what used to be called "the workman." He now wears play clothes on the job ... Gone is the honest old chambray workshirt, truly handsome garment. *That* has landed on the viable shoulders of a hardworking little sub deb at a school college campus. (Evans 1963)

As an unpublished portfolio, "The Clothes" marks a transition in Evans's career and subject matter—from workers and their uniforms on the streets of New York, to students at Yale University in New Haven, where he was appointed as a professor in the School of Graphic Design in 1964. "The Clothes," as a body of work, demonstrates that at this pivotal point in his later career it was the migration of

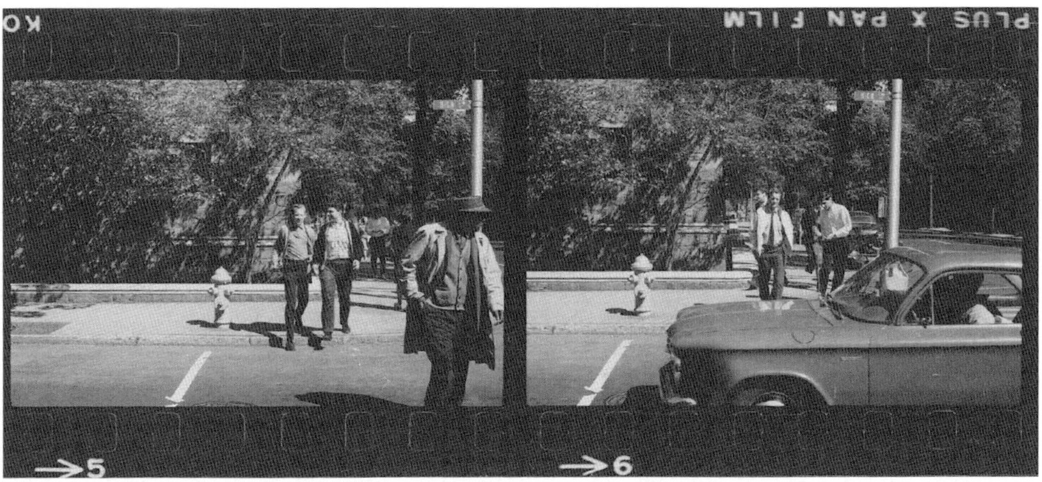

Fig 5 Walker Evans, 405 studies of men's fashion on New York City's streets and Yale University's campus, New Haven, Connecticut. Made for unpublished *Fortune* portfolio, "The Clothes," 1963. Film negatives 35 mm. The Metropolitan Museum of Art, Walker Evans Archive, 1994 (1994.253.645.1–405). © Walker Evans Archive, Metropolitan Museum of Art.

workwear that charted the photographer's new direction.

In his inaugural lecture at Yale, Evans defined the term "lyric documentary" to characterize his work as a photographer, which he held as a combined measure of the poetical and the rational, the personal and anonymous. It is arguable that lyric documentary, as a term, is predicated on the concerns of "The Clothes" as a portfolio, as an attempt to capture the readable quality of clothing in pictorial form. It serves as a reminder of how photographs can pose as traces of those often silent and unseen cultural shifts in our relationship to certain categories of clothes and the ways that they are worn. "The Clothes," therefore, reveals a sartorial vocabulary of the invisible.

A more recent study that has responded to the "thing-ness" of Evans's work—in its object-orientated focus, its interest in categories, its citation of clothing—is Geoff Dyer's *The Ongoing Moment*. A good example is his discussion of Evans's subway portraits taken between 1936

and 1941, where Dyer is attentive to the camera technology he used (a Contax 35 mm camera), its settings (a fiftieth of a second with a wide aperture), and the fact that he camouflaged the chrome parts of the casing with black paint. The most crucial aspect of the kit—the coat he wore—is also raised, like a photographer's cloak worn around the shoulders.

Such details illuminate the role of clothing in covert forms of photography. If Evans's lens operated as a surface that read what was put in front of it, then its failure to be noticed by its subjects was due to the unreadable quality of the coat it was set within. It was the blankness of that coat—its unremarkableness, its unarticulated likeness to other coats in the subway carriage—that allowed it to become a stealth carrier. Evans appreciated clothes for their ability to be visible and invisible, both in photographs and in the act of taking them.

A sense of the way that this impacts on how they are read in image form is raised by Dyer's survey of how photographers have photographed

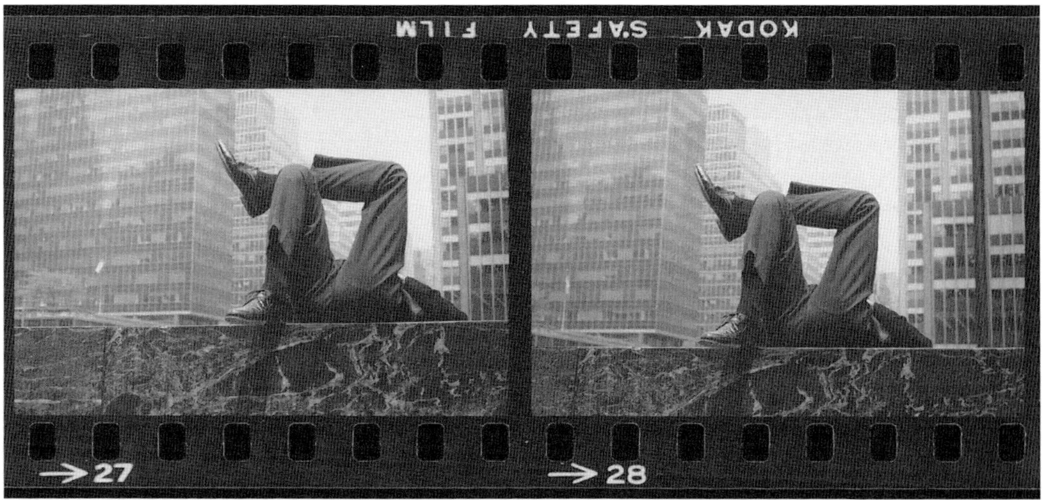

Fig 6 Walker Evans, 405 studies of men's fashion on New York City's streets and Yale University's campus, New Haven, Connecticut. Made for unpublished *Fortune* portfolio, "The Clothes," 1963. Film negatives 35 mm. The Metropolitan Museum of Art, Walker Evans Archive, 1994 (1994.253.645.1–405). © Walker Evans Archive, Metropolitan Museum of Art.

similar and often unremarkable things. Rather than concentrating on coats (although he does deal with backs), Dyer considers the hat as a kind of marker of territory. In his discussion of a photograph taken by Evans in 1936 of a barbershop interior with a hat left on a stand, Dyer claims that the hat articulates, in material form and human scale, the staging of human presence through absence. In its similarity to the kind of hat also worn by the photographer in the 1930s, Dyer regards it as tagging, a way of marking photographic territory: "You cannot photograph a scene like this, says the hat, without paying some kind of tribute to Evans" (Dyer 2005: 209).

Dyer then attempts to make sense of a broader collection of photographs of hats, accounting for the way that they have been inscribed by gender and genre. So, "The history of women and hats is the history of glamour, of fashion. The history of men and hats, on the other hand, is the history of realism, of the enduring (as opposed to the transience of the

fashionable)" (Dyer 2005: 104). It should be easy to disengage from these kinds of clichés about the order of things in photography, delineated by the kinds of classifications that were established in denial of photography's indexical nature. But the premise of these kinds of categorizations still being raised is what makes "The Clothes," as a body of work, so fascinating.

Evans termed it "documentary fashion photography," a form that blended realism and glamour, if you will; a conjoining of those very separations raised by Dyer. Evans was motivated by the fact that a hat is not simply a hat when it is photographed. He wanted to be able to encompass the full range of possibilities: how some hats are worn to be noticed and others are worn to blend in; some are worn in order to be sold, and some are just worn. Dyer recognizes the malleability of the hat, but describes it in another way—"as an all-purpose indicator of the times … itself caught up in the upheaval it describes and symbolizes" (Dyer 2005: 104–5).

This proposes a double nature for the hat, operating as a sign and featuring as a prop. It captures the duplicity of the hat and how Evans had wanted objects of apparel to function in his photographs. For Evans, a hat was sometimes a hat and sometimes it was "a sort of defiant signature" (Evans 1946). You get the sense that Evans enjoyed photographing clothing for the way it often remains fickle to the purpose of an image. The unpublished material in relation to "The Clothes" thus offers itself as a record of the upheaval in men's dress, where clothing operates dually, as visual and material anchors of a wider social flux.

It is perhaps easier to appreciate this in relation to another series of photographs by Evans about objects, published in *Fortune* as "Beauties of the Common Tool" in July 1955. Evans worked on this series of photographs of workman's tools with Robert Frank, where the tools float in a continuous tone background that masks their means of support. The photographs offer themselves as good examples of what might be described as pure object images, honorable in appearance to what Evans described as "their good, clear, 'un-designed' forms" (Baier 1977: 43). The seeming simplicity of these photographs (even though they were laborious to produce) lies at odds with those taken for "The Clothes." Clearly, a workman's tools were different in "object-ness" to the things he wore for the job. They were more substantial; there was less to them that could be construed as extraneous, or accidental.

It is important not to lose sight of the fact that these two bodies of work were produced for *Fortune*, a business magazine addressing the world of work. Robert J. Vanderlan has argued that "Evans's best work was fueled by his ambivalent relationships with employing organizations" (Vanderlan 2009: 81). Perhaps this ambivalence is also a feature of the work he produced during his time as special photographic editor on the subject of work.

If his photographs of tools were a tribute to the constancy of their forms (as many of them were superseded by other designs in other materials), then "The Clothes" is a rally against the discontinuity of clothing, a compelling advertisement for the way they constitute "work" in sartorial and pictorial form through their inappropriateness.

What is unusual about "The Clothes" is the intention on the part of Evans that it would operate as "documentary fashion photography" within the context of a business magazine: a trade-oriented, commercial periodical distinct from consumer fashion titles. To return to the categories raised by Dyer—how photographs of certain kinds of apparel are either defined by photography as either fashion or documentary— it is apparent how "The Clothes" fails to sit easily in either.

Unlike the editorial voice of postwar fashion magazines that dealt optimism, progress, and improvement, a business magazine analyzed rises in value as much as falls; it could follow new market opportunities as much as it covered those markets in decline. In this context, Evans's work at *Fortune* offered a "counternarrative of economic development" (Vanderlan 2009: 83) recognized in the dilapidated buildings and outmoded pieces of office furniture he photographed. Vanderlan claims that Evans's work published in *Fortune* "simultaneously documented decline and aestheticized decay" (Vanderlan 2009: 82). In this sense, "The Clothes" can be read as a statement about the decay of clothing categories and, less obviously, a desire to dissolve the polarity of their categorization by photography.

The representation of clothing in photography is a site where the meaning of its citation is often unsettled by the intention and effect of its description. "The Clothes" contains the product-orientated gaze of commercial imagery as much as it raises the disinterestedness that a documentary approach pays to clothing as an incidental.

In the first formal exhibition survey of Evans's work at *Fortune*, held at Wellesley College Museum, Massachusetts in 1977, Lesley K. Baier identified that many of Evans's last portfolios for the magazine deal "with the effects of time and change on [the] man-made products" (Baier 1977: 19), and that this is reflected in the titles he chose. While not the subject of Baier's exhibition or catalogue (probably because it remained unpublished), the other recorded title for "The Clothes" is "Sartorial Reality"—seemingly straightforward, but suggestive of some kind of skew; a sense that the reality it proposes is problematized by being aligned to the specificity of clothing. The other characteristic that Baier raises in these later portfolios is a kind of grandeur that Evans "recognized in the visual aspect of the object," "dealt openly in theme, images and text" (Baier 1977: 19).

"The Clothes" deserves to be better known, particularly for the way that it portrays Evans's progressive view of how clothing could be photographed and categorized. Evans described his career at *Fortune* as a time when he dressed "in disguise, earning my living as a reporter" (Evans 1974: 64). Perhaps greater attention needs to be paid to the role of clothing in how Evans worked, too. Perhaps the ability to notice, aided by a camera, is predicated on the technology of going unnoticed.

Alistair O'Neill is Senior Research Fellow in Fashion History and Theory at Central Saint Martin's College of Arts and Design, London.

References

Baier, L. K. 1977. *Walker Evans at Fortune: 1945–65.* Massachusetts: Wellesley College Museum.

Baker, J. 1965. "Commercial Sources for Hart Crane's *The River.*" *Wisconsin Studies in Contemporary Literature* (Winter–Spring), 6(1): 45–55.

Curtis, J. C. and S. Grannen. 1980. "Let Us Now Appraise Famous Photographs: Walker Evans and Documentary Photography." *Winterthur Portfolio* (Spring), 15(1): 1–23.

Chenoune, F. 1993. *A History of Men's Fashion.* Paris: Flammarion.

Dyer, G. 2005. *The Ongoing Moment.* New York: Vintage.

Evans, W. 1946. "Labor Anonymous." *Fortune,* November 1946.

Evans, W. 1963. "The Clothes: A Note on Sartorial Actuality." Typescript draft (1994.250.47), Walker Evans Archive, Metropolitan Museum of Art.

Evans, W. 1974. *Walker Evans: Photographs from the Let Us Now Praise Famous Men Project.* Austin: University of Texas.

Evans, W. 1988 [1938]. *American Photographs.* New York: Museum of Modern Art.

Evans, W. 2004 [1966]. *Many Are Called.* New Haven, CT: Yale University Press.

Evans, W. and J. Agee. 2001 [1941]. *Let Us Now Praise Famous Men.* Boston: Houghton Mifflin.

Evans, W. and L. Kirstein. 1938. *American Photographs.* New York: Museum of Modern Art.

Gefter, P. 2009. *Photography After Frank.* New York: Aperture.

Harrison, M. 1991. *Appearances: Fashion Photography Since 1945.* London: V&A Publishing.

Mellow, J. R. 1999. *Walker Evans.* New York: Basic Books.

Raban, J. 2005. "Thinking About Documentary: Notes Towards a Lecture." *Michigan Quarterly Review* (Fall), 44(4): 554–69.

Scott, W. R. 2007. "California Casual: Lifestyle Marketing and Men's Leisure Wear, 1930–1960." In R. L. Blaszczyk (ed.), *Producing Fashion: Commerce, Culture and Consumers.* Philadelphia: University of Pennsylvania.

The Times. 1975. "Walker Evans: Significant American Photographer" (April 12) Obituary, p. 14.

Vanderlan, R. J. 2009. "Walker Evans at *Fortune.*" *Raritan* (Winter), 28(3): 81–107.

Photography from A&C Black

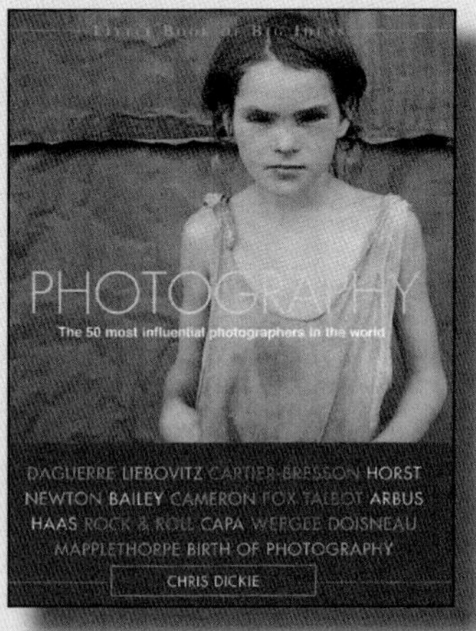

'A handy pocket-sized reference book and an interesting read'
- *Practical Photography*

Photography
The 50 Most Influential Photographers in the World
Chris Dickie
£9.99 hb
2009 / 128pp / 127 x 184mm
9781408109441

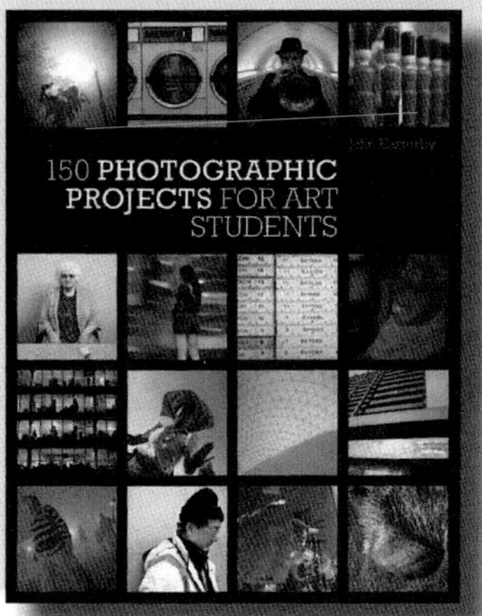

'Inspiring ... The advice is clear and helpful throughout'
- *Black + White Photography*

150 Photographic Projects for Art Students
John Easterby
£14.99 pb
2010 / 128pp / 215 x 280mm
9781408123836

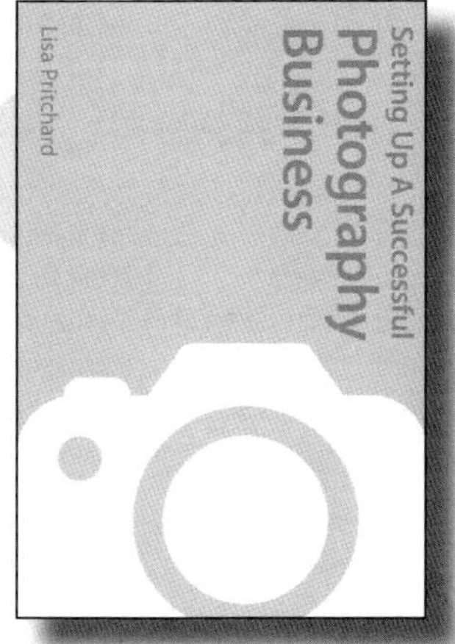

'A very good book using the input of working professionals well'
-*Terry Sims, City & Islington College*

Setting Up A Successful Photography Business
Lisa Pritchard
£12.99 pb
Jan 2012 / 144pp / 156 x 234mm
9781408125779

www.acblack.com/visualarts

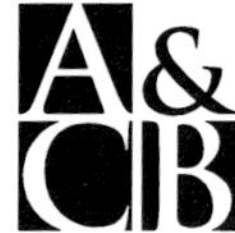

Photography & Culture

Volume 5—Issue 1
March 2012
pp. 21–36

DOI:
10.2752/175145212X13233396184991

Reprints available directly from
the publishers

Photocopying permitted by
licence only

Battlefield Souvenirs and the Affective Politics of Recoil

Wendy Kozol

Abstract

This essay explores the ways in which archives that bear the traces of military violence set up affective demands for those who turn to photographic archives in pursuit of evidence. I compare my intimate encounter with a relative's archive of Second World War battlefield souvenirs with the US national encounter with the torture pictures from Abu Ghraib. Bringing these two seemingly disparate archives into conjunction reveals battlefield archives to be sites that elicit complex negotiations around subjectivity, citizenship, and witnessing. Using my relationship with my relative's archive as an anchor through which to resist imposing a "moral" judgment that enables an alibi of disavowal, I propose witnessing strategies that instead encourage a self-reflexive engagement with spectatorship and historical accountability.

Keywords: battlefield souvenirs, archive, witnessing, Abu Ghraib, affect

The prominence of "good war" narratives about the Second World War today obscures more difficult histories of military combat such as that of American soldiers in the Pacific theater who looted the dead bodies of the enemy for souvenirs. Confronting that history became acutely personal for me when I discovered a previously unknown collection of photographs while helping to clean out a relative's house after his death. My relative, whom I will call Donald, was a first-generation American citizen who lied about his age to join the army at seventeen and was immensely proud of his army service in the Pacific.[1] Photo albums and framed pictures on the walls of his home provide a visual glimpse into the homosocial world of the army in which masculinity mixed with militarism in performances of citizenship (Figure 1). In contrast to this public display, deep in a back closet we found a collection of Japanese photographs that includes pictures of a military base, photographs of groups of soldiers, a postcard from Mt. Fuji, and a picture of a young woman (Figure 2). Many of the images have writing on the back in Japanese, and all have stamps declaring that US military

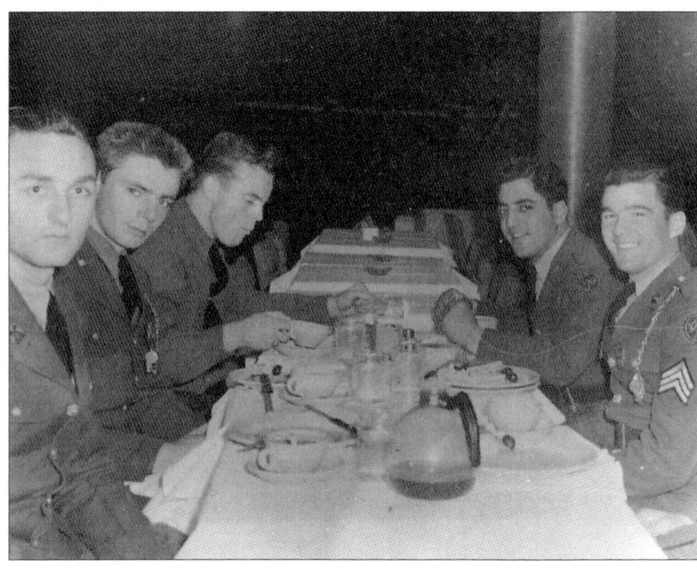

Fig 1 Unidentified friends of Donald's, 1942.

censors had processed them. Some have the words "Eniwetok Atoll" in Donald's handwriting. We also found a Japanese flag with dark stains, which I thought might be blood.[2] Here were the now quiescent signs of someone's intimate contact with enemy combatants, which may have included pillaging dead bodies for souvenirs.

Historians and anthropologists describe the taking of souvenirs from dead soldiers on Second World War battlefields as acts of looting through which soldiers attempted to dehumanize the racialized enemy (Dower 1986; Weingartner 1992; Harrison 2006, 2008). Simon Harrison (2006: 819), for instance, observes that trophy hunting during wartime increased among Euro-American militaries in the late nineteenth and early twentieth centuries predominantly in conflicts that sharply delineated

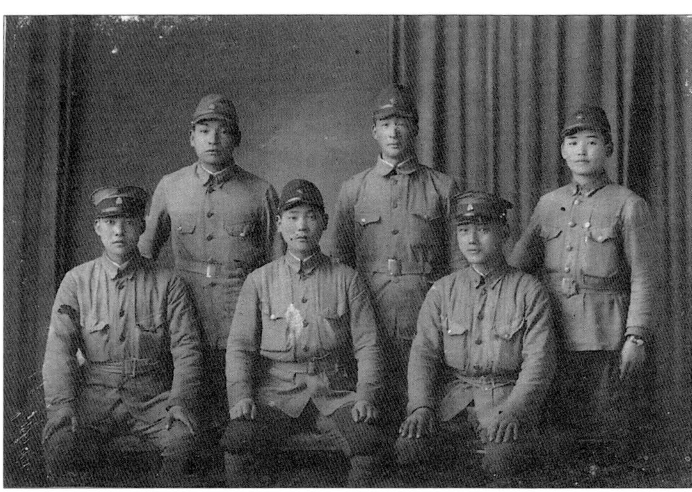

Fig 2 Anonymous group of Japanese soldiers. Photograph from unknown soldier's archive.

racial differences. During the Second World War, American government propaganda and popular culture routinely characterized the Japanese as treacherous, devious, and bestial. Scholars argue that this heightened racist discourse accounts for the much higher incidents of looting, bodily desecration and other atrocities in the Pacific than in Europe.[3] American troops who looted enemy corpses took items ranging from personal objects like wallets, letters, and family photographs to military gear such as swords, flags, and helmets. Unlike helmets or swords, personal items are "objects that any person might carry, and which relate to his or her private identity as a human being. International law defines the unauthorized taking of personal belongings of this sort from prisoners of war, or from the bodies of the dead, as looting or robbery" (Harrison 2008: 777). Looted artefacts then circulated among American troops behind the front lines through both trade and sale (Weingartner 1992; Harrison 2006, 2008).

Today, flags, photographs, swords and other material traces of battlefield looting can still be found in the personal archives of American veterans.[4] Viewers who encounter these archives are apt to recoil in expressions of shock, horror, or shame at this seemingly transparent evidence of trophy hunting. Indeed, my own reaction was one of dismay provoked by my assumption that Donald had himself pillaged dead bodies for souvenirs. I do not want to believe Donald was capable of committing the kind of violent acts implied by this disturbing archive. And yet, the Pacific War, and in particular the battles at Saipan and Eniwetok where he fought, were among the most brutal of any Second World War battlefields (Dower 1986). Donald never spoke of this archive, so there is now no possibility of knowing how he acquired it. This repressed history unsettles my memories not only of Donald but also of the connections between kinship and citizenship, for inheriting these objects also means inheriting the histories of violence

that haunt them. Accompanying the temptation of disavowal, for me, is an awareness of how the gaze motivates a curiosity about past violence that risks turning the archive into a spectacle for historical consumption.

Competing with these insights is the emotional tug of remembering Donald's pride in his military service. The affective hail of national citizenship was especially meaningful for first-generation Americans like Donald, who could not even say his prayers in English and was teased by army buddies for not being "American" enough. My dilemma is that I want to look with compassion at pictures that proudly display his military service without falling into a racialized narrative about the "good war" in which the US triumphed over a savage enemy. On the other hand, to focus on the battlefield souvenirs as evidence of the devastations inflicted by the US onto the soon to be defeated enemy risks reproducing the dominant postwar Japanese nationalist narrative that elides that nation's brutal colonial history (Dower 1997).

In response to these conflicting reactions, this essay explores the politics of recoil and related responses to battlefield archives. "Recoil" here references turning away with an emotional intensity suggestive of the backward force that can occur when firing a gun. Denial, for instance, is an emotive reaction that can distance the viewer from recognizing that witnessing is not about finding a "fixed" past in the archive but rather about participating in the ongoing production of historical knowledge. As Ann Laura Stoler notes, whether institutional or personal, archives function as metaphors for "a corpus of selective forgettings and collections—and, as important for the seduction and longings" (2007: 269). Using the recoil to stand for a host of affective responses, this essay considers some of the forgettings and longings embedded in encounters with battlefield souvenirs.

Historians, journalists and other writers have pored through government and media archives from the Second World War for documentary evidence about military strategies, battles, and the experiences of both civilians and soldiers, yet few have written about battlefield souvenirs. In contrast, an emergent area of study within anthropology and material culture has begun to analyze battlefield souvenirs, art produced out of military armament, and other commemorative practices (see e.g. Saunders 2004; Saunders and Cornish 2009). To date, however, this scholarship has not addressed the dialogic relationship between archival desires and historical witnessing. Whoever took and circulated these Japanese artefacts did so for reasons that undoubtedly contained some combination of desires associated with masculinity, nationalism, and racism. In grappling with historical and contemporary acts of archivization, it is notable that I have no access to either the soldier who carried these materials into battle or the one who took them away. These limitations pose important caveats for contemporary viewers searching the archives for evidence of military violence. More to the point, my own desires to look critically while remembering a loved one reveal the problematics of historical memory and accountability that shape encounters with the archive.

The ethical challenges of historical witnessing have urgent resonances today as we confront a variety of images from the war on terror, including the torture pictures from Abu Ghraib. On the face of it, Abu Ghraib seems to offer the opposite dilemma for witnesses. Whereas the photographs that comprise Donald's archive lack explicit violence, the visibility of torture in the Abu Ghraib pictures seems to convey information transparently about atrocities, victims, and perpetrators. Yet, here, too, contradictory pulls emerge for witnesses of military violence, particularly for American viewers, for whom these photographs thrust issues of citizenship and accountability to the forefront. Scholars such as Dora Apel (2005) and Nicholas Mirzoeff (2006) have insightfully explored the orientalist,

heteronormative, and nationalist narratives structuring the representational strategies of the torture pictures. Moreover, as Jasbir Puar (2005) argues, claims of shock or outrage typically distance the spectator through exceptionalist narratives that privilege the gendered, sexual, and racial logics of American imperialism. In critiquing both the torture photographs and their reception, the objective is, to underscore the point, not simply to ascertain the "facts" of atrocities in the assumption that there is a better truth behind the image. Instead, as Ariella Azoulay (2008) compellingly insists, scholars and viewers must confront the ethics of looking at photographic archives of state-sanctioned violence that promise to reveal evidentiary truths. Taking up Azoulay's charge, this essay explores the ways in which archives that bear the traces of battlefield violence set up affective demands for those who turn to archives in pursuit of evidence. I compare my intimate encounter with Donald's hidden archive with the national encounter with the Abu Ghraib archive that I share with other American citizens, in the recognition that the "moment of encounter" (Jill Bennett 2005) can foster forms of ethical witnessing.

By ethical witnessing, I refer here to the process of critically engaging with the historical complexities of representing social violence, including the ways in which the viewer is implicated in those complexities.[5] Visuality, after all, positions viewers of military violence within nationalist frames (among others) in ways that structure the possibilities of "knowing" for the citizen-witness. Carrie Rentschler, for instance, argues that "To treat witnessing as an ethical act requires viewers to attend to themselves and not primarily as victims. Citizens need models of witnessing that are politically powerful but not based on claims of victimization" (2004: 302). Bringing these two seemingly disparate archives into conjunction reveals some of the ways that battlefield archives elicit myriad negotiations around subjectivity, citizenship, and witnessing. In this essay, I examine features such as resistance to narrative, unknowability, affective resonances, and subject formation in order to grapple with both viewer complicity and the persistence of scopic violence in the archival encounter. Using my relationship with Donald's archive as an anchor through which to resist imposing a "moral" judgment that enables an alibi of disavowal, I suggest witnessing strategies that instead encourage a self-reflexive engagement with spectatorship and historical accountability.

Archiving Battlefield Souvenirs

Multiple desires across time, geographies, and familial inheritances generated the collection and preservation of Donald's archive. Traveling from soldiers on the battlefield to circulation routes behind the lines, this group of artefacts subsequently made its way to an American veteran's home. Family members and I discovered the photographs and the Japanese flag stuffed in an unmarked manila envelope buried deep in an over-full closet. Eerily reminiscent of Donald's own photos in size and compositional strategies, the pictures feature groups of soldiers, military encampments, patients at a military hospital, and a postcard of Mt. Fuji from a young man addressed to an eldest brother. In addition, a number of photographs depict Japanese planes half sunk in a lagoon. This latter group suggests that someone may have been gathering information about damage to Japanese aircraft for military intelligence. Beyond the images themselves, however, there is no information about the Japanese soldier who initially collected them, or even whether they all came from one collection. Likewise, I can only speculate about how Donald acquired this archive.

For over two decades, scholars have been interrogating the powerful role of archives in the contested maintenance of both social and state formations (e.g. Burton 2005; Stoler 2007). Antoinette Burton defines the archive as a "set of complex processes of selection,

interpretation, and even creative invention … processes set in motion by, among other things, one's own encounter with the archive itself, and the pressure of the contemporary moment on one's reading of what is found there" (2005: 8). Archives, in this formulation, are sites of oscillating personal and public desires in which the search for historical knowledge raises questions, in turn, about the archive's role in producing such knowledge. Jacques Derrida's influential discussion of archive fever theorizes the archival encounter as one of affective excess or, as he writes, "To burn with a passion, it is to run after the archive, even if there's too much of it … it is to have a compulsive, repetitive and nostalgic desire for the archive" (1998: 91). Given Donald's pride in his military service, it is significant that he repressed this collection and the events surrounding his acquisition of it. If shame sullied his own memories of his military service, then what was his "compulsive, repetitive, and nostalgic desire" to keep these souvenirs? Equally pressing to me is why he kept this archive all these years. As Derrida points out, nostalgia is less about a longing for the past than an interpretative framing of present and future desires. For Donald, did this archive remind him of the Japanese soldier as a vicious enemy, thus helping to keep alive the racism central to nationalist justifications for war? Or, did the photographs of family members and soldier buddies that look remarkably like Donald's own pictures function as aides-memoires of the Japanese soldier's humanity? Did he even look at these pictures in later years, or were they tucked away, a forgotten moment that marked his identity so long ago?

The unanswerability of these questions, the "not knowing" that accompanies Donald's archive, complicates Margaret Higonnet's claim that the "battlefield souvenir is a nexus of narrative" (2008: 73) in which the object functions metonymically in the nostalgic processes of historical memory. Instead, as Anjali Arondekar (2009: ix) argues, we must also attend to aporias in the archival record, gaps that block the possibility of narrative construction and thus dislodge conventional methodological assumptions about archival research. Unknowability persists in relation to various kinds of violence that hover over this archive. Most explicitly, an American soldier, perhaps Donald, obtained these photographs and the flag by taking them off a prisoner or a dead body. Here, though, I want to be cautious about reading these souvenirs as remnants of looting because military procedures for identifying bodies during wartime involves removing articles from these bodies. At the other end of the spectrum, of course, the collection of body parts was a gruesome practice that American soldiers participated in during the Second World War. Donald's archive remains ambiguously situated within this spectrum of collecting practices.

The lack of more information results today in an archive of unidentified people and unknown stories of loss, pain, and death. Donald's archive thus bears the traces of military violence that remain unknowable and hence ungrievable. While my impulse, as Donald's relative, is to express shame or disavowal, the aporias in the archive even block negative desires because I just cannot "know."[6] In the face of this silence, how do I, as a historical witness, turn the shock of recognition at the violent possibilities suggested by this archive into something more than disavowal or prurient curiosity?

Complicating that question further, the photographs themselves have an opacity with regard to specific acts of battlefield violence. Sixty years later, the Japanese soldier's pictures look remarkably like Donald's photographs and those of countless other soldiers. Repetitious pictures of men in uniform in pairs or groups, along with pictures of camp life and family members, signify ideals of militarism and masculinity (see Figures 1 and 2). Similarly, heteronormative desires associated with national ideals seem to be asserted through the photograph of a young woman whom I first assumed was the soldier's

girlfriend or wife. A colleague later identified this as a commercially produced photograph of a popular film actress.[7] Photographs of movie stars typically functioned in the mid-twentieth century to secure for young unmarried male soldiers a place in the gender and sexual hierarchies of the nation. Yet, of course, the soldier's sexuality remains unknown today. As much as the Japanese soldier's pictures portray ideals of masculinity, heteronormativity, and patriotism, reading subjectivity into these images risks committing its own kind of gender-normative violence.

Beyond the unknowable subjectivities and unknown actions that haunt the Japanese soldier's archive, violence structures subsequent circulations after it left his possession. While most of that history is now lost, one postcard provides a glimpse into the use value of battlefield souvenirs. On the back of a Japanese postcard, Donald wrote a note to his younger brother. It seems surprising that he would choose to send this postcard at a time when racist stereotypes of the Japanese were so pervasive, especially since the picture on the front humanizes the subjects in a nostalgic reverie of summer (Figure 3). A drawing features two young women standing on a bridge watching the interactions of two boys sitting on the fence. Their summer clothes, the blue sky, and the casual poses create an impression of leisure and prosperity. It is hard to imagine what kind of reception the postcard had when it arrived at Donald's brother's house. A rather pedestrian note apologizes for not writing a letter, explaining that he ran out of things to say after sending letters to their two sisters. Significantly, Donald's act of writing erases the Japanese soldier's unknown intentions in keeping this postcard, thus displacing one soldier's subjectivity with another's. Furthering the violence of the original acquisition, the discursive violence enacted when Donald wrote the note home becomes an act of citizenship in which the memory of wartime violence haunts the banality of the message. Importantly, these archival acts

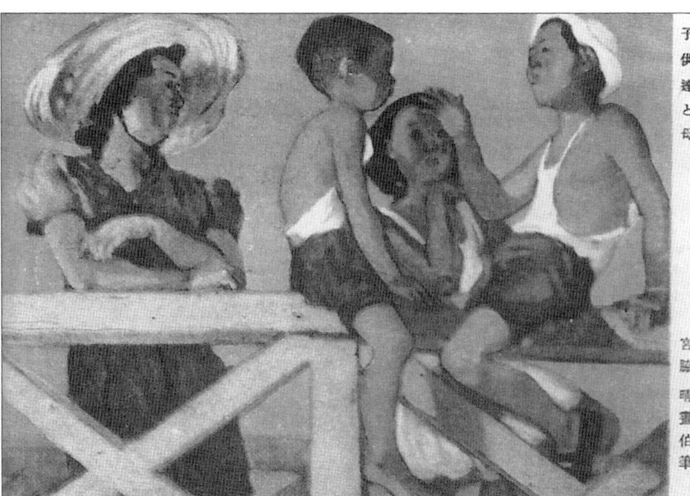

Fig 3 Postcard from unknown soldier's archive. Donald's message to his younger brother is on the reverse side.

did not just reflect the mid-century American racist discourse that characterized the Japanese as subhuman; rather, acts of looting and circulation worked to sustain the racialization foundational to US war efforts (Harrison 2006: 832).

The challenge, as this suggests, is to resist the impulse to read the archival materials as if they can explain individual motivations. Instead, the racist foundations for battlefield practices like looting reveal the relational nature of motivations. Motivations are socially mediated and as such can be defined as affects driven by forces beyond that of individual emotions or choices. Recognition of the relationality of motivation offers insights into social practices such as souvenir collecting, but not into the historically inaccessible actions or desires of either Donald or the Japanese soldier. Archive fever, in other words, references the sociality of the desires sustained by acts of archivization.

After the original acts of looting and circulation, desires associated with preservation no doubt changed over time, in the process destabilizing original meanings attached to the archive. Harrison addresses this point when he notes that while battlefield trophies undergo a "radical change in meaning" over time, "At another level their meaning has remained constant: everyone for whom these objects have had value have viewed them as remains, tokens of the bodies of the soldiers who once carried them" (2008: 785). Similarly, Sharon Sliwinski argues that even as meanings shift in different contexts, the photograph (to quote Barthes) is "chafed" by reality such that subsequent uses and meanings of the image depend upon its original significance (2009: 309). To push this insight further, which realities are chafing against these souvenirs? In Donald's archive of battlefield souvenirs, meanings are both apparent (we know or think we know something of their acquisition and significance) and inaccessible (in all the ways we can't know what actually happened). Beyond these limitations faced by any witness, for me the possibility of looting that haunts this archive chafes against another reality of a familial inheritance of citizenship.

In the absence of specific knowledge about these battlefield souvenirs, interpretative frames easily settle over the archive. Given the volume of academic and popular writings on the Second World War, affective responses can most readily activate now-prominent victimization and triumphalist narratives about the Second World War (Dower 1997). In Donald's archive, for

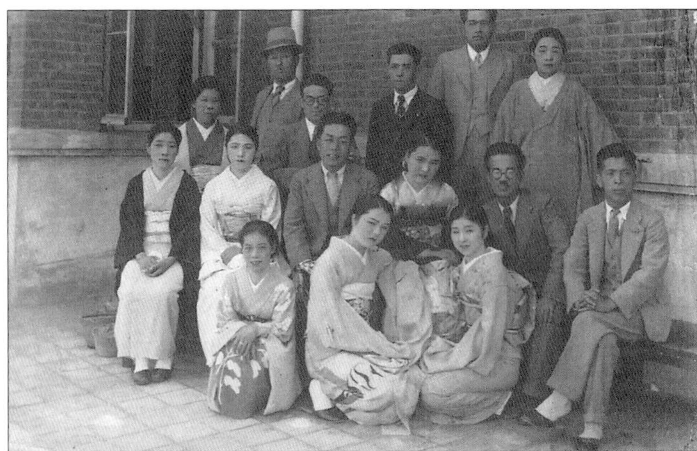

Fig 4 Photograph from unknown soldier's archive.

instance, one group portrait features civilian men in business suits and women in stylish kimonos, all roughly the same age (Figure 4). The subjects' urbane appearance, standing in front of a brick building, suggests that this may be Manchuria or someplace else in China. If this is the case, then this seemingly benign group portrait depicts a colonial scene that, through the conventional genre of portraiture, elides the oppressive imperialist state set up by the Japanese in this region. Just as acknowledgement of atrocities committed by American troops is a critical methodological tool to disrupt US triumphalist histories, recognition of this colonial history unsettles Japanese nationalist attachments to a narrative of victimization. Beyond the search for a truthful source for this photograph, as Sliwinski argues, the more significant point to consider is the "extraordinary vicissitudes of affect." How, she asks, "does the image come to be marked by affect but also serve as the medium of its transmission" (2009: 309)? Even as historically dominant narratives readily offer interpretative frames, the Japanese soldier's archive also exerts an affective pull toward imagining a more complex subjectivity for the soldier who took this portrait into battle with him. Rather than serving merely as repositories of evidence about

preexisting subjects, Arondekar (2009) urges historians to consider how encounters in archives produce the very subjectivities that the historian and witness seek. While I greatly appreciate Arondekar's important concerns about historical methodologies, I would like to turn her theoretical insight around to explore the ethical potential of imagining subjectivity. In this case, does the group portrait speak only of a history of colonial oppression or does it also indicate experiences of loneliness, loss, separation or other desires? Similarly, the postcard's idyllic scene generates an affective tug toward comforting notions about soldiers' desires for home, safety, intimacy, and innocence. Compassion for an unknown young man far from home facing violence and death certainly risks reinforcing the Japanese narrative of victimization that has dominated that nation's postwar historiography, but it can also open up possibilities for witnessing that move beyond these binary narratives.

In emphasizing the aporias that shape and constrain this archive, in other words, I want to explore the historical value of witnessing as an act of imagining subjectivity, even if it risks its own violent imposition. After all, conjuring subjectivities in the photographic archive hauntingly exposes the costs of citizenship for both men. What happens to historical witnessing if we try to imagine the subjective desires of dead soldiers? What if we put into conversation the ideals of masculinity that promoted military heroism for these young men against the recognition of trauma and atrocities that we can never know? Or consider the appeal of national citizenship through military service that represses not only battlefield traumas, but also the ways those experiences persisted unspoken and unexamined in an American soldier's life and the lives of his family members? Unknowability poignantly opens up space to consider the ways in which archival desires not only resulted in the collection and preservation of this particular archive, but also more broadly continue to structure historical witnessing.

This, in turn, raises the question of my own accountability to the histories embedded in this archive. An intimate connection to someone who may have pillaged dead bodies for souvenirs haunts my understanding not only of Donald's citizenship but also of my own. Yet, what can accountability look like sixty-five years later? The possibility of restitution to the family of the Japanese soldier, if they could be found, is not mine to pursue as the immediate family has "ownership" of these artefacts. Even were I to have that opportunity, restitution is an equivocal practice of accountability. Japanese testimonials demonstrate that the return of material effects has been meaningful for those recipients who interpret such returns as "signifying the homecoming of the soldiers' spirits" (Harrison 2008: 777). The significance for those returning these artefacts, however, has a more vexed, if now muted, politics. Despite media depictions of restitution as bridge-building or acts of goodwill, Harrison argues that veterans or their families seeking closure often desire a "mutually benevolent dissociation from [the Japanese]" (777).[8] In this way, restitution can result in disavowal of more problematic histories of citizenship.

This leaves me in the archive with visual witnessing as the only possible means of accountability. Looking at Donald's photographs of military service provokes for me affective responses that combine familial intimacies with an awareness of the traces of violence that linger on these souvenirs. Citizenship thus becomes a contradictory and haunted space, which can instantiate critical perspectives on soldiering and nationalism. Turning to the torture pictures from Abu Ghraib to confront once again the politics of the recoil provides an opportunity to interrogate further the ethical stakes in historical witnessing.

Abu Ghraib

Debates about military violence, voyeurism, and accountability emerged in 2004 when photographs of American soldiers torturing prisoners at the Abu Ghraib prison circulated among national and international audiences. While viewers expressed varying degrees of outcry, anger, and even shame about this visual evidence of sustained prisoner abuse, social critics navigated between the poles of indexicality and representation to offer powerful critiques of both the images and the abuse. Apel (2005) and Mirzoeff (2006), for instance, have examined how tropes of abjection and domination in these images work to consolidate hegemonic ideals of US imperial power. What still needs interrogation is the impact of archival desires on the demands of citizenship that occurs when American viewers confront the torture photos. In considering the dialogic tensions between positionality and spectatorship in the Abu Ghraib archive, this section explores how the selective production of subjectivities constructed in and through the archive shapes the conditions and possibilities of ethical witnessing for citizen-viewers.

As with Donald's Second World War archive, pictures of the shackled bodies and covered heads of Abu Ghraib prisoners constitute an archive never intended for a public audience. The Abu Ghraib archive began as soldiers' personal photographic practices and then circulated as battlefield souvenirs in multiple contexts. Current reports estimate that there are around 1,800 photographs of prison abuse at Abu Ghraib (Davenport 2004). Soldiers used digital cameras and often intermixed torture pictures with photographs of daily military life and tourist snapshots—ordinary, even banal pictures similar to those taken by travelers to send home to family and friends (Mirzoeff 2006). In contrast to good war narratives of the Second World War, photographs taken at the Abu Ghraib prison circulated amid fiercely divisive debates about the legitimacy of the war on terror. For many, scenes of torture by American troops joined with mounting incidents of civilian deaths and friendly fire as further evidence of the war's illegitimacy.

If historical narration, as Allan Sekula argues, "becomes a matter of appealing to the silent authority of the archive" (1987: 121), the political authority mobilized within the Abu Ghraib archive seems to privilege individual actions, yet in fact reveals repetitious exercises of power. Far from a few aberrant soldiers run amok, as some in the Bush administration claimed, the archive unequivocally demonstrates the pervasiveness of violence, including shared signs of domination evident in the repetition of gestures and poses.[9] In rejecting claims of exceptional behavior, as Puar (2005) insists, it is more productive to see the historical continuities between military atrocities, their political functions, and the visual apparatuses that sustain acts of domination. Photographic archives of torture, ranging from nineteenth-century displays of colonial conquests to American photographs of lynching and Nazi documentation of atrocities, reveal similarities in visual strategies and function.[10] One of the notable things about torture photographs is not their exceptionalism but how routinized the practice is across various historical locations, indicating a social pleasure for those in power in representing dominance and subjection that surpasses fears of exposure (Keenan 2004). In

the Abu Ghraib archive, the entertainment value for those taking, posing for, and looking at torture, evident in the smiles and even the sheer number of images, foregrounds the connections between the pleasures of voyeurism and the pleasures of domination.

Torture photographs can be understood as battlefield souvenirs to the extent that, like the collecting practices that led to the formation of Donald's archive, these are objects taken in war zones as memory-objects or souvenirs. Yet, they also remain distinctive from other kinds of battlefield souvenirs because the visual field does more than act as an aide-memoire; instead, photographing the torture participates in the discursive and material abjection of the enemy (Apel 2005; Puar 2005; Mirzoeff 2006). As social critics (e.g. Murphy 2004; Sante 2004; Sontag 2004) note, the Abu Ghraib photographs function as trophies in which smiling American soldiers proudly display their prowess to the camera as they stand over the naked bodies and hooded or obscured faces of Iraqi prisoners. The staging of terror (Hesford 2005) apparent in the exaggerated theatricality of so many carefully posed pictures is evident in the picture of Spc. Lynndie England and Spc. Charles Graner linking arms as they stand behind a "sodomitical pyramid of bodies" (Mirzoeff 2006: 28) (Figure 5). Echoing the conventions of tourist photography, this distorted version of the honeymoon couple posed next to a monument, as Mirzoeff (2006) notes, reinforces the heteronormative and racist power of imperial dominance (see also Puar 2005). In other words, by mobilizing orientalist discourses that equate racial difference with sexual deviance, the soldiers inscribe a violent heterosexuality onto a queer scenario they themselves have staged.

Beyond the taking of pictures, acts of archivization contribute to the Occupation logics that have sustained the US military presence in Iraq. Photographs of grinning soldiers looking directly into the camera amid scenes of torture

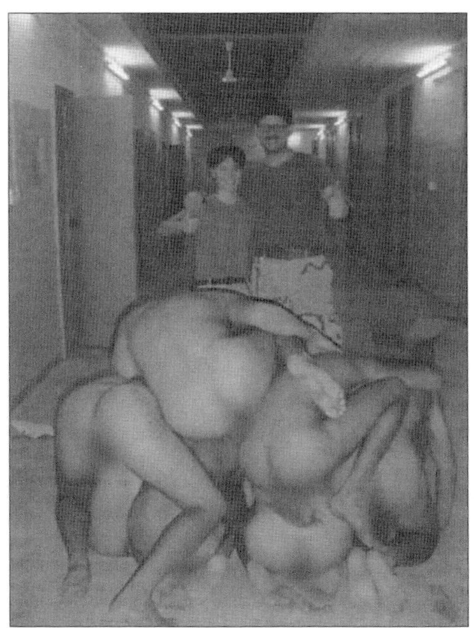

Fig 5 Spc. Lynndie England and Spc. Charles Graner in Abu Ghraib prison with unknown prisoners.

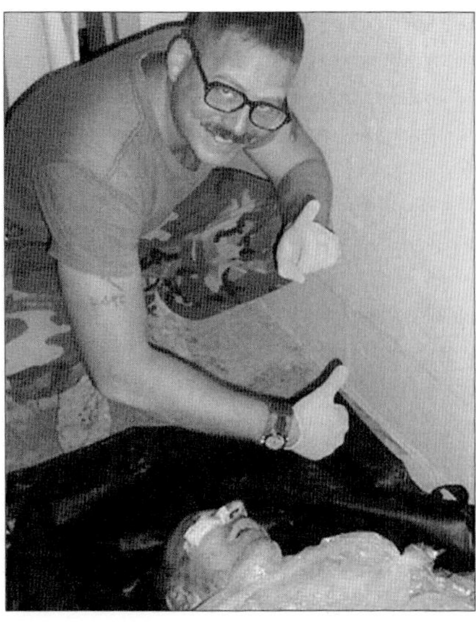

Fig 6 Spc. Charles Graner in Abu Ghraib prison with unknown prisoner.

circulated by e-mail, over the Internet, and in the prison itself (Figure 6). Apparently, one or more computers in the prison used some of these pictures as screensavers, indicating the repetitive nature of this objectification of prisoners, and the commodification of torture that this entails (Mirzoeff 2006). Far from shame, these staged pictures attempt to include the viewer as a participant in acts of scopic domination. Such framings presume that viewers will appreciate the images for their intended meaning, just as tourists send photos to friends and family to share in the pleasures of their travel experiences. In this way, archival desires generated through picture-taking, collection, and circulation also implicate viewers in the scopic violence of military occupation.

News organizations have often blurred prisoners' faces to comply with Geneva Convention prohibitions, but the result is that Iraqi prisoners appear in many of these pictures without faces, identities, or other markers of subjectivity. Pictures show hooded, faceless prisoners whose bodies are immobilized as they are chained, trapped, pinned down, or leashed. In Figure 7, a man stands precariously on two boxes, bent over while chained by the ankle to the wall. The long, empty corridor and the absence of his

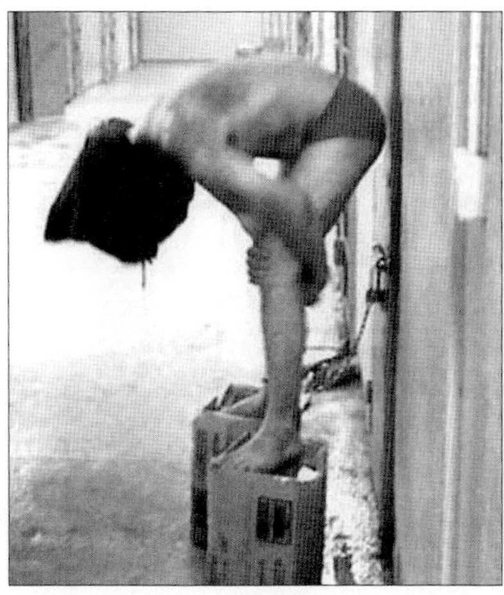

Fig 7 Unknown prisoner at Abu Ghraib prison.

face foregrounds the isolation and vulnerability of this nearly naked prisoner with apparent injuries on his body. Throughout the archive, pictures display Iraqi prisoners as only victims without agency, subjectivity, or citizenship. In Figure 8, the representation of prisoners' lack of agency is achieved not only by this man's nakedness and the arm gesture that signals his defenselessness, but also the clothed figures of the soldiers with dogs, who powerfully frame both the foreground and background, blocking any visual escape from this horrific scene. The Abu Ghraib photographs strip Iraqis of their rights and identities to become defeated and often faceless prisoners. Akin to Donald's archive of the unknown Japanese soldier, whatever indexicality the Iraqi prisoners' faces may have held in other contexts is now lost as the archive severs subjectivity from one historical context in order to serve new ideological demands. Subjectivity—that of the photographer, the camera's subjects and the viewer—gets produced in various sites that include the images as well as acts of collection, preservation, and spectatorship. In this regard, the archive produces subjectivities within a visual logic not necessarily tethered to the material bodies of prisoners or soldiers.

Privileging the soldiers' subjectivities in these pictures instead preserves a racial and sexual logic

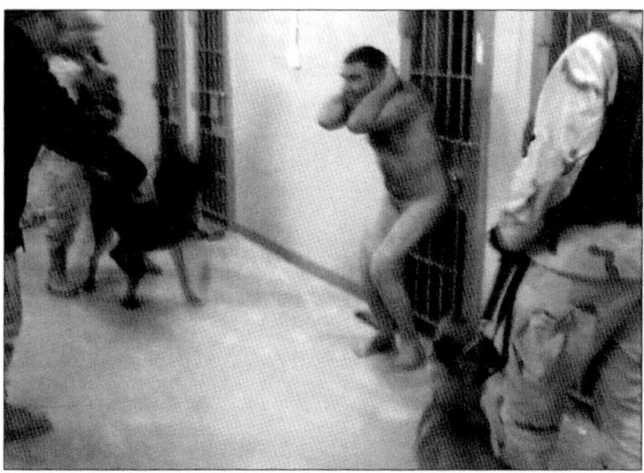

Fig 8 American soldiers with unknown prisoner at Abu Ghraib prison.

of domination that in turn complexly positions subsequent viewers who gaze at the torture archive as witnesses. In a study of the defacement of a family photograph during the Bosnian war, Sliwinski argues that:

> The contemporary spectator enters into, and indeed, becomes a participant in this narrative only at its conclusion. But this last site is itself unstable because the spectator is actually obliged to perform a dual task: to identify the subject *of* the image and to identify *with* it … The spectator, in other words, becomes both the receiver of the object's enigmatic message *and* the carrier of its affective resonances. (2009: 305; italics in original)

As an American citizen, what I find so troubling is the difficulty of escaping the visual strategies that hail me within these affective resonances. In Figure 6, for example, the close-up framing of Sgt. Graner's grinning face and thumbs-up gesture leaves little space other than to gaze with him at the abject body of the Iraqi prisoner. I do not intend by these observations to preclude the possibility that viewers can or do develop a visual empathy with prisoners' suffering, but the archive provides no access to images of Iraqis as political subjects. Instead, pictures that feature close-up framings and smiling gestures of American soldiers make it difficult to locate oneself outside of the voyeurism that is a fundamental aspect of the abuse of the prisoners. In a powerful *New York Times* article, Susan Sontag (2004) demanded that American viewers recognize their complicity as US citizens in the scopic and material violence of torture practices. Beyond this, I would like to argue, grappling with viewer complicity must also recognize the scopic pleasures of looking. Racialized, gendered, and sexualized desires embedded in the archive produce complex and potentially contradictory subject positions for the viewer. Much as I may want to disavow involvement in the torture or the war on terror, the hail of the smiling soldier and the thumbs-up gesture that claims a victorious "we" encompasses me as part of a collective American citizenship.

Attending to the politics of the recoil, or the hail, creates a witnessing position that engages with the unpredictable potentials of affect without giving in to the ways outrage or sympathy can reinscribe the viewer within systems of domination. As with the encounter with Donald's archive, my impulse is to recoil as a means of distancing myself from these acts of cruelty and all that they imply about the US occupation of Iraq. While I, like many others, might be emotionally moved by the shocking imagery, such responses risk merely confirming already established political positions on the war on terror. Instead, by pushing beyond this politically secure position, attending to the politics of the recoil can lead to a more critical stance for witnesses who recognize not only the crimes committed by the torturers but, equally important, the political complexities of citizenship in relation to this abuse. Resisting the recoil forces me into a more complex accountability that engages my own privileges as an educated, financially secure American citizen never compelled by economic, social, or cultural circumstances to serve in the military, but who benefits greatly from the national security state. Prompted by the need to go beyond the recoil, ethical witnessing thus lies in the manner in which viewing practices not only confront state-sanctioned violence but also the role of visuality, subject formations, and the archival desires that sustain those actions.

Ethics of Looking

This article has addressed the challenges of witnessing military violence through the evidentiary source of visual archives. The epistemological authority accrued to archives by dint of their ability to amass visual evidence appeals to historical desires for documents that can preserve and record militarized traumas. Instead, I argue that exposing the epistemological

conundrums in both Donald's archive of battlefield souvenirs and the Abu Ghraib photographic archive can provoke an ethical practice of witnessing. As Jane Bennett explains, ethics are "a complex set of relays between moral contents, aesthetic-affective styles, and public moods" (2010: xii). In that regard, the ethics of looking reside not simply in preserving the trace of military violence but in a reckoning by witnesses of their own archival desires.

This methodological approach calls for attention to affective resonances, along with factors such as unknowability, erasures, and narrative structures within archives of battlefield souvenirs. Central to ethical witnessing, moreover, is the issue of spectatorship, especially when regarding torture photographs that capture the viewer within their voyeuristic strategies. One prominent response to these horrific pictures of torture has been a refusal to look, based on a principled rejection of voyeurism. On a number of occasions, for instance, readers have questioned my decision to reproduce these images. As such gestures indicate, the Abu Ghraib archive incites unruly emotions; yet, I argue, the evidence of both the torture and the ways in which visual practices shape our understanding of torture are much too important to the operations of militarization to refuse to look. To look away would give credibility to the claim that these pictures are so exceptional, beyond the standards of representational decency, that we cannot study or critique them. Rather than not look, we do better to grapple with the vexing question of the pleasure of looking, for there can be a pleasure in being appalled, horrified, and disgusted, a pleasure in the sense of being right or good. Certainly, what thoughtful person could look at images of another person in pain with anything other than horror or dismay. Expressions of horror or sympathy, however, can be ways to proclaim the viewer's innocence. As Wendy Hesford argues, sympathy is an unstable rhetorical stance "that can function as an alibi for lack of action" (2005: 105). Indeed, my sympathy for Iraqi suffering risks eliding the culpabilities that accompany the privileges of citizenship. Rejecting either the controlling gaze of the knower, or the impulse to be "right" or "righteous" supports a more complex layering of witnessing responses. Instead, ethical witnessing, including the gaze at horrific violence, means grappling with one's own spectatorship. In this regard, it is the messiness of affective encounters for me as an American citizen that makes the Abu Ghraib trophy pictures, like Donald's battlefield souvenirs, both painful and necessary to witness.

Taking heed of the affective demands of the gaze at violence and trauma, Roger Simon insists that "Instead of offering the deadening mantle of guilt, [visual pedagogy] challenges us to act in the name of collective responsibility to continue the quest for justice" (2005: 31). In this regard, ethical spectatorship (Azoulay 2008) needs to engage with affective encounters within the archive in ways that do not readily resolve into comforting emotions. Moments of encounter can motivate ethical forms of spectatorship that resist disavowal, instead positioning the witness to confront preexisting assumptions about citizenship and accountability. Attending to responses such as the recoil can initiate ethical looking practices that refuse the desire to distance oneself.

Notes

I would like to thank Ann Sheriff and Suzanne Gay, who translated and helped analyze Donald's battlefield souvenirs. Sandra Zagarell, Kara Thompson, and Meredith Raimondo provided stimulating conversations about affect theory as well as helpful critiques of the essay. I am grateful to the organizers of the "Feeling Photography" conference and especially Blake Fitzpatrick's fine commentary, as well as valuable critiques by Nan Enstad, Pat McDermott, Thy Phu, and the anonymous reviewers. Steven Wojtal offered numerous thoughtful insights that helped shape this essay and I also thank the relatives who granted permission for me to use Donald's photographs.

1 Since I could not request permission from my relative, I have changed all markers of his identity.

2 The stain on the flag is not necessarily blood, although that was my initial assumption. Given the cottage industry that arose during the Second World War specializing in the manufacture of battlefield souvenirs, the stain can only serve as a trace that gestures toward a range of activities from souvenir hunting to more overtly violent acts of bodily desecration (see Weingartner 1992; Harrison 2006).

3 The Japanese government similarly propagated an intensely racist discourse about the United States that Dower (1986) argues further accounts for the brutality of fighting on both sides in the Pacific. Weingartner (1992: 62, fn. 31), however, argues that while the Japanese also mutilated dead American soldiers, it was at a lower frequency and not for the purposes of trophy collection.

4 Periodically, American newspapers report on elderly veterans or their heirs who have returned flags and other artefacts to the descendants of their Japanese owners (Harrison 2008).

5 Here, I distinguish ethical witnessing from morality, which refers to codes of conduct intended to inscribe viewers within normative culture. My argument draws on recent scholarship in visual culture studies that addresses how representations affectively move the viewer from the encounter with signs of trauma and violence to a space of critical awareness and action (e.g. Jill Bennett 2005; Bal 2007).

6 See Steinmen's (2001) memoir about her encounter with a Japanese soldier's personal flag, which she found in her father's home after his death. In this account, her reaction of shame and disavowal moves her to imagine alternative, and ennobling, ways in which her father might have obtained the flag.

7 Thanks to Suzanne Gay for this observation.

8 Harrison argues that many veterans' families seek "not only to return the object to its 'rightful owner,' but also to rid the home of an anomalous and disturbing presence" (2008: 781).

9　American military justifications for sexual and racial violence, of course, have a long history including the Tailhook scandal and the rape of a young girl in Okinawa by three soldiers, both in the 1990s; see Enloe (2000, esp. chap. 4).

10　For a discussion of the use of photography as a tool of colonial domination, see Ryan (1997). For critical evaluations of American imagery of lynching, see Allen et al. (2000) and Apel (2004). For a useful chronicle of Nazi torture pictures, see Struk (2004), as well as Hirsch's (2002) important discussion of perpetrators' photographs. See also Keenan's (2004) influential essay on perpetrators performing for the camera.

Wendy Kozol is a Professor of Comparative American Studies at Oberlin College where she teaches courses on feminist theory, visual culture, and US militarization. She is the author of *Life's America* (1994) and has coedited two anthologies: *Haunting Violations: Feminist Criticism and the Crisis of the "Real"* (2001) and *Just Advocacy: Women's Human Rights, Transnational Feminism and the Politics of Representation* (2005).

References

Allen, James et al. 2000. *Without Sanctuary: Lynching Photography in America*. Santa Fe, NM: Twin Palms.

Apel, Dora. 2004. *Imagery of Lynching: Black Men, White Women, and the Mob*. New Brunswick, NJ: Rutgers University Press.

Apel, Dora. 2005. "Torture Culture: Lynching Photographs and the Images of Abu Ghraib." *Art Journal* (Summer): 88–100.

Arondekar, Anjali. 2009. *For the Record: On Sexuality and the Colonial Archive in India*. Durham, NC: Duke University Press.

Azoulay, Ariella. 2008. *The Civil Contract of Photography*. Trans. R. Mazali and R. Danieli. New York: Zone Books.

Bal, Mieke. 2007. "The Pain of Images." In Mark Reinhardt, Holly Edwards and Erina Duganne (eds) *Beautiful Suffering: Photography and the Traffic in Pain*, pp. 93–115. Chicago: University of Chicago Press.

Bennett, Jane. 2010. *Vibrant Matter: A Political Ecology of Things*. Durham, NC: Duke University Press.

Bennett, Jill. 2005. *Empathic Vision: Affect, Trauma, and Contemporary Art*. Stanford, CA: Stanford University Press.

Burton, Antoinette. 2005. "Introduction: Archive Fever, Archive Stories." In A. Burton (ed.) *Archive Stories: Facts, Fictions, and the Writing of History*, pp. 1–24. Durham, NC: Duke University Press.

Davenport, Christian. 2004. "New Prison Images Emerge." *Washington Post* (May 6). Available online: www.washingtonpost.com

Derrida, Jacques. 1998. *Archive Fever: A Freudian Impression*. Trans. E. Prenowitz. Chicago: University of Chicago Press.

Dower, John W. 1986. *War Without Mercy: Race and Power in the Pacific War*. New York: Pantheon Books.

Dower, John W. 1997. "Triumphal and Tragic Narratives of the War in Asia." In Laura Hein and Mark Selden (eds) *Living with the Bomb: American and Japanese Cultural Conflicts in the Nuclear Age*, pp. 37–51. New York: M. E. Sharpe.

Enloe, Cynthia. 2000. *Maneuvers: The International Politics of Militarizing Women's Lives*. Berkeley: University of California Press.

Harrison, Simon. 2006. "Skull Trophies of the Pacific War: Transgressive Objects of Remembrance." *Journal of the Royal Anthropological Institute*, 12: 817–36.

Harrison, Simon. 2008. "War Mementos and the Souls of Missing Soldiers: Returning Effects of the Battlefield Dead." *Journal of the Royal Anthropological Institute*, 14: 774–90.

Hesford, Wendy S. 2005. "Rhetorical Memory, Political Theatre, and the Traumatic Present." *Transformations*, 16(2): 104–17.

Higonnet, Margaret. 2008. "Souvenirs of Death." *War and Culture Studies*, 1(1): 65–78.

Hirsch, Marianne. 2002. "Nazi Photographs in Post-Holocaust Art: Gender as an Idiom of Memorialization." In Omer Bartov, Atina Grossmann and Mary Nolan (eds) *Crimes of War: Guilt and Denial in the Twentieth Century*, pp. 100–20. New York: New Press.

Keenan, Thomas. 2004. "Mobilizing Shame." *South Atlantic Quarterly*, 103(2/3): 435–49.

Mirzoeff, Nicholas. 2006. "Invisible Empire: Visual Culture, Embodied Spectacle and Abu Ghraib." *Radical History Review* (Spring), 95: 21–44.

Murphy, Maureen Clare. 2004. "Pictures of War: Conflicts and Dates May Change but the Imagery and Inhumanity Stay the Same." *Electronic Iraq* (May 20). Available online: www.electroniclraq.net

Puar, Jasbir K. 2005. "On Torture: Abu Ghraib." *Radical History Review* (Fall), 93: 13–38.

Rentschler, Carrie A. 2004. "Witnessing: US Citizenship and the Vicarious Experience of Suffering." *Media, Culture & Society*, 26(2): 296–304.

Ryan, James R. 1997. *Picturing Empire: Photography and the Visualization of the British Empire*. Chicago: University of Chicago Press.

Sante, Luc. 2004. "Tourists and Torturers." *New York Times* (May 11). Available online: www.newyorktimes.com

Saunders, Nicholas J. (ed.). 2004. *Matters of Conflict: Material Culture, Memory and the First World War*. New York: Routledge.

Saunders, Nicholas J. and Paul Cornish (eds). 2009. *Contested Objects: Material Memories of the Great War*. New York: Routledge.

Sekula, Allan. 1987. "Reading an Archive." In Brian Wallis (ed.) *Blasted Allegories: An Anthology of Writings by Contemporary Artists*, pp. 114–27. Cambridge, MA: The New Museum of Contemporary Art and MIT Press.

Simon, Roger I. 2005. *The Touch of the Past: Remembrance, Learning, and Ethics*. New York: Palgrave Macmillan.

Sliwinski, Sharon. 2009. "On Photographic Violence." *Photography & Culture*, 2(3): 303–16.

Sontag, Susan. 2004. "Regarding the Torture of Others." *New York Times Magazine*, 23 (May): 24–29+.

Steinmen, Louise. 2001. *The Souvenir: A Daughter Discovers Her Father's War*. Chapel Hill, NC: Algonquin Books.

Stoler, Ann Laura. 2007. "Colonial Archives and the Art of Governance: On the Content in the Form." In Francis X. Blouin and William G. Rosenberg (eds) *Archives, Documentation, and Institutions of Social Memory*, pp. 267–79. Ann Arbor: University of Michigan.

Struk, Janina. 2004. *Photographing the Holocaust: Interpretations of the Evidence*. London: I. B. Tauris.

Weingartner, James J. 1992. "Trophies of War: US Troops and the Mutilation of Japanese War Dead, 1941–1945." *Pacific Historical Review*, 61(1): 53–67.

Photography & Culture

Volume 5—Issue 1
March 2012
pp. 37–52

DOI:
10.2752/175145212X13233396185035

Reprints available directly from
the publishers

Photocopying permitted by
licence only

Photographic Bodies and Biographical Narratives: The Finnish State Archaeologist Juhani Rinne in Pictures

Visa Immonen

Abstract

Although the new approaches of biographical writing and current theories on photography have similar tendencies, there are also frictions between them. They stem from the commitment of biography to concentrate on a certain person and his or her life course, in my case the life of the State Archaeologist Juhani Rinne (1872–1950). I present photographs of Rinne as a case study and focus on the tensions between biographical narrativity and photographic bodies. The pictures of the Rinne collection seem to be linked to each other only by his name and body. The concept "image-body" is used to denote this discursive setting, where a relation between lived and represented bodies is conceived in terms of knowledge and truth. Rinne's image-body draws attention to work and its constitutive position in performing academic masculinity. It resonates with discourses on nationalism and civilized men. The repeated, orderly poses combined with formal dress go beyond a simplistic dichotomy of private and public.

Keywords: biography, corporeality, narrativity, academic masculinity

Narrative Tensions in Photographs and Biographies

When writing a biography, one comes across not only written records, but also photographs depicting the subject. This is especially pertinent with the pioneering Finnish medieval archaeologist Juhani Rinne (1872–1950). Rinne made his career at the State Archaeological Commission of Finland, and became best known for his restorations of several medieval and other historical buildings, most importantly the restoration of Turku Cathedral in the 1920s (Cleve 1950; Gardberg 2006). Despite his merits, only a few brief biographical texts have been written on Rinne's life. The surviving written primary sources are also relatively scarce. There is, however, a collection of about 150 photographs of Rinne, taken in public and private situations.

During the past few decades, a movement called the New Biography has sought to theorize a traditional biographical literary genre. It shares many theoretical undercurrents with recent discussions in the study of photography, or production and use of visual material in general. They are related, for example, to embodiment, subjectivity, narrativity, and the truthfulness and uses of representations. According to Jo Burr Margadant (2000: 7; see also France and St Clair 2002), the "subject of biography is no longer the coherent self but rather a self that is performed to create an impression of coherence, or an individual with multiple selves, whose different manifestations reflect the passage of time, the demands and options of different settings, or the varieties of ways that others seek to represent that person."

The biographer, in tracing how selves are created and combined into a coherent narrative, shares a pivotal question with the study of photographs. How are biographical narratives and photographs used? How do these uses frame the ways in which lives and photographs are interpreted? Often the biographer is faced with fragments of the past which appear enigmatic due to the erosion of their first-hand everyday context. Similarly, the historical study of photographs needs acts of decoding and historical dialogue in order to bring out the significance of past images (Holland 2004: 118). The complexity of this work is often furthered by archival practices, which may rearrange previous contexts of use and homogenize differences between different photographs and their genres.

There are, however, frictions between these new theoretical perspectives on writing biographies, on the one hand, and analyzing images on the other. The tensions stem from the commitment of biography to concentrate on a specific person, and his or her life, in my case the life of Juhani Rinne, even if it is acknowledged that ultimately only a proper name designating a person is the unifying factor on which narratives are pinned (Bourdieu 1987: 3). Theories on photography and images, in contrast, tend to focus more on individual photographs or genres, or the series of photographs created by a certain photographer, rather than on a particular biographical individual or body depicted in the visual material (cf. Lalvani 1993, 1996; Canning 1999: 500; Henning 2004). In the following, I will present photographs of Rinne as a case study on these frictions and focus on the tensions between biographical narrativity and photographic bodies.

Rinne belonged to a new kind of generation of Finnish archaeologists (Immonen and Taavitsainen 2011). In contrast to its predecessors, this group embraced specialism at an early stage, and whereas earlier generations were drawn from the Finnish upper class, Rinne's contemporaries came from a wider social background. Rinne's parents were farmers near Turku, where he graduated from secondary school in 1893. Rinne began his studies at the University of Helsinki, where he graduated in 1899 as a teacher of Finnish. He completed his master's degree in 1900. In the same year, he was employed as a trainee at the State Historical Museum of Finland. Rinne's superiors were pleased with his work, and he was employed permanently. Rinne's upward career continued as he publicly defended his doctoral dissertation in 1914, and was appointed as the director of the Department of History in 1917. From 1923 to 1928, he codirected the major restoration of Turku Cathedral with the architect Armas Lindgren (1874–1929). Eventually, he was appointed as the director of the State

Archaeological Commission, and granted the honorary title of the State Archaeologist in 1929.

Bodies and Images of Juhani Rinne

The Rinne collection is kept in the archives of the National Board of Antiquities of Finland. It comprises negatives of which prints have been made and assembled into seemingly arbitrary groups, mounted on sheets of grey pasteboard. Since Rinne rose to a prominent position in public office, there are dozens of photographs of him taken in official situations. Moreover, he was an amateur photographer himself. Rinne joined the Club of Amateur Photographers of Helsinki in 1916, and acted as the club's chairman in 1919 to 1920 (Sinisalo and Tähtinen 1996: 225). Rinne's activity slightly predated the general development in Finland, where photographing became an established and popular part of culture in the 1920s (Frigård 1999: 84). In addition to photos taken at public events and at work, the collection has several depictions of his family and home, mostly from his summer villa at Mössö Island in Kirkkonummi. Hence, though the majority of the photographs are by Rinne, some were taken by his friends, colleagues, and professional photographers.

Besides being a keen amateur, Rinne's relationship with photography was also professional. Like his Finnish colleagues of the same age, Rinne favored it as a method of documentation (Dölle and Kukkonen 1992). Archaeology as a discipline strove for scientific means to describe sites, and in this task the new technology of photography had a major role. For Rinne, objectivity had even more importance, since he was the leading protagonist of the protection and restoration of historic monuments by relying on thorough archaeological fieldwork and documentation. In the restorations he directed, Rinne wanted to break firmly away from the romantic and stylistic idealism of the late nineteenth century, and argued for restorations based on "academic facts." Rinne's

technical photographs are entirely dedicated to architectural structures and other finds, and human bodies appear only occasionally in them, unlike in the photographs related to Rinne's private and public life.

The pictures in the Rinne collection seem to be connected to each other only by Rinne's name and body. His body is like a signature or a sign representing the person. In fact, it is the body, its features and accessories, and its surroundings that we first see, and through a process of recognizing these anatomic, social, and historic differences and similarities that Rinne becomes a specific individual. My aim is to analyze how the individual emerges through the presentation of the body in a range of situations. The object of my research is thus the life of Rinne and his body, and the narratives and memories his presence in various photographs evokes.

The analysis of Rinne's photographs revolves around the visual representations of his body. This, however, still requires a concept with which representations and bodily presence can be connected to each other and eventually to a biographic unity. Modern visual technologies, especially photography, seem to have an ability to sever the lived body from the world and transform it into an accurate representation of a body (Sekula [1983] 1999: 182; Kember 1996). At the same time, this act of cutting becomes rather imperceptible, because a photographic body appears as an autonomous and self-evident piece of reality, while the complex social and corporal processes enabling it to be photographed and identified remain in the background. The technology of photography emphasizes the nonarbitrary nature of representations of bodies and constitutes the relation of lived and represented bodies as pure and immediate. We know, on the basis of representations made of Rinne's body, of the represented ensemble created by its anatomy, of the texture of its surfaces and clothes, and of the way in which objects are positioned around him as an operational sphere, that his body is a male body, or the body of a scholar.

The concept *image-body* denotes the discursive setting where the relation between lived body and represented body is conceived in terms of knowledge and truth. The concept gives visibility to the way in which the lived body is posited in line with its visual representations. Representations of Rinne have become sites in which gender, class, and nationalism unfold and make possible various readings of his being. An antithetical pair for the image-body is the concept "body image" which, like the idea of "mental image," treats the body through mental representations: the body is first and foremost a cultural or personal ideal or conception which is then projected into physical being giving it form and meaning (Hunt 2007). Therefore, by switching the order of elements in the concept body image, the image-body perhaps encapsulates better the way in which a viewer creates a relation of anticipation and knowledge to photographs, in the first instance, through his or her own corporeality and its functionality, not through mental representations. The image-body is a relation between bodies established in a representation. In a way, Rinne is experienced as a body, not in the form of pure physicality, but as both objectified and subjectified by the technology of photography (cf. Holland 2004: 172).

Rinne's Private Life Through Photography

The basis of my encounter and description of Rinne's image-body is the division made, for instance, by Sigmund Freud between private and public lives. In *Civilization and its Discontents* (1930), discussing the human struggle for happiness, Freud summarizes that "The motive force of all human activities is a striving towards the two confluent goals of utility and a yield of pleasure" (Freud 1989: 48). Consequently, Eros and Ananke, love and necessity, are the

parents of civilization. They ultimately lead to the differentiation of love and sexual life at home and struggle for the community at work. Moreover, Freud's vision engenders work as the arena of men, and home as feminine, thus reflecting ideals of the nineteenth and early twentieth centuries. Men's lives and work in bourgeois families were connected to each other by notions of masculinity (Hearn and Collinson 1994: 99, 104).

In focusing on the body of Rinne, I consider his embodiment as a site where divisions between masculine and feminine, public and private, are present. I also look at the positioning of his body within discussions of social class and nationalism. However, when constructing such a narrative, there may be a risk of inflicting a narrative coherence—whether based on gender, nationalism, or work—on individual photographs and their micro-narratives. As Roland Barthes ([1980] 2000) points out, looking at photographs invokes collective as well as personal memories, and various and highly different ways of engaging with the image. How do you avoid implementing narratives within locations that may well resist such an invasion? In archival collections, photographs become prey, semantically available to scholars (Sekula [1983] 1999: 183); personal photographs are embedded in the lives of their subjects and are rich with knowledge unknown to others (Holland 2004: 117–18). In Rinne's case, this concern is even more marked, as contextual information on his photographs is so meager.

A strategy, or at least an attempt, to avoid the illusion of a coherent biographical narrative could involve a dualistic vision, where, on the one hand, representations in photographs are analyzed, but on the other hand, this content is juxtaposed with the technological dimension of photographing and archiving, involving genres of photography, and the material practices of making pictures and using as well as collecting them. Photographing does not simply represent biographical bodies, but participates in creating the bodies as biographical, since as technology, it creates specifically photographic ways of seeing and understanding bodies (Holland 2004: 161).

The duality of bourgeois life can be seen in Rinne's visual legacy within two distinct types of photographs. The first consists of images from his home and villa, inhabited by Juhani Rinne, his wife Anna Sigrid and their children, and from time to time by relatives. The second group of photographs shows Rinne in official and public settings, where he is either alone or a part of various (mostly male) groups.

In photographs of Rinne's family life, he himself rarely appears in these images, probably because he was the family photographer. In a rare photograph which included the whole family, taken at the Rinne family's villa at Mössö, Juhani Rinne, Anna Sigrid Rinne and their two young children are photographed during their leisure time (Figure 1). Juhani leans on the folded bed, or storage shelf, while she sits on the floor beside the children. The children are moving and their bodies are blurred. On the evidence of these photographs, Rinne's domestic life seems happy and unaffected, although his pose remains more formal, giving distance between the father and the family. This distance is clear in all of his family photographs.

The division between family and public life can become dangerously straightforward, and separating the two spheres entirely seems often arbitrary. There is a pair of photographs which points out this intertwined relation poignantly. In both pictures, the image-body has an almost identical seated pose in which the head is bowed

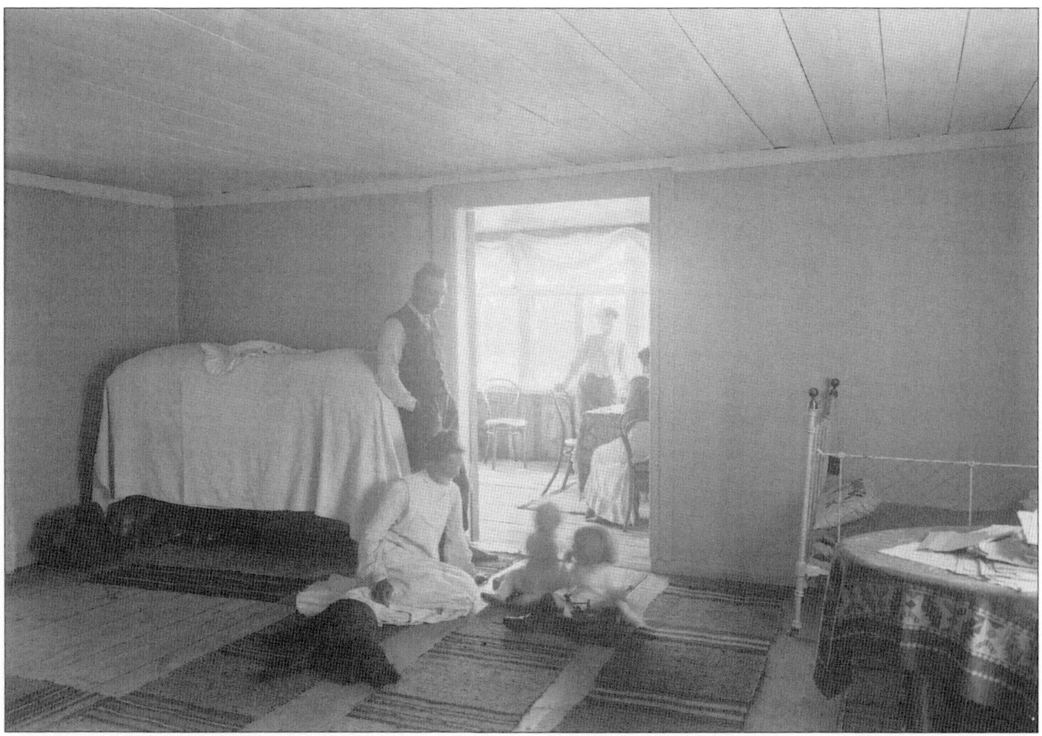

Fig 1 Anna Sigrid and Juhani Rinne with their children at their Mössö villa in 1909. National Board of Antiquities of Finland.

with concentration toward the work at hand, and both depict a gendered home environment. The first of the pair depicts Anna Sigrid Rinne in a kitchen at the family villa (Figure 2). She has a chopping board on her knees and is cutting meat. The second photograph shows her husband seated by a desk in the comfort of home, not at the public offices of the State Archaeological Commission (Figure 3). Also, Juhani Rinne devotedly concentrates on his work, reading or looking at a book, but the viewer's gaze is fixed upon a grandly framed copy of the middle panel in Akseli Gallén-Kallela's (1865–1931) *Aino* triptych (1891), where the mythical figure of Väinämöinen lustfully tries to catch the maiden Aino from his boat. The painting is one of the key works of Finnish national romanticism. A home

in possession of such a piece was undoubtedly culturally and nationally orientated. In this photograph, Rinne's public life as a scholar and professional is presented at home, the public as well as private thus supporting his persona.

Despite similarities in the pose of the wife and the husband, the difference between the image-bodies is in the spheres of anticipation and orientation established by the surrounding space and its objects, whether related to academic pursuits or preparing a meal. The photographs suggest a difference in the past of the image-bodies, and futures available for them. Unlike depictions of Juhani Rinne, this and other photographs showing Anna Sigrid do not provide hints of a life outside the domestic sphere. In fact, Anna Sigrid Behrens, before she married in 1906,

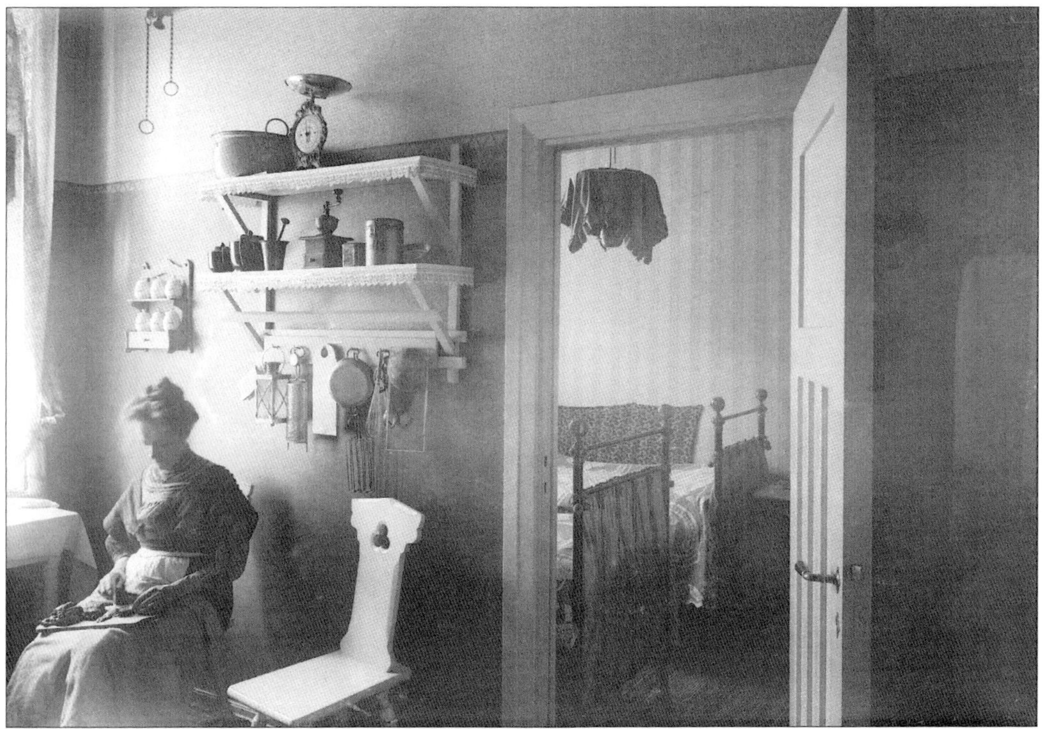

Fig 2 Anna Sigrid Rinne at the kitchen of the Mössö villa, undated. National Board of Antiquities of Finland.

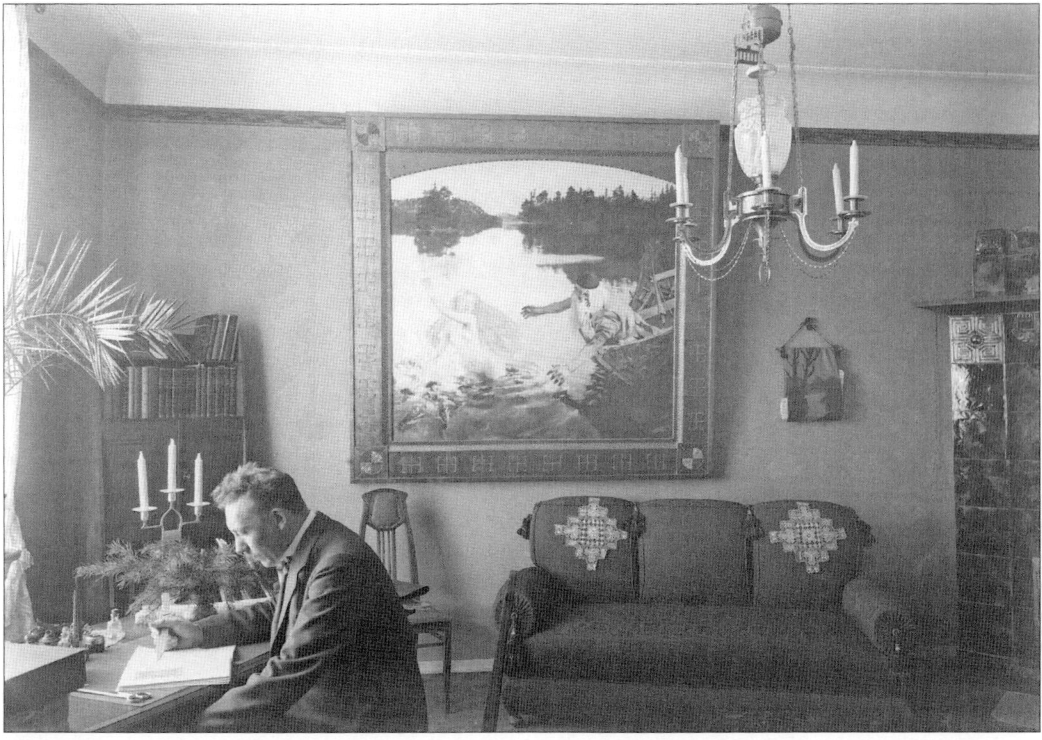

Fig 3 Juhani Rinne by his desk in the family home in 1906. National Board of Antiquities of Finland.

had studied art in order to be a painter. However, she painted only few works, which remained in the family, such as the copy of the *Aino* painting.

The photographs of the couple at home were intended for limited consumption as tokens of private lives and family emotions (Palin 1992: 358), and have not been published before. Nevertheless, both photographs are also public displays (Lalvani 1993: 450–51). Like any family photograph, they demonstrate sensitivity to ideological and institutional constructs of family. The photographs participate in presenting and producing members of the family as objects to be recognized as such, making their subtle differences visible.

Rinne's Public Life and its Depictions

The reverse of domestic life is the public life of work. In addition to constituting a field for exercising power and creating materialistic benefits, salaried work is an arena in which a subject can attain a sense of oneself, and earn her or his position in a community (Whitehead 2002: 117–18). Although photographs of both leisure and work can be thus attributed as sites where gender and individuality are negotiated, the photograph that documents the image-body in a public space differs from the representation of the domestic. In the case of Rinne, unlike his family images, public images were taken in an institutional setting, often to fulfill the needs of official documentation and publicity.

Rinne's public image-bodies appear in two kinds of photographs. Firstly, there are photographs depicting him in the midst of work, in his office or at sites in which he directed restorations. Secondly, a group of photographs documents Rinne taking part in public events and festivities. In contrast to the first group, in cases where the photographers are known, they were not family members or relatives. Moreover, these photographs were circulated and reproduced in newspapers and other publications. For instance, numerous features on the restoration of Turku Cathedral were illustrated with these pictures, and photographs depicting Rinne in his suit appear repeatedly in news articles related to his career,

and later in the biographical accounts of Rinne's life.

To tease out various meanings and context for depicting Rinne, I have chosen five images visualizing different aspects of his image-body in relation to the bodies of others. The first photograph showing Rinne's image-body at work also features two women (Figure 4). The setting is a 1910s office located in the archive of the State Archaeological Commission in Helsinki. A doorway provides a view to another room, where Rinne is searching through index cards in a filing cabinet. In the front, Mary Nielsen, standing, assists Siri Brunou in going through some papers. They both are doing volunteer work. The difference between the female volunteers and salaried men is clearly visible in this photograph and other

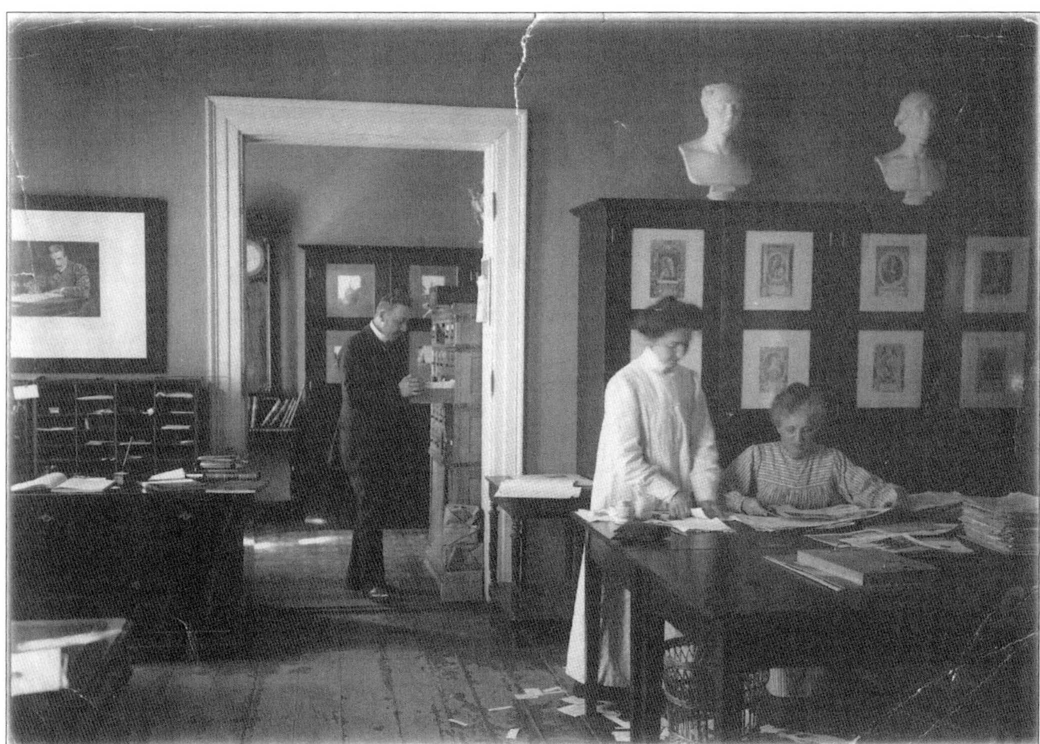

Fig 4 Juhani Rinne, Mary Nielsen, and Siri Brunou at the archive of the State Archaeological Commission in the 1910s. National Board of Antiquities of Finland.

Photography & Culture　Volume 5　Issue 1　March 2012, pp. 37–52

contemporary pictures (cf. Härö 1984: 161, Fig. 42): the volunteers sit around desks and collect and store information and finds, while the salaried staff supervise their work, and conduct their own research.

On the left side of the doorway hangs a well-known print of the nationally celebrated Finnish painter Albert Edelfelt (1854–1905), while on the right side of the doorway, there are several drawings attached to the glass windows of a cabinet, depicting Swedish kings. On top of the cabinet are busts of Carl Ludvig Runeberg (1804–77) and Elias Lönnrot (1802–84). Both Runeberg and Lönnrot are nineteenth-century national heroes: Runeberg is the national poet, and Lönnrot compiled the Finnish national epic, *Kalevala*. In the early twentieth century, similar busts and prints of historical figures were common in state offices, schools, and private homes as they illustrated the past of the nation and reminded people of its heroes. Here the busts, along with other cultural figures, emphasize the gravity of the work conducted at the Archaeological Commission.

Rinne was a member of the Finnish cultural elite, and his academic masculinity positions itself in the continuum of the nineteenth-century discourse on cultural figures, Edelfelt,

Runeberg and Lönnrot. In late nineteenth- and early twentieth-century Finland, the elite actively supported nationalism. During the period of the Finnish autonomy under Russia before 1917, the national project devised by the administrative and cultural elite focused on finding and creating a cultural unity which would allow Finland to become a nation among other nations. The attention was fixed upon the mythical deeds, assiduity, and self-sacrifice of national heroes. Rinne's image-body resonates with this discourse on nationalism and civilized men rather than sharing the militaristic discourse of war heroes, which emerged after Finnish independence in 1917 and the horrors of the Civil War in 1918.

Rinne's social and bodily affinities with the civilized elite are visible in the second photograph taken by his colleague Sakari Pälsi (who was an archaeologist, ethnologist, and influential advocator of amateur photography) in 1915. Rinne sits by his desk and has turned his face toward his work (Figure 5). He holds a pencil and appears to be writing. The desk is overflowing with papers and books; there is a cupboard and a filing cabinet. Rinne's pose almost mirrors that of Albert Edelfelt's in the print hanging on the wall of the archive (Figure 4).

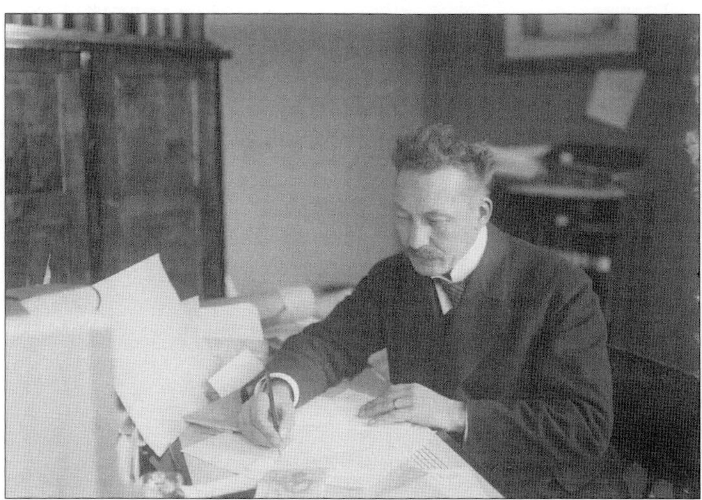

Fig 5 Juhani Rinne as the intendent of the Department of History at the State Archaeological Commission in 1915. Photograph by Sakari Pälsi/ National Board of Antiquities of Finland.

The Restoration of Turku Cathedral, and the End of Rinne's Career

Rinne was at the high point of his career in the 1920s, when the third photograph was taken during the restoration of Turku Cathedral (Figure 6). He is standing in one of the funerary chapels of the cathedral beneath a circular window. Rinne holds an object in his hands. It is probably a human bone from one of the medieval relics that he found in the cathedral during its restoration (Rinne and Kajava 1927). The photograph, showing a body at work, draws attention to Rinne's garments. Besides a white overall to protect his clothes, Rinne wears distinctive headgear. As well as being a functional, protective cap used by contemporary scholars during restorations or other fieldwork, this is also a rhetorical device not present in other situations.

Rinne's pose and dress form a contrast with the working-class men employed at the same restoration. In another photograph, a large, brick-built column surrounded by scaffolding dominates the scene (Figure 7). In addition to their crouched and sitting poses, the two men's untidy and rather loose garments, without any protective overcoats,

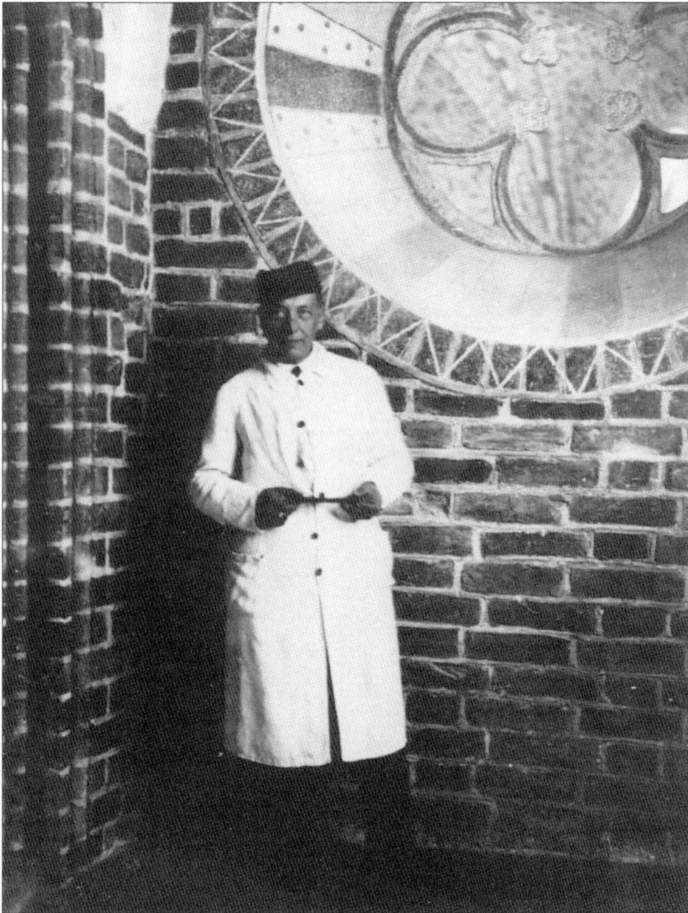

Fig 6 Juhani Rinne standing in the funerary chapel of the Tigerstedt–Wallenstjärna family in Turku Cathedral in the late 1920s. National Board of Antiquities of Finland.

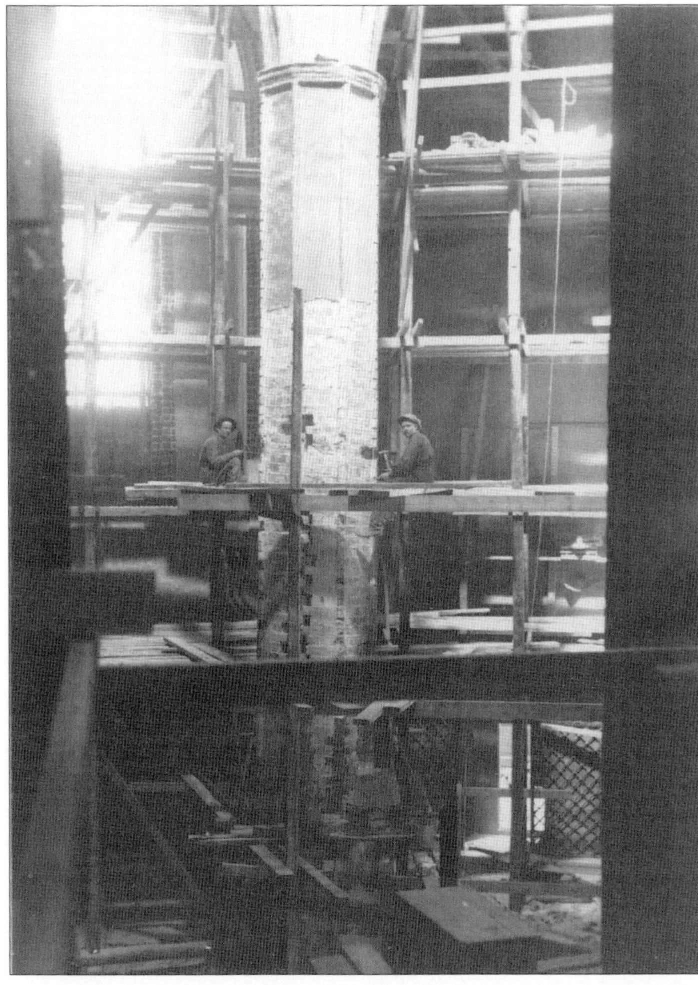

Fig 7 Two workmen by the pillar P2 during the restoration of Turku Cathedral in 1925. Photograph by K. Kiviranta/ National Board of Antiquities of Finland.

reveal them to be working-class men. Their rigid poses and the head-on stare, conforming to the contemporary visual stereotypes of the working class (Tagg 1988: 35), appear repeatedly in photographs of restoration workers.

The last photograph of Rinne at work depicts a highly formal and publicized event (Figure 8). The picture appeared, among other publications, in the newspaper *Hufvudstadsbladet* on December 5, 1928, and in Julius Finnberg's (1929: 39) popular book on the history of Turku

Cathedral. It shows a group of men wearing dark suits, standing rigidly near the main altar of the cathedral. The caption lists the names and titles of all the men present. Juhani Rinne stands on the far right. The men are conducting the final official inspection of the restoration on December 4, 1928. Turku Cathedral was re-inaugurated in June 1929 amid great festivities as part of the 700th anniversary of the founding of the city. Guests of honor at the event included President Lauri Kristian Relander (1883–1942).

Photography & Culture   Volume 5   Issue 1   March 2012, pp. 37–52

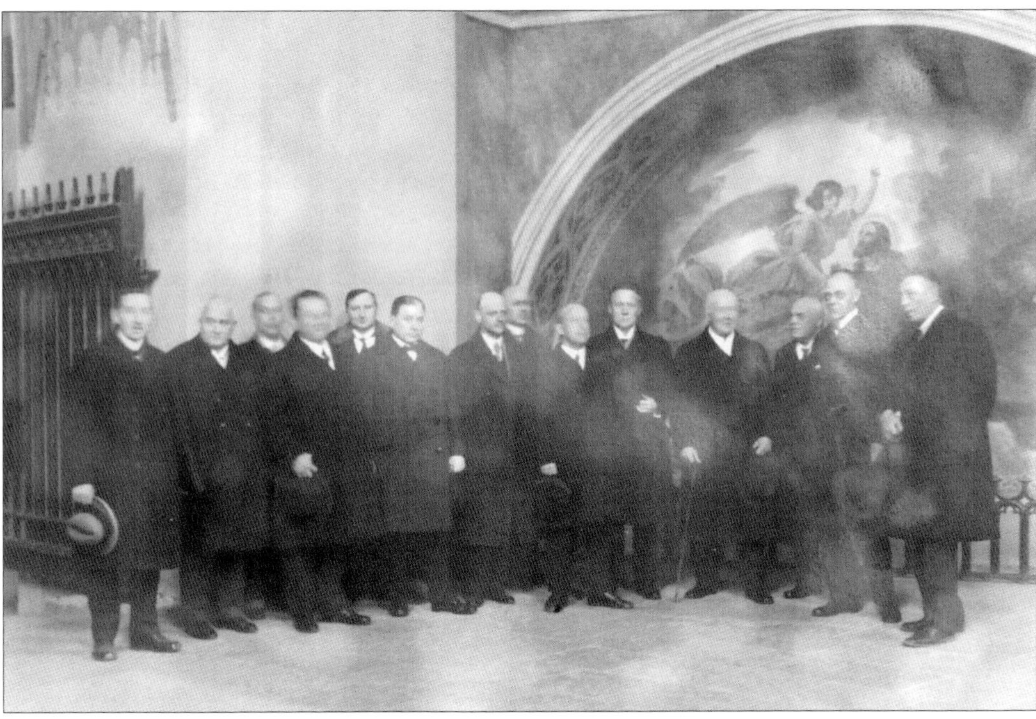

Fig 8 The final inspection of the restoration of Turku Cathedral on December 4, 1928. Provincial Archives of Turku.

In resolute ceremonialism, Rinne and the other men stand side by side seemingly as equals. The image encapsulates the dynamics of a male group making important public decisions, which differs from the polarities of control and care apparent in pictures with salaried men and volunteer women. This is a world based on persuasion, rhetoric, and the challenging of equals. The civilized conduct and compromising can, however, also be seen in another, more unsettling light, as Roslyn W. Bologh (1990) does in her analysis of Max Weber's (1904) notions of modern work and public life. Weber associates men and their instrumentalism with rational, unemotional decision-making, which is essential for development and individual accomplishments in a national state. The emergence of bureaucracy is an answer to the situation in which men are driven by the will to accomplish an autonomous and independent agency. It is needed to control relations between men. In the stately photograph, the high bureaucrats have gathered together in order to mark the national event and their single-minded uniformity.

Public ritual performances play an important role in the creation of gendered meanings, and following Don Conway-Long (1994: 68), they can be conceived as situations which produce coherence in the lived bodies of individuals and communities, e.g. in the form of ethnic and national unity. Notwithstanding the masculine homogeneity of the group, the direction of the restoration was full of tensions. Rinne and Lindgren had a completely different attitude toward the overall scheme of the restoration. Rinne did not approve the general style of

Lindgren's plan, and eventually his vision became dominant. Rinne turned into the single figurehead of the whole project, while Lindgren's contribution was downplayed. Moreover, despite being considered nationally highly significant, the funding of the restoration was constantly fought over in the national parliament. In fact, the whole project ended unfinished in 1928 due to the lack of state funding.

Rinne's image-body is in line with the national heroic and scholarly bodies, but the scandalous end of his career disrupts this respectability. In 1933, Rinne and his master builder Adolf Rahola (1884–1963) were arrested and charged with misappropriating funds designated for the restorations of Suomenlinna Fortress, Turku Castle, and the ruined church of Rauma (Gardberg 2006). Before his arrest, Rinne destroyed an unknown number of his letters and documents, contributing to the sparseness of surviving source material. The statements of his colleagues suggest that Rinne was far from innocent of the crimes that he was charged with. In fact, he drew up the accounts of the restorations with Rahola in secrecy. The lengthy minutes of the Supreme Court also show Rinne as highly ambitious, competitive, and even ruthless in furthering his administrative and academic career. He served a prison sentence, but his suspended civic rights were restored after an appeal by the Finnish bishops. Nevertheless, his contemporaries considered his deeds shameful, and he withdrew from the public sphere for the rest of his life. He died in 1950.

Image-Body and Biography

Looking at the photographs in the Rinne collection reveals how subjectivities are interwoven with knowledge. The recognition of Rinne's image-body with its specific features, and making it into an individual, is based on both subjective, tacit knowledge and historical reconstruction. This mélange gives his body an appearance of incontestability and stability,

which weaves it into a narrative of his life and deeds. The form and meaning of image-bodies are, nevertheless, a result of specific bodily performances in the past and present (Barad 2007: 155, 189), conditioned by the technology and genres of photography. Hence the intersections between pictures and texts, or historical biographies, should be approached as "attacks launched by one against the other, arrows shot at the enemy target, enterprises of subversion and destruction, lance blows and wounds, a battle" (Foucault [1968] 1983: 26). Similar struggles are waged between photographs and their interpreters.

In Rinne's case, his image-body seems to conform to the dichotomy between private and public, which is referred to as a key theme in nineteenth- and early twentieth-century bourgeois life. The distinction comes into being both through his corporeality and the genres of photography it inhabits (Foucault 2000: 375–76). While the family photographs appear affective, tender, and intimate, Rinne's public images are distanced and formal, resonating with the Finnish discourses of nationalism and scholarly conduct.

Notwithstanding the duality of Rinne's images, understanding them requires crossing over the distinction between private and public, partly because of Rinne's way of constructing his life and photographing it, and partly because of the way photography looked and was used at the time (see Palin 1992). There is a structural similarity which both the private and public pictures share. This is visible in photographs of Rinne working at home, where the civilized environment echoes his public images. Also his repeated, orderly poses combined with his formal dress go beyond any simplistic dichotomy of private and public, extending one sphere into the other.

Rinne's image-body draws attention to work and its constitutive position in performing academic masculinity. Through work, his image-body establishes itself in the system of institutionalized scholarly practices. It constantly refers to the exercise of his brain and hands, to his work, away from his body in its entirety (cf. Collinson 2007: 69). The work, gendered as a masculine task, nevertheless is crucially a bodily phenomenon, which grants Rinne entry into the ranks of other scholars as an equal member of the academic and cultural community. In this setting, Rinne's image-body becomes a site of intellectual contention, which still has to meet certain physical characteristics such as stability, credibility, and distinctive solidity (Gerschick 2005: 375).

The reading of Rinne's photographs through the image-body seems to fragment his life into intersections of corporeality, gender, and nationalism. In fact, as a scholar writing Rinne's biography, my approach emerges from the contemporary interest in these intersections. Writing them into a single narrative is based on Rinne's name, and the archival processes that have brought together the heterogeneous visual material. The uniformity is emphasized by the fact that the photographic collection is cut away from its uses during Rinne's lifetime. Particularly his family photographs lack contextual information, whereas the use of public images can be traced to an extent on the basis of newspapers and other publications.

The present approach can be criticized for being anachronistic or irrelevant for understanding Rinne's life and the lives of his contemporaries. Similarly, looking at early photographs through present bodily experiences could be seen to be erroneous. However, as the concept of image-body suggests, the relation between the lived body and represented body provides the basis for knowledge and truth. This intimate relationship makes past and present more or less inseparable. The photographs do represent biographical bodies, but this representation is made possible by a bodily connection that can appear anachronistic. The issue of articulating further the differences of the present from the past remains acute, but equally crucial is the question of how their

relationship is developed, used, and written into narratives. This brings forth the complexity of the connection between image-bodies and lived bodies.

Visa Immonen is an archaeologist who specializes in the material culture of the Middle Ages and the early modern period. He has recently completed his Ph.D. thesis, titled "Golden Moments: Artefacts of Precious Metals as Products of Luxury Consumption in Finland c.1200–1600," and is currently writing a biography of the Finnish State Archaeologist Juhani Rinne.

References

Barad, K. 2007. *Meeting the Universe Halfway: Quantum Physics and the Entanglement of Matter and Meaning.* Durham and London: Duke University Press.

Barthes, R. [1980] 2000. *Camera Lucida: Reflections on Photography.* London: Vintage Books.

Bologh, R. W. 1990. *Love or Greatness: Max Weber and Masculine Thinking—A Feminist Inquiry.* London: Unwin Hyman.

Bourdieu, P. 1987. *The Biographical Illusion.* Working Papers and Proceedings of the Center for Psychosocial Studies 14. Chicago, IL: Center for Psychosocial Studies.

Canning, K. 1999. "The Body As Method? Reflections on the Place of the Body in Gender History." *Gender & History,* 11(3): 499–513.

Cleve, N. 1950. "Juhani Rinne." *Finskt Museum,* LVII: 5–8.

Collinson, D. 2007. "Class, Work and Masculinity." In M. Flood, J. K. Gardiner, B. Pease and K. Pringle (eds) *International Encyclopedia of Men and Masculinities,* pp. 69–73. London and New York: Routledge.

Conway-Long, D. 1994. "Ethnographies and Masculinities." In H. Brod and M. Kaufman (eds) *Theorizing Masculinities,* pp. 61–81. Thousand Oaks, London and New Delhi: Sage.

Dölle, S. and J. Kukkonen. 1992. "Tutkijat kuvaajina." In J. Kukkonen, T.-J. Vuorenmaa and J. Hinkka (eds) *Valokuvan taide: Suomalainen valokuva 1842–1992,* pp. 370–71. Helsinki: Suomalaisen Kirjallisuuden Seura.

Finnberg, J. 1929. *Turun Tuomiokirkon vuosisataiset vaiheet.* Helsinki: Otava.

Foucault, M. [1968] 1983. *This Is Not a Pipe.* Berkeley, CA: California University Press.

Foucault, M. 2000. "Nietzsche, Genealogy, History." In M. Foucault, *Aesthetics, Method and Epistemology*, pp. 369–91. London: Penguin.

France, P. and W. St. Clair (eds). 2002. *Mapping Lives: The Uses of Biography.* Oxford and New York: Oxford University Press.

Freud, S. [1930] 1989. *Civilization and Its Discontents.* New York and London: W. W. Norton & Company.

Frigård, J. 1999. "Mikä uutta, mikä vanhaa, näkemyksiä valokuvasta 1900–1940." In J. Kukkonen and T.-J. Vuorenmaa (eds) *Varjosta: Tutkielmia suomalaisen valokuvan historiasta*, pp. 80–101. Helsinki: Suomen valokuvataiteen museo.

Gardberg, C. J. 2006. "Rinne, Juhani (1872–1950)." In *Kansallisbiografia.* Helsinki: Biografiakeskus, Suomalaisen Kirjallisuuden Seura. Available online: http://artikkelihaku. kansallisbiografia.fi/artikkeli/6356/

Gerschick, T. J. 2005. "Masculinity and Degrees of Bodily Normativity in Western Culture." In M. S. Kimmel, J. Hearn and R. W. Connell (eds) *Handbook of Studies on Men & Masculinities*, pp. 367–78. Thousand Oaks, CA: Sage.

Härö, M. 1984. *Suomen muinaismuistohallinto ja antikvaarinen tutkimus: Muinaistieteellinen toiminta 1884–1917.* Helsinki: Museovirasto.

Hearn, J. and D. L. Collinson. 1994. "Theorizing Unities and Differences Between Men and Between Masculinities." In H. Brod and M. Kaufman (eds) *Theorizing Masculinities*, pp. 97–118. Thousand Oaks, London and New Delhi: Sage.

Henning, M. 2004. "The subject as Object: Photography and the Human Body." In L. Wells (ed.) *Photography: A Critical Introduction*, 3rd ed., pp. 217–50. London and New York: Routledge.

Holland, P. 2004. "'Sweet It Is to Scan …': Personal Photographs and Popular Photography." In L. Wells (ed.) *Photography: A Critical Introduction*, 3rd. ed., pp. 159–92. London and New York: Routledge.

Hunt, S. 2007. "Body Image." In M. Flood, J. K. Gardiner, B. Pease and K. Pringle (eds) *International Encyclopedia of Men and Masculinities*, pp. 44–5. London and New York: Routledge.

Immonen, V. and J.-P. Taavitsainen. 2011. "Oscillations Between the National and the International: The Case of Finnish Archaeology." In L. Lozny (ed.) *Comparative Archaeologies: A Sociological View of the Science of the Past*, pp. 137–78. New York: Springer.

Kember, S. 1996. "'The Shadow of the Object': Photography and Realism." *Textual Practice*, 10(1): 145–63.

Lalvani, S. 1993. "Photography, Epistemology and the Body." *Cultural Studies*, 7(3): 442–65.

Lalvani, S. 1996. *Photography, Vision, and the Production of Modern Bodies.* New York: State University of New York Press.

Margadant, J. B. 2000. "Introduction: Constructing Selves in Historical Perspective." In J. B. Margadant (ed.) *The New Biography: Performing Femininity in Nineteenth-Century France*, pp. 1–32. Berkeley, Los Angeles and London: University of California Press.

Palin, T. 1992. "Muotokuvan vakiintuvat muodot." In J. Kukkonen, T.-J. Vuorenmaa and J. Hinkka (eds) *Valokuvan taide: Suomalainen valokuva 1842–1992*, pp. 356–61. Helsinki: Suomalaisen Kirjallisuuden Seura.

Rinne, J. and Y. Kajava, 1927. "Pyhäinjäännöksistä Turun tuomiokirkossa." *Esitelmät ja pöytäkirjat: Suomalainen tiedeakatemia*, 1927: 35–9.

Sekula, A. [1983] 1999. "Reading an Archive: Photography Between Labour and Capital." In J. Evans and S. Hall (eds) *Visual Culture: The Reader*, pp. 181–92. London, Thousand Oaks and New Delhi: Sage.

Sinisalo, H. and R. Tähtinen. 1996. *Suomen valokuvaajat 1842–1920.* Helsinki: Suomen valokuvataiteen museon säätiö.

Tagg, J. 1988. *The Burden of Representation: Essays on Photographies and Histories.* Basingstoke: Macmillan.

Weber, M. [1904] 1970. *The Protestant Ethic and the Spirit of Capitalism.* London: Unwin University Books.

Whitehead, S. M. 2002. *Men and Masculinites: Key Themes and New Directions.* Cambridge: Polity.

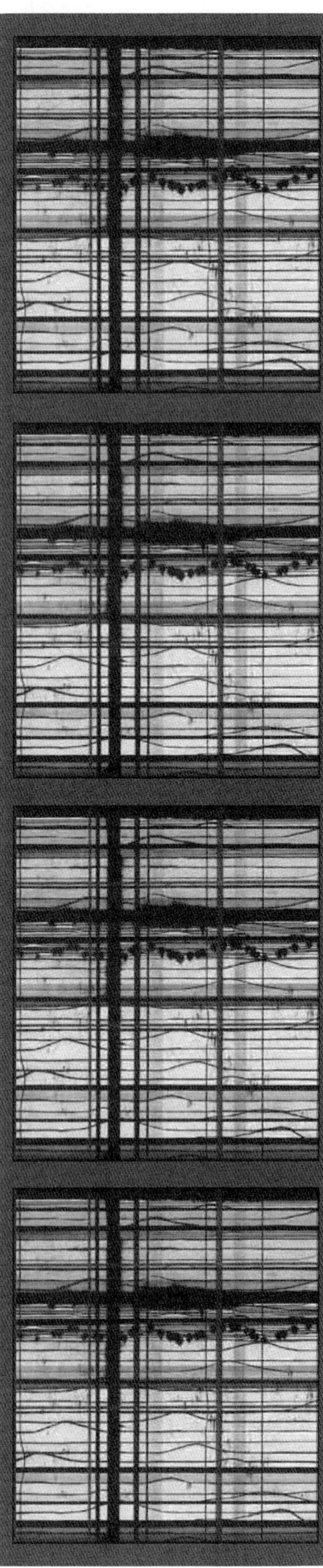

The Handbook of Visual Culture

Edited by Ian Heywood & Barry Sandywell

Consultant Editors: Michael Gardiner, Gunalan Nadarajan and Catherine Soussloff

The Handbook of Visual Culture embraces the extraordinary range of disciplines which now engage in the study of the visual – film and photography, television, fashion, visual arts, digital media, geography, philosophy, architecture, material culture, sociology, cultural studies and art history. Throughout, the *Handbook* is responsive to the cross-disciplinary nature of many of the key questions raised in visual culture around digitization, globalization, cyberculture, surveillance, spectacle, and the role of art.

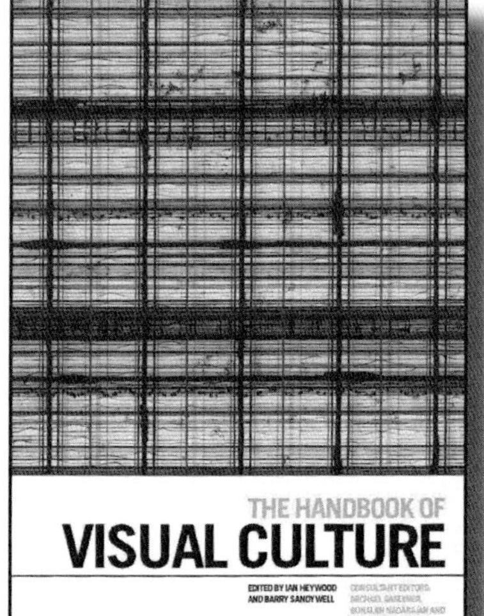

The *Handbook* guides readers new to the area, as well as experienced researchers, into the topics, issues and questions that have emerged in the study of visual culture since the start of the new millennium, conveying the boldness, excitement and vitality of the subject.

CONTENTS SUMMARY

General Introduction • PART I:History and Theoretical Perspectives • PART II: Art and Visuality • PART III: Aesthetics, Politics and Visual Culture • PART IV: Practices and Institutions of Visual Culture • PART V: Developments in the Field of Visual Culture • Contributors • Bibliography • Index

January 2012 • 816pp • 50 bw illus
HB 978 1 84788 573 9 **£80.00 • $140.00**
E-book edition also available

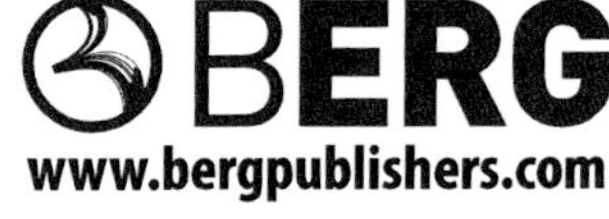

Photography & Culture

Volume 5—Issue 1
March 2012
pp. 53–76

DOI:
10.2752/175145212X13233396185071

Reprints available directly from
the publishers

Photocopying permitted by
licence only

Fields of Consciousness: The Ghost in the Machine

Mark Gisbourne

Abstract

The aim of the article is to question the extent to which modern information technologies in photography and other media increasingly disseminate and determine both the material and intellectual formation of contemporary consciousness. The study questions the relationship of mind and mechanism in establishing neuro-aesthetic arguments of cultural consciousness, that is to say how the actual neuro-physiology of the brain is affected and shaped through the workings and continuous formation of cultural consciousness. The study, by concentrating on the sources and the works of the artist Warren Neidich, reveals a systematic pattern and artistic practice that expresses a commitment to developing our understanding of what is now commonly called neuro-aesthetics or the formation of a contemporary neuro-culture. By using historical source materials (most often photography and reproductive media), cast into the context of Neidich's contemporary exhibition and cultural investigations, observations are drawn in reference to the artistic practices of the artist as to the methods he adopts and their neuro-aesthetic outcomes that are suggested. The article therefore constitutes an overview of what is still a highly contentious area of social and cultural research. The outcome or conclusion(s) of the study does not proffer firm answers but extends and opens up further the debate around discourses of mind, consciousness, and perception, as to the genuine validity of neurological aesthetic argumentation.

Keywords: photography, cognition, perception consciousness, neuro-aesthetics

The contentious debate as to an aesthetic relationship between mind–mechanism–representation has not gone away, that is in spite of scientific researches in physiology and neurophysiology that have recently dressed matters up in terms of mapping the brain and a causal biochemistry. Yet given a recent return of somatic dominance there nonetheless still remains much to be said about the mental role of a creative culture in the living biochemistry of modern being. This is not to argue that nineteenth-century Drieschian-derived ideas of "vitalism" and its legacy can any longer offer a nonmaterialist hiding place for theories of mind and consciousness.[1] Theories of mind have largely been reduced today to two areas, namely the biological sciences and/or experimental cognitive psychology.[2] It is the discursive and interactive relationship between biological science and the different psychologies of consciousness that for the most part frames the current debate. In areas of cognitive consciousness, the emphasis is now firmly placed upon the "embodied," that is to say in living conditions of "being" that foments representation: to represent means quite literally an embodiment of signs that are brought to mind only in and through reflective consciousness as lived experience.[3] The subjective Cartesian formation of the mind–body question, and its many subsequent philosophical interpretations, has been increasingly sidelined somewhat ironically (given Descartes's mechanistic view of the body), by an extension of materialist mechanisms (scanning machines), and the explications of neuroscience that accompanies their use.[4]

But the way that the brain works and the related questions born of how representation within consciousness takes place remain a vexatious territory that is still fundamentally unresolved. It is clear that the representation of the world through sign and symbols is a given and everyday reality, but to what extent can it be said that consciousness and its physiological component can be altered by the sensory experiences of the world through the changing conditions of cultural representation? It leaves open the question of whether consciousness is nothing more than an extension of structural physiology with a purely biological foundation (that is to say predetermined by brain chemistry), or whether there is a spectral or non-definable hermetic substance that changes the conditions

of consciousness through interactions with numerous sensory experiences in the world, something that shapes, sharpens, and thereafter alters the physiological arguments of pure mechanism. Put another way, does the visual language experience of representation (I use the word "language" advisedly) alter in any way the simple physiological processes of working consciousness? If it is the first question posed, this leaves aesthetics and discussions as to the aesthetics of consciousness in a perilous position. If it is the second, the representational aspects of aesthetics remain open and in a continual state of change and development. And as an aside, in simple historical terms, this also questions whether there could ever be a fixed "cultural canon" of those conventional but shifting representations through artistic experience, as either expressed or implied by continuous transformations of states of cultural consciousness.

In more conventional aesthetic terms, it touches upon one of the oldest of philosophical-aesthetic concerns, namely whether different material forms of representation take on the appearance of change (merely as a sort of repetitive cultural and pictorial mutation), or conversely, that cultural change is a continuous and changing condition of appearance as those successive temporal representations take place.[5] In short, in what ways does living culture alter and/or expand upon the aesthetic aspects of our consciousness? How do representations through perceived experiences in and of the world effect an interaction between consciousness and the body? And, where do representations stand in regards to the return or "eternal recurrence" of images and ideas that daily saturate our lived experience? The artist Warren Neidich has long been concerned with these contentious issues, and has also written a related book of essays, emphasizing different cultural effects on neural networks as they relate particularly to experiences of film and photography.[6] I intend in this essay for the most part to concentrate on Niedich's photographic and film/video-based work, incorporating aspects and use of his different performance-experience-experimental contents that consistently appear within what is a challenging and diverse body of artworks.

It is quite clear that photography and film combine aspects of mind and mechanism. The camera has the status of a tool in terms of representation and visual language, a tool that has a use value that mediates representations through applications of mind as consciousness. But it is commensurate to argue that pictorial representation is a continuous visual language that sculpts and shapes our ongoing perception of the world. The bifocal aspects of the mind and mechanism are grounded as a necessary form of mutuality that are ineluctably manifested within lived experience. Neidich's work in recent years has concentrated on two *vital* concerns.[7] The first I will discuss is a large and developing series of the artist's work, which he has called "Blanqui's Cosmology" (1997–2005), a work that investigates questions around issues of origin as

regards the modern subject in photography, and specifically ideas as it relates to repetition and recurrence. He asks what meanings are exposed (as simile) by repetition and recurrence. The second area of discussion will be Neidich's diverse series of conceptual works in different media that investigates the history of consciousness (1996–2010). Their analogous relationship is self-evident as both the inside and outside (perception and perceived) of mind and mechanism, cosmological projections of consciousness (consciousness fused with mechanism) on the one hand, and the internal assimilations that form a fluid creative state of sensory consciousness on the other. As applied to culture and the history of photography, mind and mechanism is always in a state of confrontation with resistance.[8] Among the myriad aspects of cultural objects and their conditions of experience in the world, the state of their resistance to any singular assimilation or interpretation is well established. It becomes the basis for arguing that the conditions of consciousness are shaped by any number of provisional interactions.

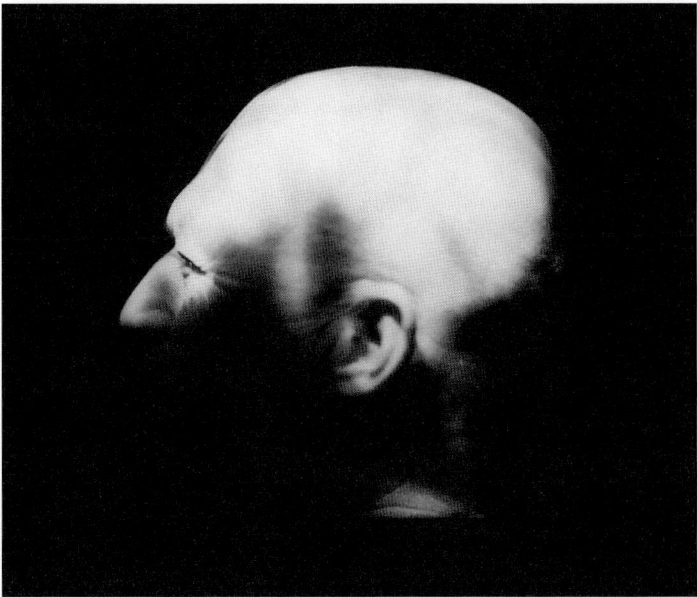

Fig 1 *Douglas,* 1996, "Blanqui's Cosmology" 1994–2007, 20 × 24 in. silver print.

The role of the camera as mechanism in capturing the conditions of culture at a given moment is neither uniform nor singular, but always subject to the prevailing provisional and historical states of consciousness. This is not to say that they cannot be mapped, but at best used only to define a transitional state of apparent reality at a given period of time. The role of resistance in culture and the objects of culture (born of "intentionality" as origin) are encoded in such a way so as to make them take on the hidden visible (or, inferred contents) of photography. It is not surprising therefore that the corollary of the "negative" has been essential to the historical development of the photograph and of film, a mechanistic inversion that expresses itself through the obverse image.

Neidich's reference to the writings of Louis Auguste Blanqui (1805–81), a nineteenth-century French radical, a Republican socialist-activist, who spent much of his life incarcerated, may not seem immediately relevant to the task in hand. However, Blanqui's text dealing with the cosmology of revolution, *L'Éternité par les astres*, makes it immediately relevant. Apart from his importance to historical political science, Blanqui's text draws an analogy between the continuous cosmological contents of the universe, the formation of stars, novas and supernovas, the coming together and the cosmic dissolution of galaxies, to common mentalities within human consciousness that can be linked to photography.[9] If physical laws (mechanism) govern the universe, they do so in a state of unending revolution: perpetually in being as light in darkness, as death in life and life in death. Repetition and cosmic recurrence form an undefined frame in which the variable possibilities of the universe remain infinite. The cosmos is in

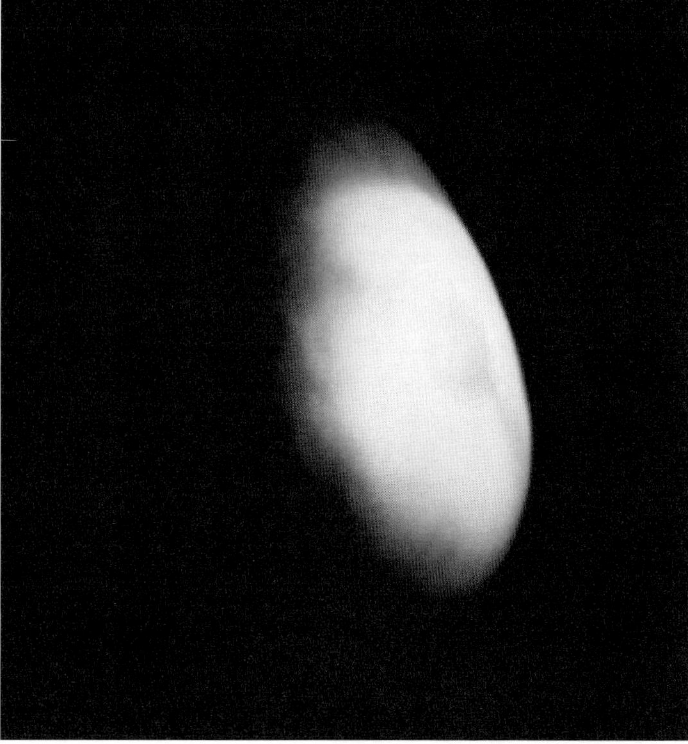

Fig 2 *Solar Eclipse*, 1998, "Blanqui's Cosmology" 1994–2007, 20 × 24 in. silver print.

a state of eternal recurrence whose condition is that of revolutionary contentiousness. The same cosmological analogy of light in darkness can be said also to mark the material and psychological origins and practices of photography.

Blanqui's inference of eternal recurrence or repetition, preceding as it does Nietzsche's use of the term in *Daybreak* and *Thus Spake Zarathustra* a decade later, argues the idea of repetition as both an infinite and eternal variation.[10] Photography and its instrument, the conventional camera (mechanism), similarly denies the possibility of a repeated temporal excision of an image (the same), but gives repetition to images through the use of reproductive copies. The camera is a mechanism that captures light through darkness; photography is therefore born of light.[11] All forms of sensory perception and assimilations of consciousness through representation also depend on light; the world around us is not a sheet of darkness. It was the same Blanqui idea of eternal repetition as infinite variation and differentiation that later attracted the attention of Walter Benjamin (1892–1940). It attracted Benjamin for two reasons: the mechanistic, insomuch as repeatable images can be derived or copied from a single negative; and a more complex sense of repetition, which he saw as an extenuated form of continuous alterity. For repetition or recurrence is never "the return of the same" but a movement within which something other has become inscribed within the same. Benjamin's interest in mechanical processes is well known, not least his texts on photography and mechanical reproduction.[12] However, his interest in eternal recurrence and Blanqui's text was part of his near encyclopedic but unfinished research investigations, called *The Arcades Project*. The project was Benjamin's attempt to encapsulate or frame the epistemology that generated and explained states of formed cultural and social consciousness operating in nineteenth-century Paris. A city traditionally associated with the foundation of photography, nothwithstanding

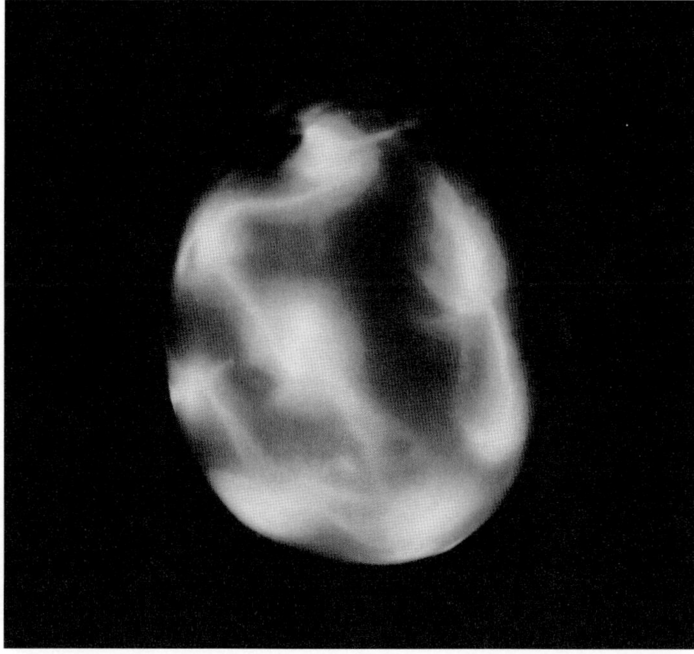

Fig 3 *Super Nova*, 2001, "Blanqui's Cosmology" 1994–2007, 20 × 24 in. silver print.

the immediacy of developments in England. In what Benjamin calls the "ingenuous reflections of an autodidact" he quotes an extended paragraph from Blanqui's *L'Éternité par les astres*:

> So each heavenly body, whatever it might be, exists in infinite number in time and space, not only in the *one* of its aspects but as it is at each second of its existence, from birth to death … The Earth is one of these heavenly bodies. Every human being is thus eternal at every second of his or her existence. What I write at this moment in a cell of the Fort du Taureau I have written and shall write throughout all eternity—at a table, with a pen, clothed as I am now, in circumstances like these. And thus it is for everyone … the number of our doubles is infinite in time and space. One cannot in good conscience demand anything more. These doubles exist in flesh and bone—indeed, in trousers and jacket, in crinoline and chignon. They are by no means phantoms, they are the present eternalized. Here nonetheless lies a great drawback: there is no progress … What we call "progress" is confined to each particular world, and vanishes with it … the same drama the same setting, on the same narrow stage … believing itself to be the universe, and living in its prison as though in some immense realm, only to founder at some early date along with its globe …[13]

In his reading of the text Benjamin asserts a "phantasmagoria of a history," a phantasm or imposed teleology and of imagined novelty and false consciousness. The German writer made great play of the fact that Blanqui's cosmology was based on the "mechanistic general sciences," and since materials and elements are finite, and if cosmic nature must repeat their combination ad infinitum, it follows that there is inevitably a perpetual aspect and necessary phenomenon of eternal recurrence. Benjamin went further and devoted a whole collated section of *The*

Arcades Project to "Boredom and Eternal Return," quoting from many other passages of the Blanqui cosmological text. And, Benjamin throughout and in other writings extended the astral analogy of the stars as repetition and reproduction of light, an argument that becomes part of his thought as to the informing principle of photography as it developed. Benjamin's argument was that "The universe in its entirety works like a gigantic photographic machine."[14] And, since all aspects of mind, consciousness, and mechanism are necessarily part of that cosmological universe, we can never be ultimately separated from it. In that respect they form the macrocosm that dwarfs the microcosm posed by the immediacy of mind–body question, and which in turn must become seen as no more than a system within a provisional and eventually self-exhausting solar and planetary system.

Warren Neidich's "Blanqui's Cosmology" is a contemporary mapping of what might be called a continuous presence through eternal recurrence. It departs from the reference to the early procedures of photography, namely time, light, and the modern subject. At the same time the long-exposure photographs attempt to map a sense of period consciousness, the hidden visible that photographs are able to reproduce, and the influence of photography in shaping a whole series of scientific, psychological, and parapsychological (formerly called psychical research) nineteenth-century discourses that emerged around the use of the camera as mechanism. Working with 1,200 shaved-headed portrait subjects over a protracted period of many years, both men and women, Niedich used a light pen drawing upon the head of each subject and developed the photograph through long exposure in a darkened space. Two elements were immediately foregrounded as important ideas by the artist: the choice of the head signifies the seat of consciousness, and the performance content, whereby he physically interacts with the sitter while making the light

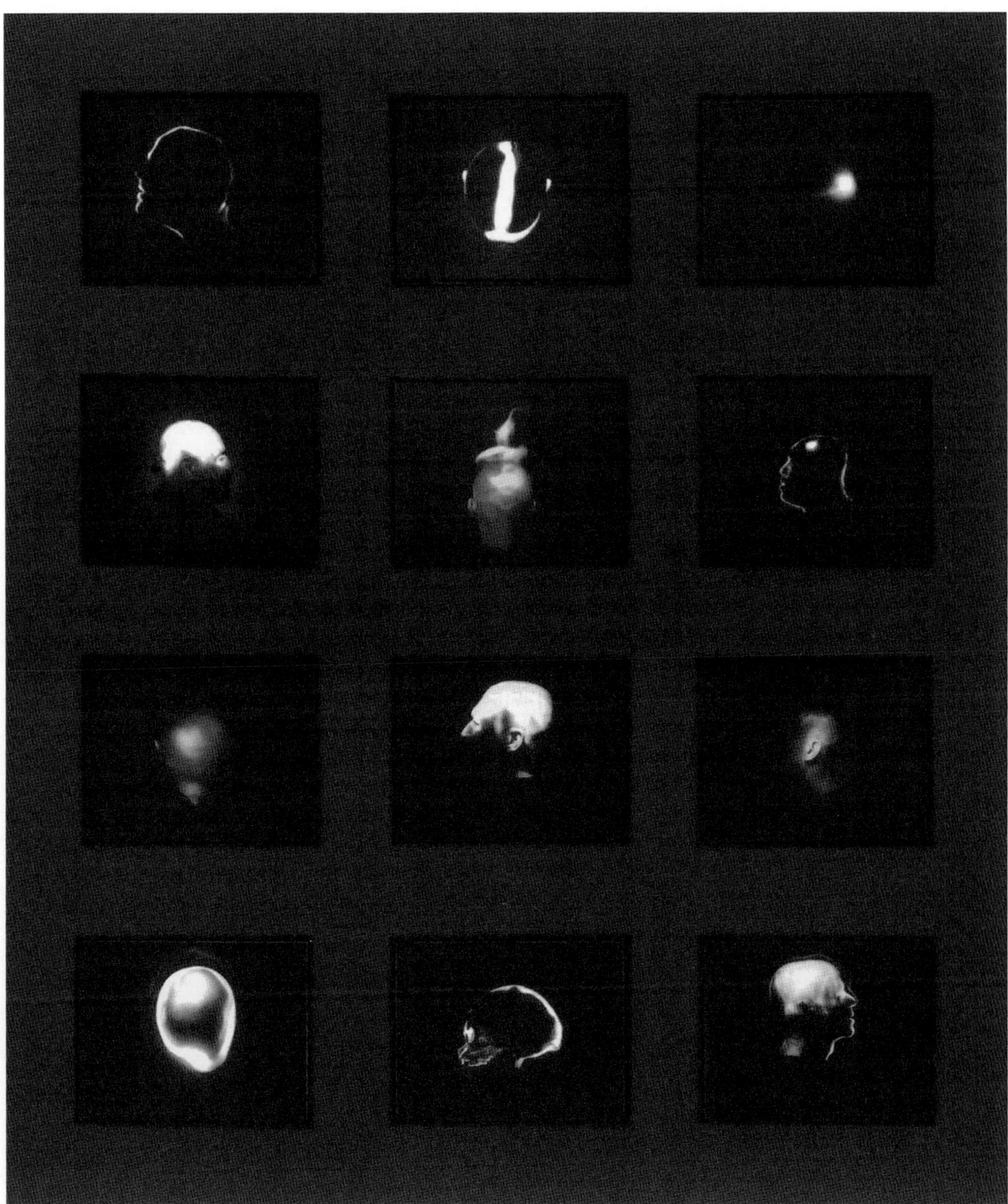

Fig 4 "Blanqui's Cosmology" 1994–2007, installation at Magnus Mueller Gallery, 2008.

pen drawings. An aspect of performance and the free participation of subjects is a common feature in many of Neidich's photographic and video works. At the same time, the portraits refer visually, perhaps, to early ideas of photographic portraiture technology, the calotype and the daguerreotype—the first mechanical photographic systems of light exposure to darkness and which offered reproductive images.[15] The cosmological metaphor of light and dark exposed and expressed through the early procedures of the camera as an extended form of representation.

At the same time, "Blanqui's Cosmology" reveals embedded and extended references to the uses and discursive applications that early procedures in photography provoked. The most obvious was that of physiognomy, through the early use of photography in cranium studies and cerebral localization,[16] and indirectly thereafter to the pseudoscience of phrenology.[17] By the second half of the nineteenth century, the photographic images of heads and skulls served also as primary illustrations to studies in eugenics,[18] and were even more rapidly expanded in their use following Galton's naming of the science in 1883, allied to further photographical advances in technology.[19] Peripherally, early photography was extended into numerous other areas: pathological psychiatry (then called alienism) through images of congenital idiotism, cretinism, the nineteenth-century science of anthropological degeneracy, and as the founding illustrative pictorial documents of criminal anthropology.[20]

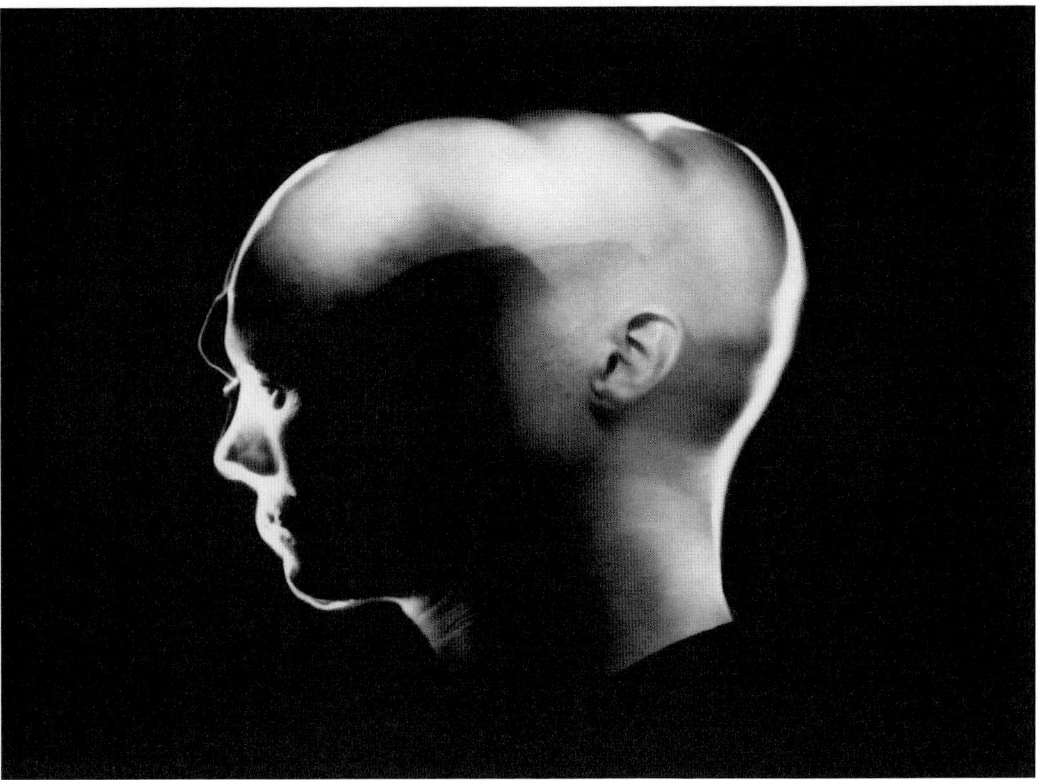

Fig 5 *Mutant 1*, 2005, "Blanqui's Cosmology" 1994–2007, 20 × 24 in. silver print.

The creative performance aspects integral to the creation of Neidich's photographic images also evoke something of the photographs of pseudo-performances of hysterics at Charcot's Salpêtrière,[21] presentation experiments that were later discredited by showing through theatrical repetition that they were increasingly the product of psychological suggestibility.[22] The use of photography in experiments of animal magnetism (later called hypnotism) was also extensive throughout much of the nineteenth century.[23]

Early photographic uses in physiology were also common, particularly in myology, where electrodes and electric shocks were tested on mental patients to establish how muscle systems worked.[24] Texts on physiognomy were frequently dedicated for the use of artists. Just as common was photography's nosological use in asylums to pictorialize largely imagined categories of mental illness. Boundaries between science and what later became seen as mere pseudoscience were not clearly delineated.[25] Positivist experimentation (facts and images) were misguidedly seen and largely taken as a truth equivalent, following on from an old physiognomic idea that outward appearance must accord in some way as a truth to an interior reality.[26] Applications in astronomy (the universe as the primary source of light and dark) had some practical use and photographic validity, at least in an abstract sense, since any physical sense of provable material verification was low. But photographic applications and manipulations in areas of Spiritualism and other areas of psychical research, such as photographs of ectoplasmic events, ghost appearances, and other strange kinetic phenomena are plainly nonsensical when seen in retrospect.[27] This said, however, Spiritualism and psychical research (parapsychology) bore intimate proximity with the early parallel developments of dynamic psychology, and by extension with increasingly numerous investigations into the workings of unconscious and conscious mental mechanisms. And, at the same time, Niedich's "Blanqui's

Cosmology" also bears intimate pictorial relation to the implied physical interiority of the body, something that was expressed by Röntgen's development and use of X-rays (electromagnetic radiation) from the mid-1890s.[28]

Neidich's evocation in "Blanqui's Cosmology" has a deliberately intended intellectual elasticity, the word "elasticity" suggesting both actions of expansion and contraction as resistance. Hence the repetition or recurrence of discursive tropes of history are not intended by the artist to be read or to serve a didactic purpose, but rather to express the necessary role of resistance itself; it follows from a supposition that resistance leads to changes of functional field within cultural and mental consciousness. If we remember that Blanqui's ideas of astral cosmology were primarily written and framed in terms of political activism, and that he pursued revolution and the overthrow of the aristocratic and bourgeois order of his day as a necessary end in itself. It was a revolution that was to be simultaneously materialist as well as one that transformed human consciousness.[29] It is the reason, perhaps, why the Marxist Benjamin frequently linked Blanqui to Nietzsche in his writings, though it is patently evident they come from totally different traditions of intellectual-political thought.[30] Thus encoded within issues of recurring consciousness, when "Blanqui's Cosmology" was installed by Neidich in an exhibition, it followed the same pictorial convention of light in a darkened space and was installed in a manner that seemed redolent of an installation mediating the space between art and science, between comparative taxonomy and a grid-like conceptual minimalism. Also, given that there are 1,200 component photographs, the work offers enormous possibilities of interchangeable installation, and as a result the work intentionally repeats the cosmological potential of Blanqui's original thesis. A repetition that does not "return as the same" but as a recurrence within which the subtle movement of the other has been inscribed.

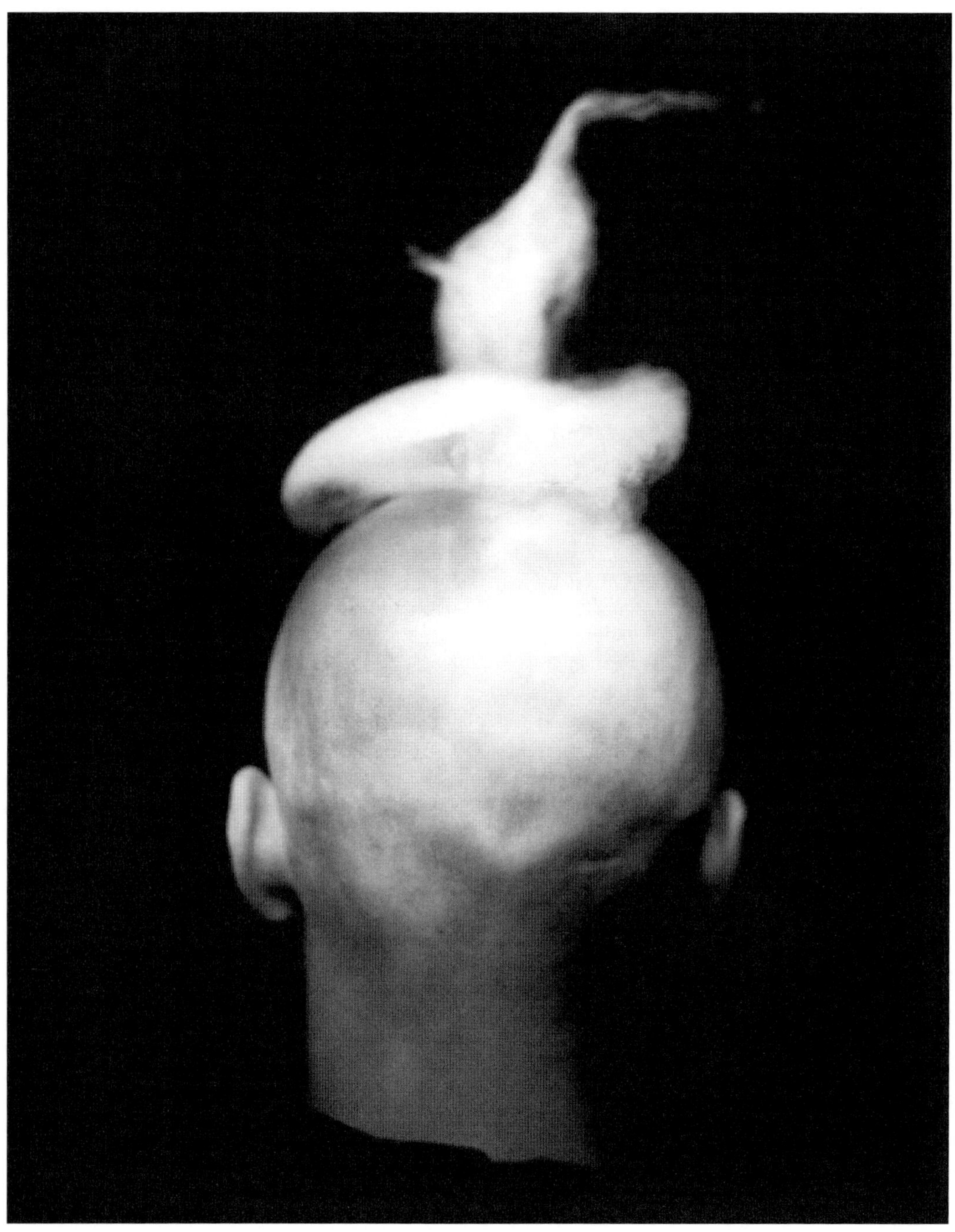

Fig 6 *Ectoplasmic Release*, 1996, "Blanqui's Cosmology" 1994–2007, 20 × 24 in. silver print.

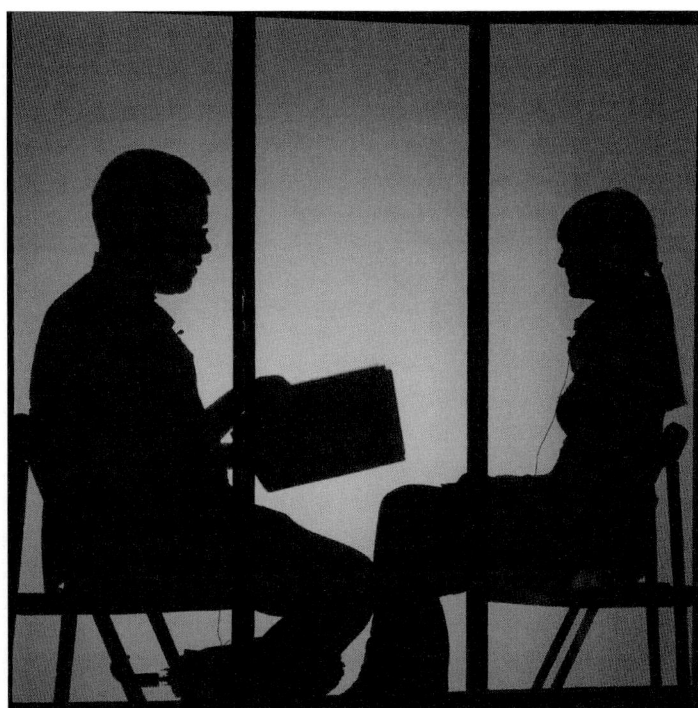

Fig 7 *In the Mind's I*, "The Noologist's Handbook," 2011, performance still, Emily Harvey Foundation, NYC.

Issues of mind, mechanism, and cultural consciousness are similarly encapsulated in many different ways in the series of works that Neidich has called "The History of Consciousness." They constitute a large number of projects that have preoccupied him over the last fifteen years. While the ideas and their material realization are never uniform, they almost always involve aspects of cultural interaction. The works engage with an either/or of elements forming a sense of interactive physical-conceptual consciousness, and often require different types of direct participation and/or performance. A recent project has been *In the Mind's I* (2009–10), a series of interactive performances between Neidich and an artist or critic in a staged setting.[31] Seen only in silhouette in a darkened space set against different and changing color monochrome backgrounds, the artist asks his fellow participants to bring along personal objects and thereafter imagine them within the context of a proposed exhibition. The personal objects chosen by the participants are unknown to Neidich prior to the meeting. In the form of an interview, better described as a shared performance, a discussion of the objects' personal meaning and their motivated contents is revealed. In one respect it follows the idea of memory as restaging a set of former conditions of personal consciousness and identity; that is, as they originally and currently relate to the objects. Yet on another level it constitutes a form of projection, drawing upon a particular exhibition space setting, in a setting as imagined, described, and projected through the participant's own choosing.

The purpose was to create an exhibition of the mind, conceived solely in the mind's eye without a material or commercial manifestation. No exhibition was to actually exist save that of the purely imagined exhibition, and the only

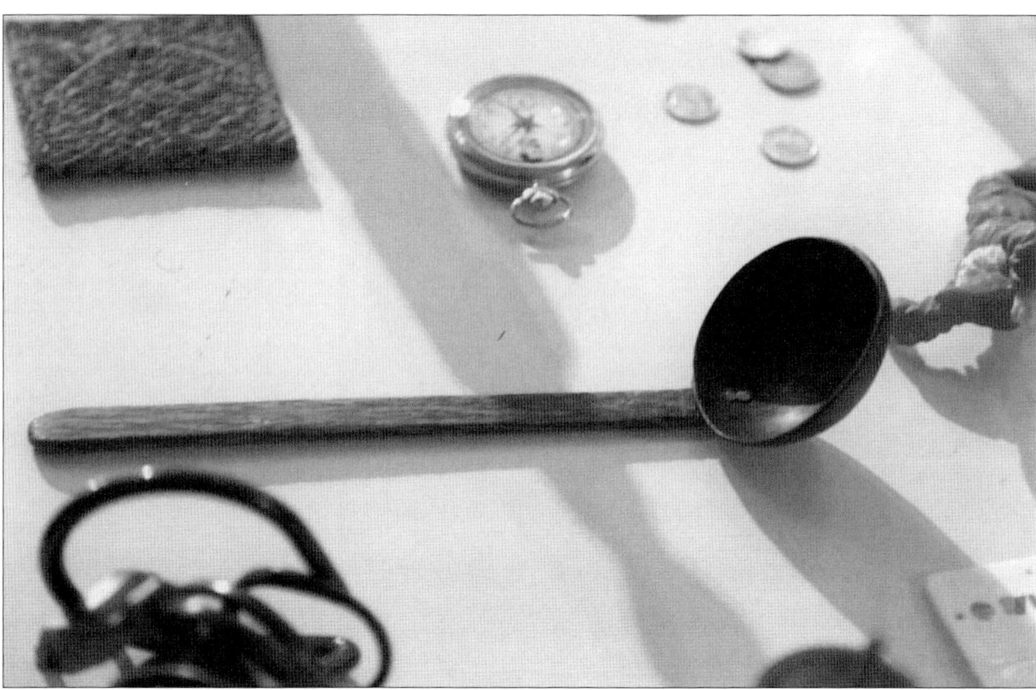

Fig 8 Assorted objects for performance of "The Noologist's Handbook," 2011, performance still, Emily Harvey Foundation, NYC.

supposed contents or objects that remained were those referring to the exhibition's existence through the videoed performance and the film-documented discussions of the two participants and audience attendees at the performance. The film-staged setting, framed as it is in terms of a imagined visual presentation, allowed the viewer to share only in what might have been, and the artist participant retained his integrity over that which he personally imagined, thereby challenging the conventional idea of a materialized art exhibit. However, since the objects used were not immediately identifiable other than to the direct participants, the viewer has to project the exhibition simultaneously within his or her own imagination. But not only does this idea question issues of potential authorship in a non-delineated boundary between the maker

and the viewer—where, in real terms, does the actual exhibition reside?—but it also raised fundamental questions as to where the boundary between art and the artist exists, that is to say in the idea of the exhibition or in its realization, and further still who might be in a position to realize it? In terms of conceptual strategies, there have been many creative ideas of origin, but in the light of appropriation, other conceptual strategists have realized them; one might think of the recent instance of the development of Facebook. The question of "origins" and the source of ideas become problematized as a result. In certain respects, the work not only references Neidich, earlier associations, and familiarity with *Art & Language*,[32] but also recalls and extends several issues of "dematerialization" common to conceptual art in the 1960s and 1970s.[33]

What distinguishes Neidich's approach, however, is that he creates the grounds of a continuously shifting consciousness from maker to making, from making to made, from made to reception, back into immaterial memory as recollection; there is a sort of intellectual and cosmic circularity about what has taken place. If art can never be free of itself in being art, it can at least be free of a singular subjectivity that limits its cultural parameters to the maker and thing made. That Neidich often does this through the uses of film and photography owes as much to his familiarity with the facilities of mechanism as it does to any separately operating system of imagined consciousness. The view that mechanism and consciousness are mutuality interactive and constitute a "forming" relationship that is subject to cultural experiences, is an intellectual and axiomatic position for the artist.

A fascination with the history of photographic apparatuses and technologies has always been an ever-present aspect of Neidich's artwork. This was evident in an exhibition installation called *The Mutated Observer Part 1* (2001) in Los Angeles, in which the apparatuses of early photography were placed in relation to the discursive contents which brought about and enlarged the artist's view as to the newly triangulated environment of mechanism (brain), mind, and eye.[34] The installation included some early photographic elements of the then ongoing project "Blanqui's Cosmology." A particular emphasis was placed, in the exhibit, on understanding the history of photography in the context of Lyotardian "postmodernism," namely

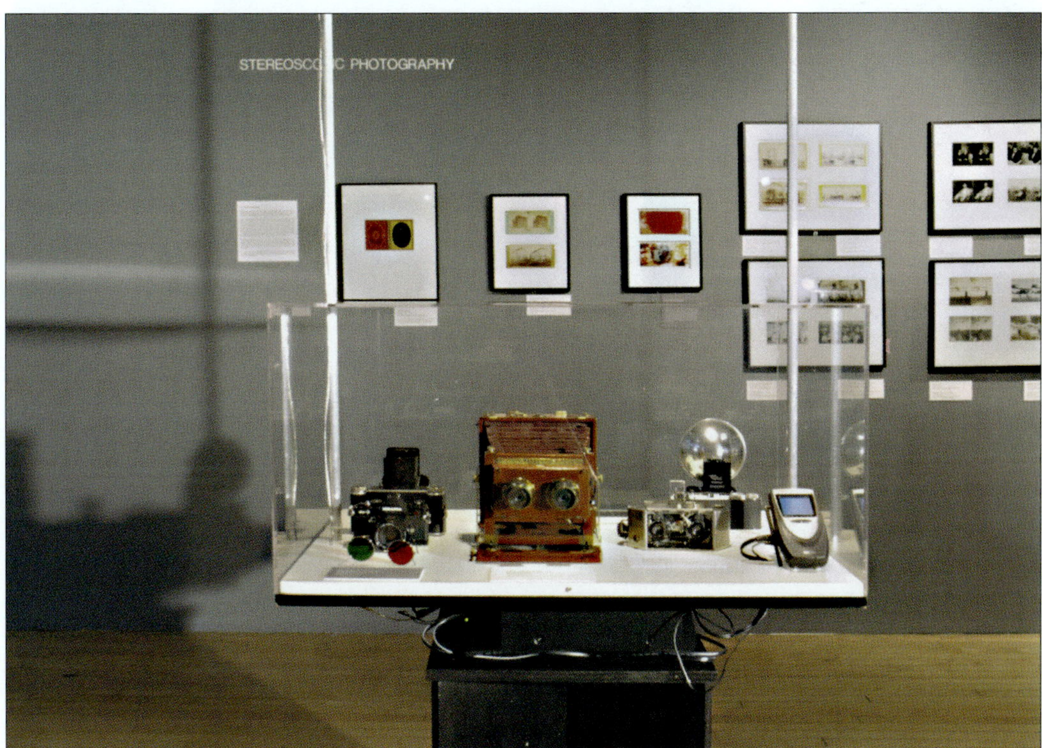

Fig 9 *Mutated Observer Part I,* 2002, installation view, California Museum of Photography.

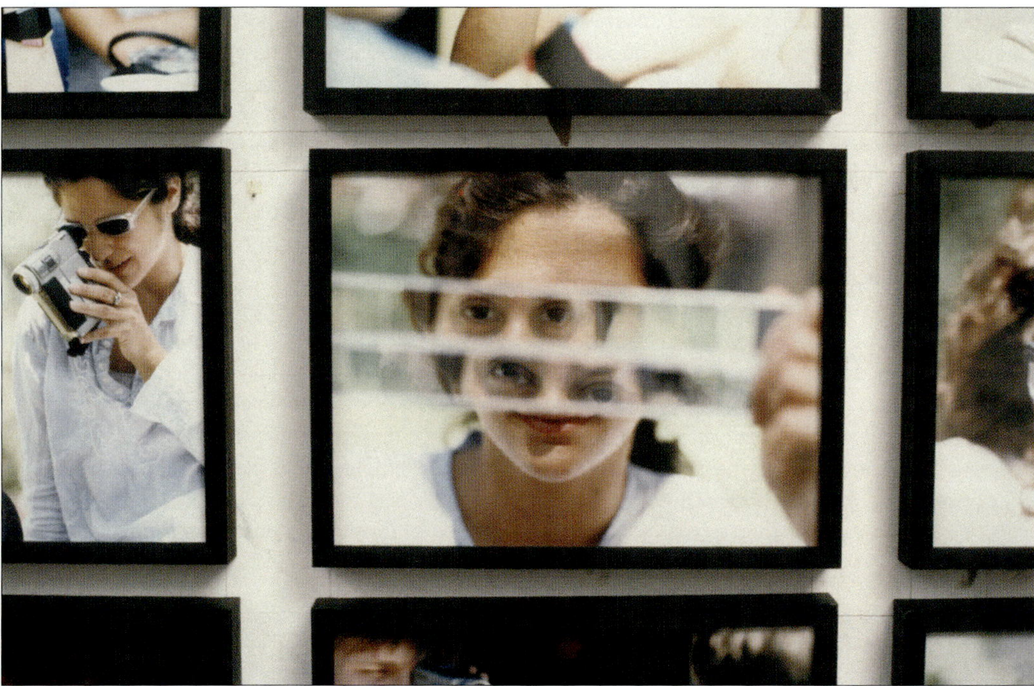

Fig 10 *Shot Reverse Shot* (detail), 2002. Twenty type-C prints, 16 × 20 in.

the idea that: "A work can become modern only if it is first postmodern. Postmodernism thus understood is not modernism at its end but in the nascent state, and this state is constant."[35] Called "hybrid dialectics," Neidich posed the question of whether the advent of photography had altered the eye to mind relationship to that of consciousness. Installed in vitrines as if an "art and science" intervention, the exhibit introduced a complete reshuffling and destabilizing of nineteenth-century epistemological categories, generating a new set of relations that included conversation maps, painted and drawn elements, as well as suggesting a necessary reconfiguration of what might be understood by media history.

The recursive approach which appeared to define the function, but which expressed an infinite condition by using finite components, was the key to understanding the problematizing aspects of Neidich's installation. Since recursion is itself a form of semantic repetition inherent to photographic reproduction, and repetition is an incomplete recurrence, it is embedded in the use of language and by extension in visual language.[36]

A history of consciousness is not necessarily a history of recorded thought but rather a history of sensory thinking, that is to say a mapping of various behavioral tendencies within the processes of thinking; it stresses the fact that all thought is embodied and in consequence inevitably performative. In *Mutated Observer Part 2* (2002), installed at the same museum one year later, Neidich extended the question of the idea of mechanism as apparatus (the camera) to its operative realities in the social space, and in a series of video and photographic installed elements entitled *Remapping 1–6, Blind Man's Buff* (dream sequence video image projected from

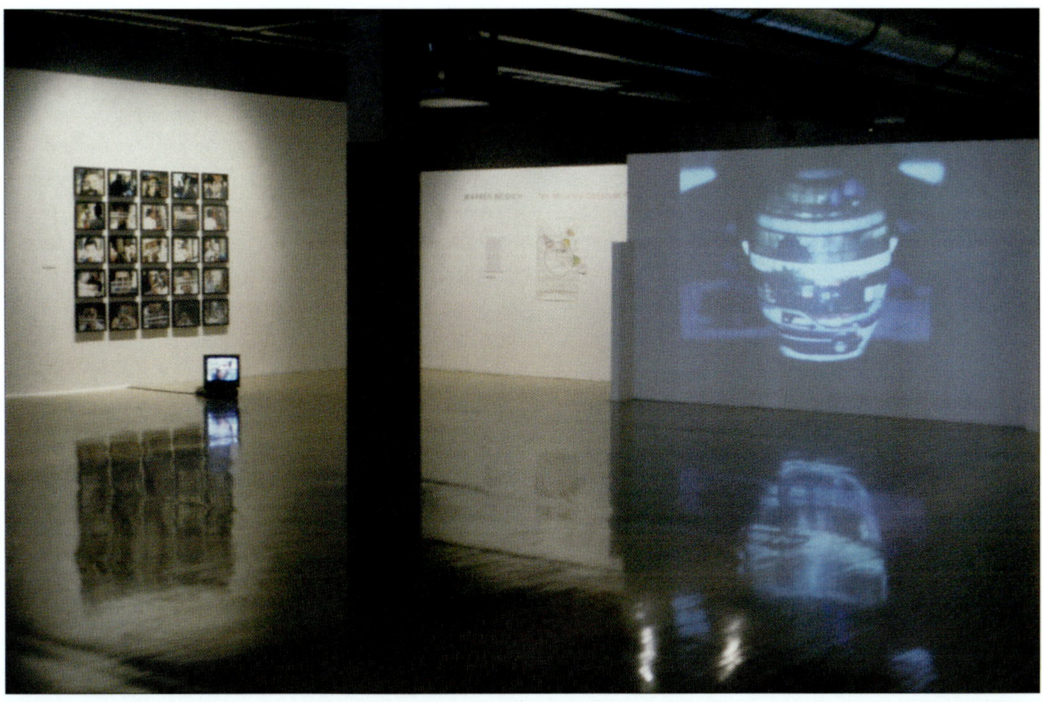

Fig 11 *Mutated Observer Part II,* 2002, installation view, California Museum of Photography.

a screen to the top of a person's head), and in *Shot Reverse Shot and Beyond the Vanishing Point.*[37] The idea of diagrammatic cultural and aesthetic mapping (often by means of wall drawings) is another continuing feature of this artist's works. It is frequently related to ideas of the performance-lecture, as in Neidich's performance presentation at the Temporäre Kunsthalle, Berlin, in 2009—a lecture that was developed in some respects from a Stockholm audio performance-lecture during an IASPIS residence in Stockholm in 2009, which also included a large-scale wall drawing. Yet the desire to delineate and survey the conditions of continuously dynamic consciousness is tied closely to the artist's concern with sustaining sensory thinking rather than the mere production of thought; sensory thinking is closely allied to aesthetic intuition rather than deterministic rational thought. It picks up on the immediacy

of embodied experience as against distilled and prolonged conceptual reflection. Notions of the dynamic (the speed of synapses in contemporary life) and the constantly shifting grounds of our contemporary perception are, for the artist, directly analogous to our contemporary understandings of brain function. In this respect, Neidich might be said to dislike certain aspects of stasis, because not only does it reflect for him the tendencies of earlier forms of consciousness, but carries or at least implies the inhibition of entropy.

In the film and photographic mediated world of today, performance as acting and cultural role-playing exists in all our lives; there are no neutral spaces where we are free of continuous role play. The expanded nature of cultural role play is the price paid to participate in our increasingly mediated world. In consequence, it has opened up far-reaching issues around the discursive problems of identity in contemporary life. Warren Neidich embraces the idea of role play and performance and its temporal-transitional documentation, since he believes it is essential to his view as to creating the ability of verifying the existence of cultural neuro-aesthetics; those arguments that the neural networks of the brain are subject to adaptation in relation to mediated cultural experiences.[38] In a work he called *Earthling* (2006), he adopted a very simple but provocative approach by using the conventions of mass media, newspapers, video film, and photographic reproduction. Clearly, Neidich's intention was to show that, as he puts it,

> New forms of temporality and spatiality become embedded in architecture, design, fashion, design, and aesthetic practice and as such create a new kind of network, for instance in the visual cultural field These new network relations in the real world, which might be called the real-imaginary-virtual interface, can reconfigure neural networks in the brain These networks are dynamic: and as they reconfigure the matter of the brain they produce new possibilities for the imagination and creativity …[39]

Photographed in a series of cafes across Europe and America, the artist asked the cafes' customers if they would hide their faces behind headline images in national and international newspapers and magazines. The artist then cut out the eye sockets of the famous or at least newsworthy faces and/or symbolic-iconic images presented photographically on the newspaper's or magazine's front pages. Aligning the eye or eyes of the anonymous cafe customer (the temporary actor of role play) behind the headline images, the customers were then photographed. On the face of it, we might assume that the different newspaper and magazine media were chosen to reveal the subject interests of each customer, and as a consequence organs of social appropriation and identity in some way associated with the person hidden behind them. But Neidich disavowed this stereotypical and, he thought, bland idea that the participants were to be determined simply by what they read and consumed, since the newspapers and magazines were collected and provided by the artist. The site of the cafes evokes complex dialectical relations to the history of culture as both familiar places and non-places, a transitory location of self-presentation deeply embedded in culture conventions and often associated with personal locality, but just as conversely with touristic transience. It cannot be ignored that in terms of cafe culture, art and artists have had a long association with such places.[40] But Neidich's intention was to excise precise moments of shifting temporality, to convene and parody the sometimes farcical sound bites and oversimplifications that contemporary newspapers and magazine headlines always present. Concerns with how consciousness assimilates the pseudo-texts of popular media, its tendency to alienate and reduce the reality of images to one-dimensionality, echoes (as Marcuse long ago observed) a measure of the ever increasing forms of hidden social and political control through repetition and homogenized information formulae.[41] This offers a political framework and understanding for much of Neidich's art, that is to say inasmuch as it touches directly upon the forming and manipulation of personal subjectivity within consciousness. At the same time, *Earthling*, with its humorous science-fiction comic-book redolence, also reveals the ever more complex strategies adopted by contemporary psychology in manipulative presentation, its superficiality (formulae), its theatricality (body-face-pose), its disembodiment and substitution (its "faux" suggestion of time and place that strips it of any substantial or contextual meaning), its ubiquity (everywhere and nowhere), its indigestibility (sound bites and headlines to be swallowed whole), its games of genealogical pretence (for it denies the actual contents of a meaningful subject) as regards establishing a

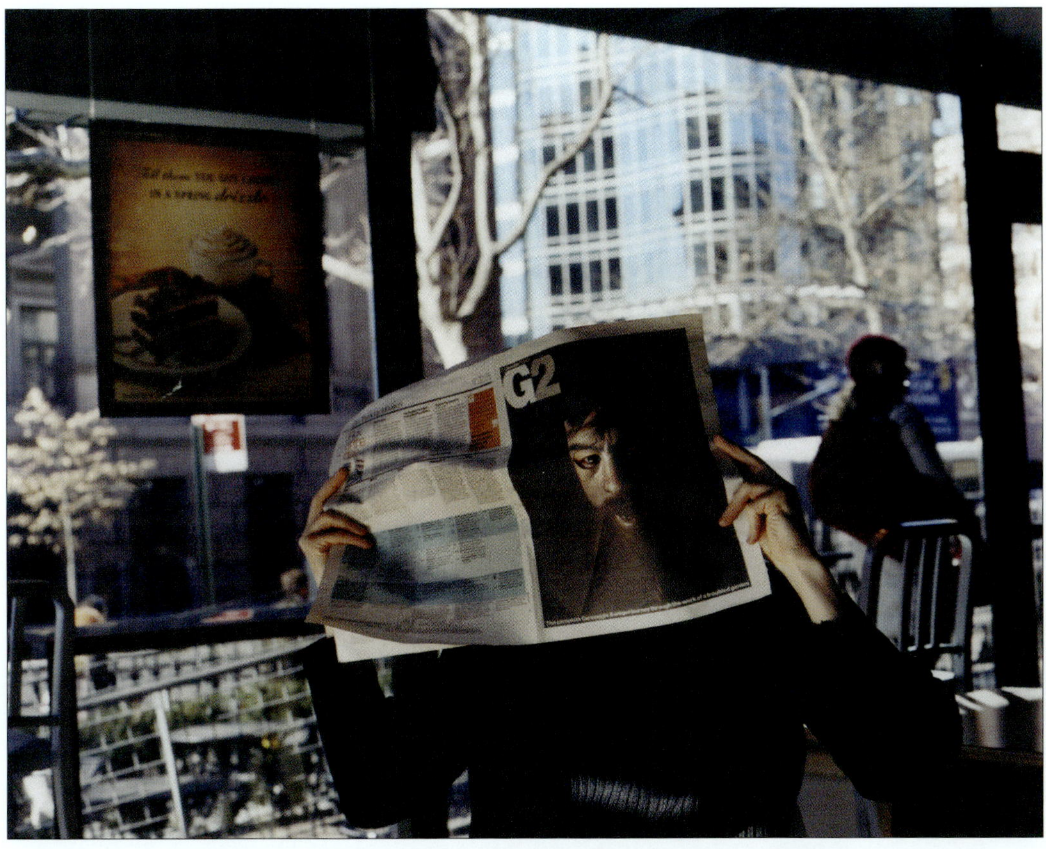

Fig 12 *The Guardian, New York,* "Earthling," 2004, type-C print, 30 × 40 in.

sense of the development of an individual identity and/or picturing the true nature of a society, and so on into a future of seemingly endless disembodied synchronicity.[42] It is repetition and return that arguably serves no purpose other than the economics of expanded consumption.

I began this essay by speaking of the brain, mind, and consciousness in relation to contemporary modes of representation as they are presented by the use of photographic images; the simile between photography, the cosmos, and consciousness. The raw and literal presentation of modern media gives no better example than the direction in which modern forms of photographic representation (photography, film, Internet) are

being driven. They have at times a complete lack of self-reflexivity and value structure, and mirror in many respects recent invasive political attempts at getting mediated photographic images under control (particularly on the Internet). Warren Niedich's thesis that these tools of media monopoly constitute, at the same time, instruments which form the various states of consciousness and as a result alter the neural networks of the brain's biochemistry. If this is the case, it supposes many challenges in terms of the political, social, and cultural field, and suggests an ever increasing form of cultural mind control on an enormous scale. Neidich has taken matters further over the last decade, for if consciousness

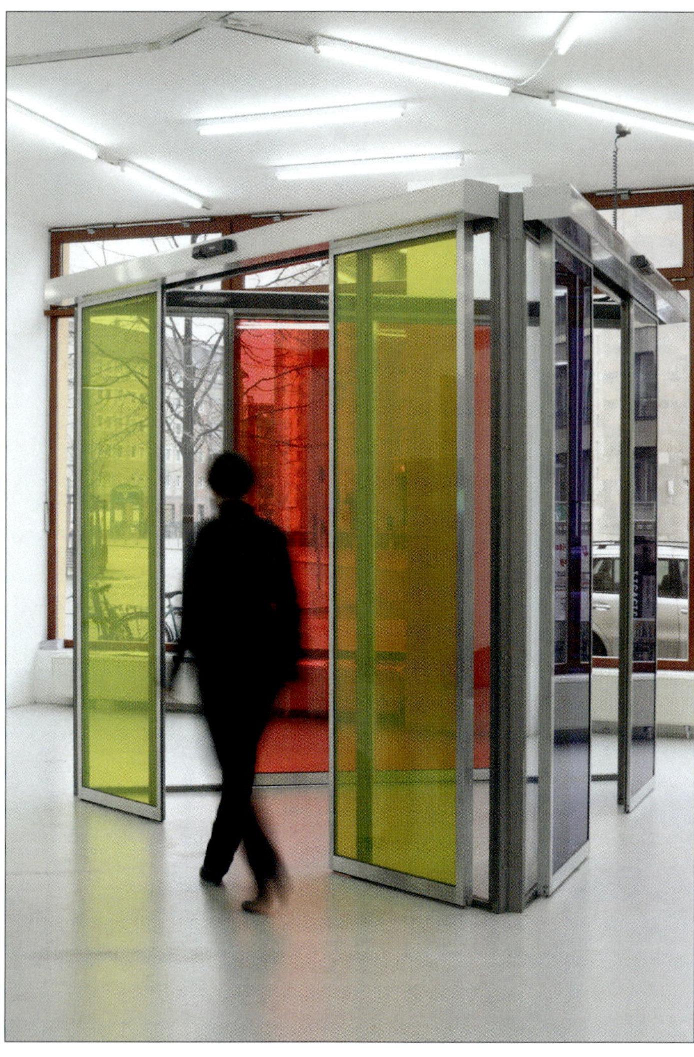

Fig 13 *Infinite Regress*, installation view, Magnus Mueller Gallery, Berlin, 2008. Steel, electronic sliding doors, and colored glass, 10 × 10 × 10 ft.

is of brain and mind it also has to be considered as having a spatial aspect that might just as easily be subject to manipulation.

In works like *Infinite Regress* (2008), Neidich addressed ideas of perception and consciousness in space with a transparent, three-sided pavilion installation. In this instance, sensor-operated doors in the three primary colors opened and closed as viewers passed by, in or through the pavilion.[43] Once triggered and in order to heighten awareness, the doors continued to open and close for two and a half minutes. At one level, it recalled and exaggerated such phenomena in the transitional spaces of public access, stations, airports, department stores, etc., highlighting social phenomena that operate upon consciousness, but which are rarely scrutinized. While it draws on Light Art traditions of artists such as Turrell and Irwin, it avoided their ephemeral sense of conceptual transparency and expanded upon it, asserting itself as an object.[44] Given the sensor mechanism as the doors continued their opening and closing, the three primary colors used were in a state of continuous overlapping, and in consequence generated a visual blending and dissolving of the colors as they interacted with one another. The work can be said to have operated in the visual and intellectual space between Light Art and Dan Graham's phenomenological spatial constructions.[45]

An interest in chromatic perception also lay behind *Rainbow Brushes* (2007–2011) recently exhibited in his one-person exhibition "Acceptable Differences: Pluripotentiality and Painting" at Belgrade Cultural Center, where a series of large paintbrushes, more often used as "paste" brushes in the hanging of wallpaper, were adapted to present the rainbow colors found in Rubens's famous Het Steen painting, *Landscape with a Rainbow* (1636), which is in the Wallace Collection in London. The colors were arranged on paper and the brushes pulled across it, leaving a series of rainbow-colored after-traces that constituted the painting that accompanied each brush as installed in the exhibition. In appearance, though in a different scale, they were not unlike Morris Lewis's earlier vertical poured presentations. However, Neidich's more conceptual orientation showed his long interest in the foundations of color perception, and was an attempt to illustrate that color owes as much to historical artistic practices in the shaping of our cultural consciousness as it does to the "physical" prismatic principles argued by Newton's Optics. Of course, color is also linked closely to theories of light, for without light there can be no color. The mass or volume of an object generally remains constant, but its colored appearance is always modulated in relation to light. The point Neidich made related specifically to how artistic practices and experimentations with color have changed radically the status and perception of color, and as a result changed understanding

in terms of our cultural comprehension of a color consciousness.[46] From Isaac Newton's color "physical" wavelength Optics, to Goethe's psychological theories of color in "Farbenlehre," Chevreul's chemical theories of colors, Runge and Romantic philosophy, and theosophical and spiritual connotations in Blaue Reiter, historical consciousness has been in a continual state of flux as regards the interpreting and meaning of the colors of the rainbow.[47] Color is continuously determined by prevailing historical periods that have redefined it in relation to contemporary perception and consciousness. Neidich's installation, presented through altered color configurations, was a direct challenge to the determined mechanistic "normative" approaches of Newtonian science. The symbolic role of the rainbow has, in the post-Romantic age, largely been subjected to the aesthetics of the sublime. However, originally, in earlier times, the "rainbow" was always connected to the aesthetics of wonder and rare experiences through curiosity and poetic bafflement, and frequently evoked in relation to cosmological analogies.[48] Color theory and brain function are among the most complex areas of contemporary cognitive studies of consciousness, where many contemporary cognitive neurologists speak of the phantoms of the brain.[49] Scientific evidence of neural pathways adapting and remapping themselves to changing physical and environmental conditions is increasingly prolific. Warren Neidich would assert that this research, and prima facie historical evidence that cultural consciousness reshapes our perceptions, gives tangible reality to adaptations within the biochemistry of actual being. He suggests that since mind today is shaped by culture, rather than nature, "as such the history of the representation of the rainbow might be looked at as an ontology of mindedness. Their historical trajectory can be considered a projected image of the condition of the mind itself."[50] It also further implies the idea that while the subject of "rainbow-mindedness," like other

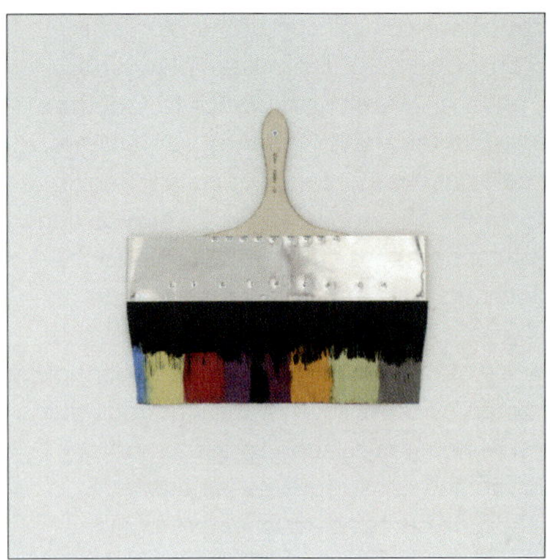

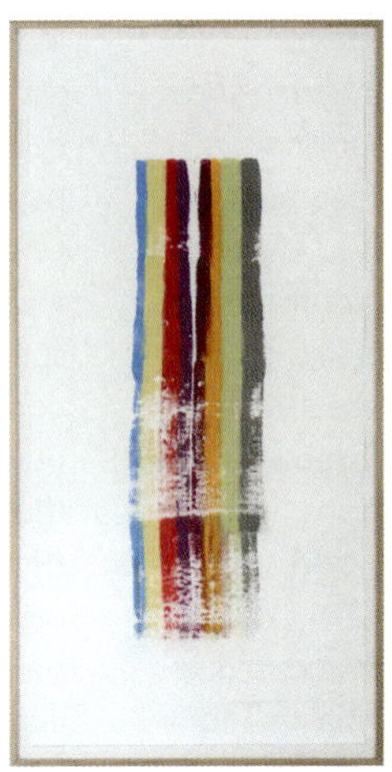

Fig 14 *Rainbow Brushes*, 2008–2010. Left image: acrylic paint on horse hair brush, 13 × 5 in.; right image: acrylic paint on paper, 9 × 3 ft.

returning phenomena inevitably reappears over time, it is never quite the same—some other aspect or mind configuration has also been newly inscribed within the ongoing conditions that are continually shaping our cultural consciousness.

It may appear as if I have underplayed the role of sensory perception in this essay. But perception as mechanism (as optics) finds their meaning in the workings of mind and consciousness; sensory perception is the purveyor of experiences of our world. Perception receives, collects, takes possession, and apprehends, but what one perceives is commonly an interplay between past experiences, often tied specifically to particular cultures, and to the general interpretations existing around the perceived. A history of perception is not the same as a history of consciousness: perception is the mirror that is ultimately shaped by mind through consciousness. In the contemporary moment it is the neural field of mind and mechanism that largely grounds our present-day understanding of the issues; if Neidich is right, it is possible to foresee that this may not always be the case so simply answered. If the universe is in a state of eternal recurrence and repetition, it suggests that in the future there may well be shades of quite another color.

Notes

1 Hans Adolf Eduard Driesch (1867–1941), a biologist and embryologist-philosopher who founded "Neo-Vitalism," largely argued through an updated adaptation of Aristotle's theory of "entelechy." The notion of "entelechy" being the "potentiality" at work in areas of motion, causality, physiology, and human ethics, as distinct from their actuality in the working system whereby phenomena take on reality.

2 In recent philosophy of biology (1970s to the early 1990s), the primary debate about reduction has focused on the question of whether (and in what sense) classical genetics can be reduced to molecular biology. Another less prominent strand of discussion concerns whether evolutionary theory is inherently anti-reductionist because of the principle of natural selection. See http://plato.stanford.edu/entries/reduction-biology/.

3 Francisco Varela, Evan Thompson, and Eleanor Rosch, *The Embodied Mind: Cognitive Science and Human Experience* (Cambridge, MA and London: MIT Press, [1993] 2000).

4 It is ironic because Rene Descartes (1596–1650) in the 1640s defined the body as a *machine*, distinguishing it from *mind,* which he saw as the seat of consciousness, and thereby founding his philosophy of mind–body dualism. Modern research scanning machines for brain-mapping argue an increasingly integrated relationship.

5   In Presocratic philosophy, Parmenides of Elea (fifth century BCE) argued that nothing changes, only the appearance of things change, and that the everyday perception of reality and its different forms was a mistake—the underlying principle being one immutable whole or truth (*aletheia*). Its more contemporary relevance can be linked to Heidegger's essay on Parmenides (1942–43), but equally relevant to his "The Origins of a Work of Art," in Martin Heidegger, *Poetry, Language, Thought* (New York: Harper, 1971). Conversely, Heraclitus of Ephesus (c.535–c.475 BCE) claimed that everything changes and is constantly in a state of flow, in a perpetual state of transformation. Heidegger again addressed this subject in his Heraclitus Seminar (1966–67).

6   Warren Neidich, *Blow-Up: Photography, Cinema and the Brain* (New York: D.A.P. Publishers, 2003).

7   I emphasise the word "vital" not in its Drieschian "spiritual" sense of a separate internal perfecting principle, but its literal meaning of belonging to and relating to life, its energy and function; contributing to life, containing life: living. But also necessarily as capable of life, in terms of a contemporary meaning of entelechy as mind and consciousness: a unity of mind and mechanism that realizes or makes actual what is otherwise merely potential.

8   Vilém Flusser, "The Gesture of Photography," in *Towards a Philosophy of Photography* (London: Reaktion Books, 2000), p. 33: "The acts of resistance on the part of culture, the cultural conditionality of things, can be seen in the act of photography, and this can, in theory, be read off from the photographs themselves."

9   Louis August Blanqui, *L'Éternité par les astres* (Paris, 1872).

10   Friedrich Wilhelm Nietzsche (1844–1900), *Daybreak: Thoughts on the Prejudices of Morality* [*Morgenröte. Gedanken über die moralischen Vorurteile*] (Cambridge and London: Cambridge University Press, [1881] 1982); and *Thus Spoke Zarathustra: A Book of All and None* [*Also sprach Zarathustra: Ein Buch für Alle und Keinen*] (Harmondsworth: Penguin, [1883–85] 1961).

11   Eduardo Cadava, *Words of Light; Theses on the Photography of History* (Princeton and London: Princeton University Press, 1997).

12   Walter Benjamin, "The Work of Art in the Age of Mechanical Reproduction," in *Illuminations* (London: Fontana, [1973] 1992), pp. 211–42; and "A Short History of Photography," in *One Way Street and Other Writings* (London: Verso, 1985), pp. 240–57.

13   Walter Benjamin, *The Arcades Project* (Cambridge, MA and London: Harvard University Press, 1999), pp. 25–6. "Men of the nineteenth century, the hour of our apparitions is fixed forever, and always brings us back to the very same ones."

14   Cadava, op. cit., p. 33.

15   Traditionally, 1839 is set as the historical moment that initiates photography (though not without earlier experimentation), its founders being the Frenchmen Louis Daguerre (1767–1851) and Joseph Niépce (1765–1833), and the Englishman William Henry Fox-Talbot (1800–77). Recently, several artists including Chuck Close and Adam Fuss, among others, have reintroduced the daguerrrotype process into their artworks.

16   Franz Joseph Gall (1758–1828), neuro-anatomist and physiologist, was the first scientist to develop and publish theories of brain localization. Around 1800, he developed a system in Paris called cranioscopy, a method to determine the personality and development of mental and moral faculties on the basis of the external shape of the skull. It was later given the name of phrenology, and it is important to stress that Gall was a serious scientist who was not responsible for turning the system into the pseudo-parlour game that it subsequently became.

17   Johann Gaspar Spurzheim (1776–1832) coined the term "phrenology" and was a great popularizer of the movement after he arrived in Paris in 1807. He died of typhoid in Boston in 1832, where his skull, brain, and heart were preserved, and was so celebrated that the Bostonians gave him a public funeral and commissioned a cemetery monument for him at Mount Auburn, Cambridge, Massachusetts.

18   Anne Maxwell, *Picture Imperfect: Photography and Eugenics, 1870–1940* (Brighton: Sussex Academic Press, 2008).

19   Francis Gall (1822–1911). The term "eugenics" was first coined in Gall's *Inquiries into Human Faculty and its Development* (London: Macmillan, 1883), p. 199.

20 For a pictorial overview, see *L'âme au corps:
    arts et sciences 1793–1993* (Paris: Grand Palais,
    Paris, Réunion des Musées Nationaux, Gallimard/
    Electra, 1993) and *Wunderblock: Eine Geschichte der
    modernen Seele* (Vienna: Messepalast, 1989).

21 Jean Martin Charcot (1825–93), known as the
    founder of modern neurology, and whose students
    included Sigmund Freud, Joseph Babinski, Pierre
    Janet, William James, Pierre Marie, Alfred Binet,
    Georges Gilles de la Tourette, and numerous
    others who form the founding figures of modern
    dynamic psychology and psychoanalysis. He is most
    known, however, for the photographed "hysterical"
    performances that were later debunked. See J.
    Bogousslavsky (ed.), *Following Charcot: A Forgotten
    History of Neurology and Psychiatry (Frontiers of
    Neurology and Neuroscience)* (Basel: Karger Pub.,
    2010).

22 Hippolyte Bernheim (1840–1914), Head of the
    Nancy School of Psychiatry and Neurology, was
    an influential figure who developed psychological
    theories of suggestibility, and was a critic of Charcot
    and his methods. See *Suggestive Therapeutics: A
    Treatise on the Nature and Uses of Hypnotism [De la
    Suggestion et de son Application à la Thérapeutique]*
    (New York: G. P. Putnam's Sons, [1883] 1889), and
    *New Studies in Hypnotism [Hypnotisme, Suggestion,
    Psychothérapie: Études Nouvelles]* (New York:
    International University's Press, [1891] 1980).

23 Dr. James Braid (1795–1860) first coined the
    term "hypnotism" for what was formerly called
    animal magnetism in his lectures of 1841–42, and
    is seen as the founder of hypnotherapy. The word
    "hypnotism" means, literally, "nervous sleep" (sleep
    of the nerves).

24 Guillaume-Benjamin-Amand Duchenne (de
    Boulogne) (1806–75), *De l'Électrisation localisée et
    de son application à la physiologie, à la pathologie et
    à la thérapeutique* (Paris, 1855); *Mécanisme de la
    physionomie humaine, ou Analyse électro-physiologique
    de l'expression des passions applicable à la pratique
    des arts plastiques* (Paris, 1862); and *Physiologie des
    mouvements démontrée à l'aide de l'expérimentation
    électrique et de l'observation clinique, et applicable
    à l'étude des paralysies et des déformations* (Paris,
    1867).

25 Dr. Jules Baillarger (1809–90) was probably one
    of the first to make portraits of the mentally ill in
    the early 1840s in Paris, immediately following the
    founding of photography. But the best-known early
    portraits were taken by Dr. Hugh Welch Diamond
    (1809–86) at the Surrey Asylum in England in 1848–
    58. Diamond was an amateur photographer who
    began photographing three months after Fox Talbot
    unveiled his new calotype photographic system, and
    was the first Secretary of the Photographic Society
    (founded 1853) and the editor of its journal. See
    Sander L. Gilman, *The Face of Madness: Hugh W.
    Diamond and the Origin of Psychiatric Photography*
    (New York: Citadel Press, 1986).

26 Cesare Lombroso (1835–1909) was the founder
    of criminal anthropology and his theories stated
    that criminality was inherited, and that someone
    who was a "born criminal" could be identified by
    physical defects which confirmed a criminal, as in a
    savage or atavistic being; the measurement system
    he developed was called anthropometry. Lombroso
    was among the most famous men in Europe in
    the second half of the nineteenth century, and his
    Research Institute still exists in Turin. The subject
    of criminal degeneracy and subsequently Social
    Darwinism was a huge area of research in the years
    following Benedict Augustin Morel's (1809–73)
    coining of the term "degeneracy" in 1857 (*Traité des
    dégénérescences physiques, intellectuelles et morales
    de l'espèce humaine et des causes qui produisent
    ces variétés maladives*), as it related to progressive
    mental degeneration. He was also the alienist who
    coined the term "dementia praecox" (1860), later
    renamed "schizophrenia" by Eugen Bleuler (1911).

27 Societies of Psychical Research and their
    publications were founded across Europe and the
    USA in the 1880s and 1890s (London, 1882).
    G. W. H. Myers, and the philosophers William
    James and Henri Bergson, were all members. The
    distinction between dynamic psychology and
    psychical research (now called parapsychology)
    was not clearly established. For photographic
    examples of the research, and so-called ectoplasm
    photography, see *Im Reich der Phantome: Fotographie
    des Unsichtbaren*, ex. cat. (Mönchengladbach:
    Stadtisches Museum Abteiberg, 1998).

28 Wilhelm Conrad Röntgen's (1845–1923)
    first developed X-ray was of his wife's hand
    on December 22, 1895, and the first public
    presentation was in a lecture on January 23, 1896.

See Bettyann Holtzmann Kevles, *Naked to the Bone: Medical Imaging in the Twentieth Century* (Camden, NJ: Rutgers University Press, 1996).

29 Blanqui took part in the armed insurrection in Paris in 1839 (May 12–13), and was a leading member of the Société des Saisons; as a result he was sentenced to death in 1840, later commuted to life imprisonment. The oath of allegiance to the Société stated that members were to kill the aristocracy of birth and the bourgeois aristocracy of money that had replaced it.

30 In this we need not be surprised, since Benito Mussolini (1883–1945), Italy's fascist dictator, was profoundly influenced by both Blanqui and Nietzsche, and an epigraph of Blanqui adorned *Il Popolo d'Italia*, the Italian fascist newspaper.

31 The participant-performances took place at Maison Gregoire, Brussels, December 5, 2009; Kunsthalle Athena, Athens, May 2010; and at LAXART, Los Angeles, July 30–31, 2010.

32 For an overview perspective on art and language, see Charles Harrison, *Essays on Art & Language* (Cambridge, MA: MIT Press, 2003).

33 See *Live in Your Head: Concept and Experiment in Britain 1965–75*, ex. cat. (London: Whitechapel Gallery, 2000).

34 It took place at the California Museum of Photography, Riverside, 2001. The use of the term "mutated" was significant since it is generally seen as a value-free, non-teleological premise. Mutation means simply to change shape or form, usually argued as the process of natural selection, and it emphasizes a process, as distinct from evolution, which argues differentiation and gradual development.

35 Jean-François Lyotard, "Answering the Question: What is Postmodernism?," in *The Postmodern Condition: A Report in Knowledge* (Manchester: Manchester University Press, [1979] 1984), pp. 71–82; quote on p. 79.

36 Rene Cori, Daniel Lascar and Donald H. Pelletier, *Recursion Theory, Godel's Theorems, Set Theory, Model Theory* (Oxford: Oxford University Press, 2001).

37 Op. cit. The same works were later extended and installed in New York, in "Storefront for Art and Architecture," 2002.

38 Deborah Hauptmann and Warren Neidich, *Cognitive Architecture: From Biopolitics to Noopolitics: Architecture & Mind in the Age of Communication and Information* (Rotterdam: 010 Publishers, 2010).

39 "Warren Neidich in Conversation with Hans Ulrich Obrist," in *Earthling* (New York: Painted Leaf Press, 2005), pp. 13–21, quote on p. 14.

40 Less common today, artistic culture and cafes largely belong to an earlier "*flaneur*" time period, where the supposition of a continuous temporality was more secure. See Marc Augé, "From Places to Non-Places," in *Non-Places: Introduction to An Anthropology of Supermodernity* (London: Verso, 1995), pp. 75–120.

41 Herbert Marcuse, *One-Dimensional Man* (Boston: Beacon, 1964). He argues that the ideology of advanced industrial society produces false needs, false consciousness, and one-dimensional mass consciousness. This was extended to society in the online essay "One-Dimensional Society": "A comfortable, smooth, reasonable, democratic unfreedom prevails in advanced industrial civilization, a token of technical progress. Indeed, what could be more rational than the suppression of individuality in the mechanization of socially necessary but painful performances; the concentration of individual enterprises in more effective, more productive corporations; the regulation of free competition among unequally equipped economic subjects; the curtailment of prerogatives and national sovereignties which impede the international organization of resources." Available online: http://igw.tuwien.ac.at/christian/marcuse/odm1.html.

42 Michel Foucault, *The Order of Things: An Archaeology of the Human Sciences* (London: Tavistock Publications, 1970). An important discursive argument (though now largely assimilated) that opened up the discourse on the history and shifts that take place in the history of scientific consciousness.

43 The installation and exhibition took place at Magnus Müller Gallery, Berlin, 2008.

44 Peter Weibel and Gregor Jansen (eds), *Light Art from Artificial Light: Light as a Medium in the Art of the 20th and 21st Centuries* (Ostfildern: Hatje Cantz, 2006).

45 Bennett Simpson and Chrissie Iles (eds), *Dan Graham: Beyond* (Cambridge, MA and London: MIT Press, 2009).

46 John Gage, *Colour and Culture: Practice and Meaning from Antiquity to Abstraction* (London: Thames & Hudson, 1993).

47 John Gage, *Colour and Meaning, Art, Science and Symbolism* (London: Thames & Hudson, 1999).

48 Philip Fisher, "The Rainbow and Cartesian Wonder (The Aesthetics of the Rainbow)," in *Wonder, the Rainbow, and the Aesthetics of Rare Experiences* (Cambridge, MA and London: Harvard University Press, 1998). "In the aesthetics of experience the rainbow stands alongside many other candidates for wonder, for example, the night sky filled with stars" (p. 33).

49 Vilayanur S. Ramachandran, *The Emerging Mind (Reith Lectures)* (London: Profile Books, 2003); see also Vilayanur S. Ramachandran, Sandra Blakeslee and Oliver Sacks, *Phantoms in the Brain: Human Nature and the Architecture of the Mind* (London: Fourth Estate, 1999). Ramachandran's recent neurological studies of synesthesia argues the cross-activation of different sensory functions in the brain.

50 Warren Neidich, *Acceptable Differences: Pluripotentiality and Painting*, exhibition catalogue (Warren Neidich in collaboration with local artists and experts, Cultural Center of Belgrade Art Gallery, January 12–30, 2011), p. 15.

Mark Gisbourne is an ex-postgraduate lecturer at the University of London and Sotheby's Institute (affiliated Manchester University Master's Programs), an international curator, and author. As an art historian and critic, his academic writings and art criticism are found in many international art publications. His books include *Berlin Art Now* (Thames & Hudson, English and German editions, 2006), *Double Act: Two Artists One Expression* (Prestel, German and English editions, 2007), *TERRAE "Manel Armengol"* (Turner Books, English and Spanish editions, 2010), *Martin Assig; Vasen, Gipfel, Menschen* (Schirmer/Mosel, English and German, 2010). He has also made numerous contributions to recent books and catalogues, including essays on Photography and Brasilia, Polish Contemporary Art, Socialist Realism in the GDR (an essay contribution for the Soviet Socialist Realism exhibition currently in the Palazzo delle Esposizioni, Rome), and written essays for institutions in New York, St Petersburg, and Beijing. He lives and works in Berlin.

**Photography &
Culture**

Volume 5—Issue 1
March 2012
pp. 77–80

DOI:
10.2752/175145212X13233396185116

One Photograph

Life on the Floor

Marjolaine Ryley

My grandmother still recounts, with some delight, how horrified she was the first time she visited my "dropped out" parents. "How very sad it was," she recalls, that my bed consisted of "a mattress on the floor." My parents had begun squatting in 1974 and I was born in a communal squat in South London. Squatting; the very word seems to imply a primal human impulse to shrink down and hug the ground, an alien experience for most of us urban chair-dwellers. What did a childhood spent "on the floor" mean to me? In *Villa Mona—A Proper Kind of House* I questioned the experience of visiting a family holiday home in Belgium, where the interior spaces were defined through the layout of the furniture and the "proper" rituals of bourgeois life. So very different was spending time at Villa Mona compared with my home environment that my mother remembers me declaring: "Furniture is something I aspire to!"

Yet I have come to view my "life on the floor" in a different way. My current work *Growing Up in the New Age* was born during a residency at Braziers' International Artists' Workshop, Braziers' Park. Spending two weeks removed from my normal life, residing in a commune, surrounded by bountiful gardens and the fields of the Oxfordshire countryside and immersed within a highly creative environment, long-buried memories from my childhood emerged. Shades of green, sunlight, water, rambling gardens, mud, woven rugs, vegetables, flowing skirts, and charcoal-blackened pots—all writ within my own eyelids. Shortly after going to Braziers' Park, I wrote the following text:

> You lay, belly down, the sun feeling its way between the stems of long grass, wasps buzzing dangerously nearby, camera before you. You felt yourself remember in some deep recess of your soul, yes that was the word that came to mind, your soul was being revived, stirred, called. You were remembering the person you had chosen to ignore. So how could that spirited, anarchistic child full of self-assurance, joy, energy and a dictionary of swear words no child should know, have turned into a conformist member of society with a nine-to-five job and a mortgage. You are living the wrong life. There it was as clear as the shooting stars that you had watched the night before as you lay on the grass, staring up at the clear skies with two other momentary kindred spirits. And just as the gypsy

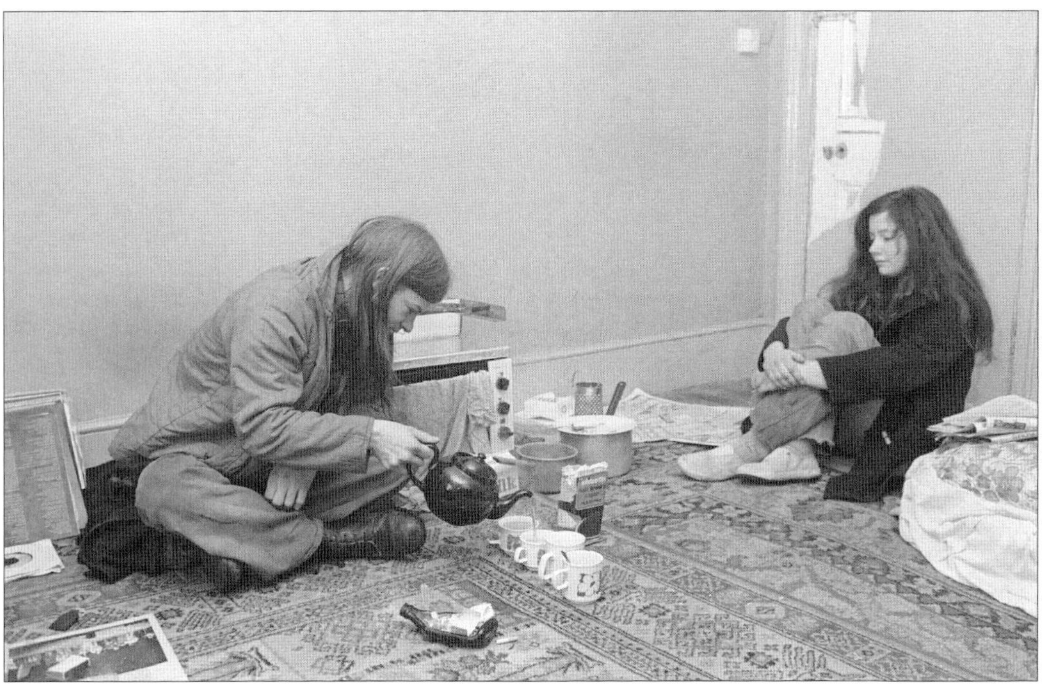

Fig I Dave Walkling, *Kevin and Anna*, Anerley, South London, 1979.

fortune-teller you had dressed as on the theme night of "Come as Your Alternative Profession" seemed eerily to have the gift of "sight" as she read people's cards, so you now had the gift of insight, the gift that so many had sought through these very same means.

It appeared that there was something in my parents' furniture-less way of life that I had perhaps been too quick to judge, an elusive key to personal freedom, and one that I had nearly thrown away. Whatever the cost I had to get out and, metaphorically speaking, to let go, drop out, and lie back down on the floor again.

Growing Up in the New Age is my searchlight. It illuminates parts of the past, some beautiful, effervescent, magical. Haunting and tantalizing visions of past utopias are fleetingly revealed. And then the light disappears for a while and into darkness it all falls. That past can become very dark indeed; it was not all a paradise lost, but an emotionally twisted time, full of complex social struggles, disintegrating relationships, spirtual awakenings, and journeys to the edge of madness. And then a familiar alchemy takes place as these histories are absorbed and reborn in my writing and photogaphs. They free my past. There is no need for concrete answers. It is enough just to gaze.

Along this journey the searchlight fell upon the photographic archive of Dave Walkling. This photograph was taken by him in 1979 while he was living as a squatter. He shows us two young people (who look about the same age as my parents would have been) living life on the floor. Yet this beautiful ritual of tea with a "proper" teapot seems to elevate them above floor level. Or perhaps the status of the floor itself is transformed: into a magic carpet which gently levitates. For me this remarkable photograph is an image of freedom (both spiritual and material), not of poverty. This image might just reassure my grandmother. Do not be sad; look—they were happy on the floor.

Marjolaine Ryley is an artist working with photography, moving image, text, and archival materials. She teaches part-time at the University of Sunderland. Dave Walkling is a photographer who has documented countercultural South London in the 1970s and 1980s, building up an extensive archive. Field Study 15, *Growing Up in the New Age* brings together the work of both Ryley and Walkling, exploring the interwining strands of their work and lives. More images can also be viewed on the project's website: www. growingupinthenewage.org.

Photography & Culture   Volume 5   Issue 1   March 2012, pp. 77–80

CREATIVE INDUSTRIES
Critical Readings

Edited by Brian Moeran and Ana Alacovska

A LIBRARY MUST-HAVE!

Creative Industries: Critical Readings brings together the key writings – drawing on both journals and books – to present an authoritative and wide-ranging survey of this emerging field of study.

The set is presented with an introduction and the writings are divided into four volumes, organized thematically:

Volume 1: Concepts – focuses on the concept of creativity and the development of government and industry interest in creative industries.

Volume 2: Economy – maps the role and function of creative industries in the economy at large.

Volume 3: Organization – examines the ways in which creative institutions organize themselves.

Volume 4: Work – addresses issues of creative work, labour and careers.

This major reference work will be invaluable to scholars in economics, cultural studies, sociology, media studies and organization studies.

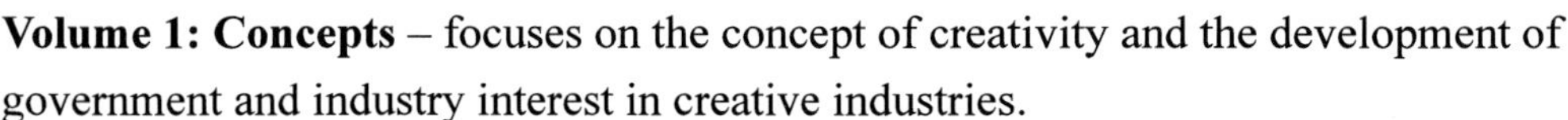

OCT 2011 • 1,600 pp • 244x172mm
HB SET 978 1 84788 778 8 **£550**

Also available:

ADVERTISING: Critical Readings
Edited by Brian Moeran

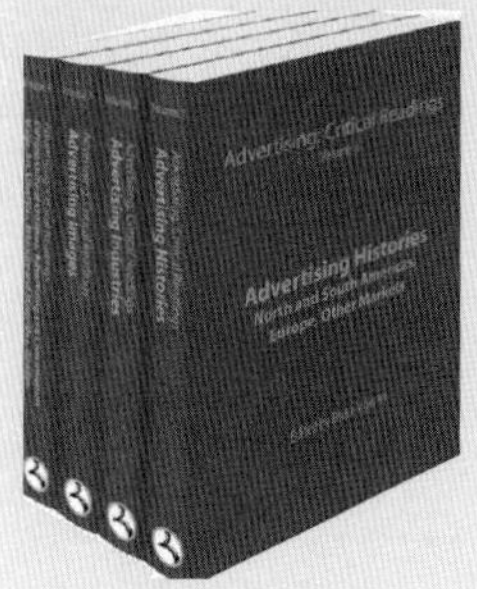

A multi-volume collection for scholars of the key writings - from Communications, Business as well as Media writing - on Advertising.

Vol I: History; Vol II: Industry; Vol III: Communication; Vol IV: Culture.

2010 • 1,600pp • 244x172mm
HB SET 978 1 84788 550 0 **£595.00**

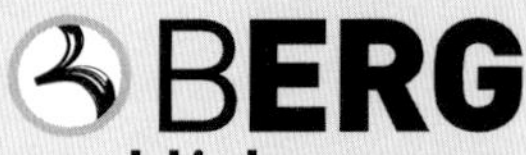

Order online at www.bergpublishers.com

Photography & Culture

Volume 5—Issue 1
March 2012
pp. 81–88

DOI:
10.2752/175145212X13233396185198

Reprints available directly from
the publishers

Photocopying permitted by
licence only

Portfolio

"Resort 1"

Anna Fox

Keywords: documentary photography, photographs of the
English seaside, Butlin's, large-format practice, new color
photography, collaborative practice, John Hinde Studio

"Resort 1" is a series of photographs, the result of two years'
practical exploration and research in 2009–11, concerned with
photographing the contemporary face of Butlin's, Bognor Regis.
Observing and recording some of its most recent developments,
I have considered the new ways in which the Butlin's resort is
providing a leisure environment for public consumption.

Initial research for the project was conducted using a number
of different methods: gaining access to the Butlin's archive and
examining photographic material there; discussions with past
employees and holidaymakers, investigating personal memory;
discussion with the current commercial owners, identifying their
ambitions for the resort; examination of past documentary
representations of the British seaside; and practical research with
different film types, cameras, and production techniques.

One key body of photographic work that stood out as
profoundly different in the historical research was the work made
by the John Hinde studio in the late 1970s, created as a result of
a commercial commission from Butlin's. These highly staged and
colorful photographs were made on a large-format camera by a
team of photographers and assistants and with the collaboration
of the company, which assisted in the setting of scenes and the
coordination of models. One of the Hinde photographers talks
about how the walls of each set were paper-thin and if you
leaned on them, you were likely to fall through. Although today
the walls between sets are not so flimsy there is still a sense, as
you roam the site, that you are moving from one theater stage to
another and certainly in the few chalets that remain (soon to be
replaced by another new hotel) the walls are not in the slightest bit
soundproofed.

After a series of early visits with one assistant, a medium-
format camera, portable flash, and color negative film, I came up
with a series of portraits made at the relatively recently launched
adults' weekend parties that happen on weekends about once a

month. These portraits possess a sense of the carnivalesque and, through the use of directed flash, isolate the characters in their burlesque costumes against darkened backgrounds of the resort environment. Frequently, men dressed as women and huge stag and hen parties rolled from bar to bar advertising themselves via slogans and phone numbers on their T-shirts. My intention had been to work in the manner I had developed for earlier portrait work, such as *Zwarte Piet* (1994–99) and *Back to the Village* (1999–2006), a manner which helped to emphasize the performative aspect of the subject.

Later analysis and reflection of these early shoots, as well as discussion with Butlin's (one of the main sponsors of the project), led me to reconsider this approach particularly for the exhibition series, which is distinct from the proposed content of the two albums, "Resort 1" and "Resort 2," which will form the basis of the publication and represent the family breaks and adults' weekends in separate volumes.

I started to photograph more of the family holidays and was acutely aware of the difficulties of making documentary photographs in this context. In a sense, the guests at the adults' party weekends, exotically dressed up, were waiting to perform for the camera, while the family holidaymakers were only planning to pose for their own private snapshots. It also became clear that the adults' weekends and the family holidays could not appear in the same space as they were such contradictory events; although they physically did happen in the same venue, this was always at different times.

My next step was to take the 5 × 4 camera and color film, with a small team of assistants, to shoot the family holidays. I have always been fascinated by the large-format documentary work made by Chris Killip; the detail achieved, while so close to the subjects, gives his photographs

a striking presence. This new approach proved incredibly difficult and the images I made rarely achieved the quality of the Killip or Hinde work. The final stage in the shooting research process was to bring in lighting director Vicki Churchill and a digital Hasselblad to back up the 5 × 4 (to ensure that an image was created in each selected location). This type of production became like a movie set and more assistants were required to manage lights as well as digital capture. The team and the team management were vitally important; first assistant Andrew Bruce and lighting director Vicki Churchill were key to both framing the image and managing the rest of the team. This was the first time I had worked in such a group and the nature of the process was quite different from the far less static approach I have been used to.

The final photos exhibited were all created in this way, with the subjects in the images being well aware that they were part of a created scene. Shooting on the 5 × 4 and digital Hasselblad gave me the scope to work in the darkroom to create large-scale prints (largest 6 × 8 ft) with incredibly sharp definition. Some digital post-production was also explored and three of the images were digitally joined using multiple negatives. The definition and scale helped to exaggerate the theatrical sense of the place, with the largest images actually appearing as if they were extensions of the gallery.

Anna Fox is Professor of Photography at University for the Creative Arts, Farnham. "Resort 1" and "Resort 2" were commissioned by Pallant House Gallery, Chichester, where it was first exhibited and sponsored by Butlin's, University for the Creative Arts, and Goldenshot. The exhibition is now on tour and opened at the James Hyman Gallery in London on October 11, 2011. "Resort 2" will be shown in 2012.

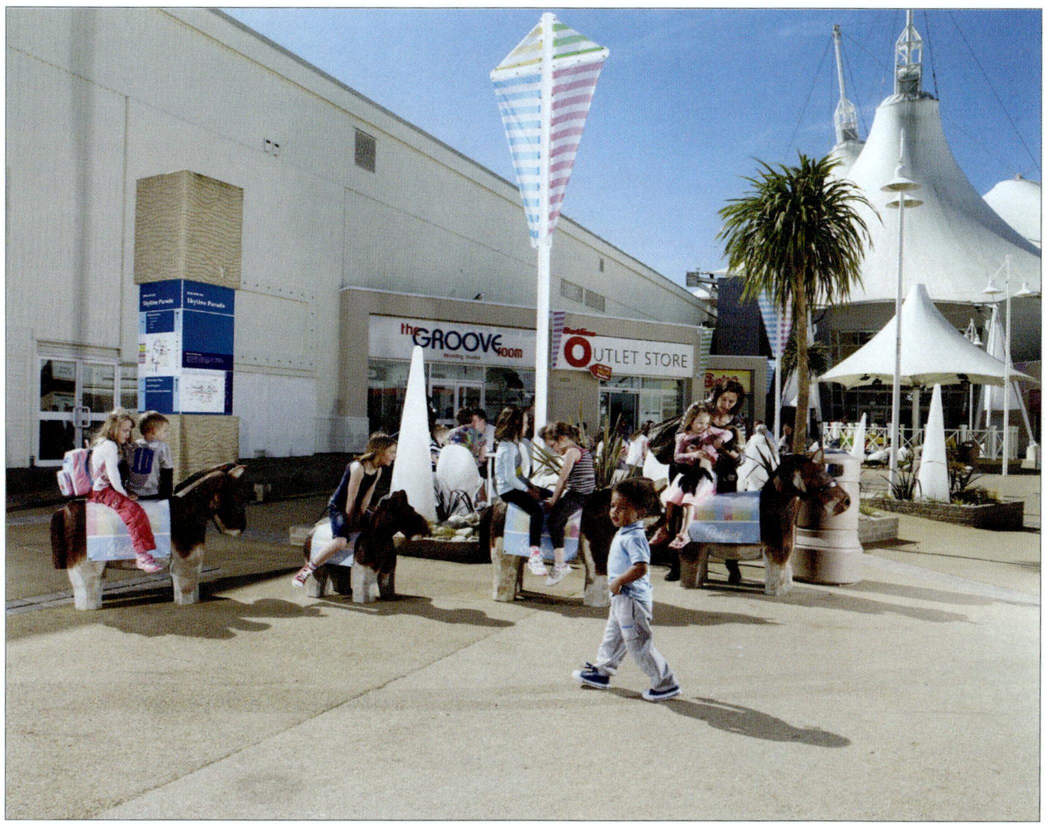

Fig I Anna Fox, *Wooden Donkeys*, 2011. From the series "Resort I," photographs of Butlin's at Bognor Regis. Courtesy of James Hyman Gallery, London.

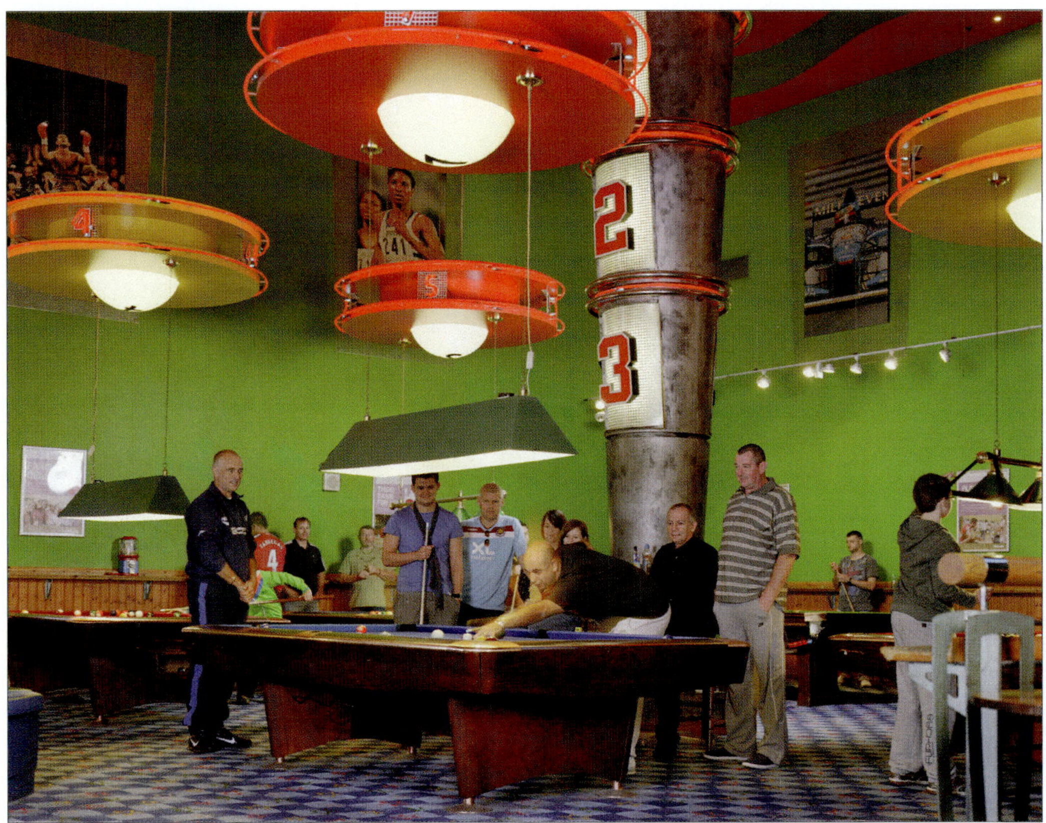

Fig 2 Anna Fox, *American Pool Hall*, 2010. From the series "Resort 1," photographs of Butlin's at Bognor Regis. Courtesy of James Hyman Gallery, London.

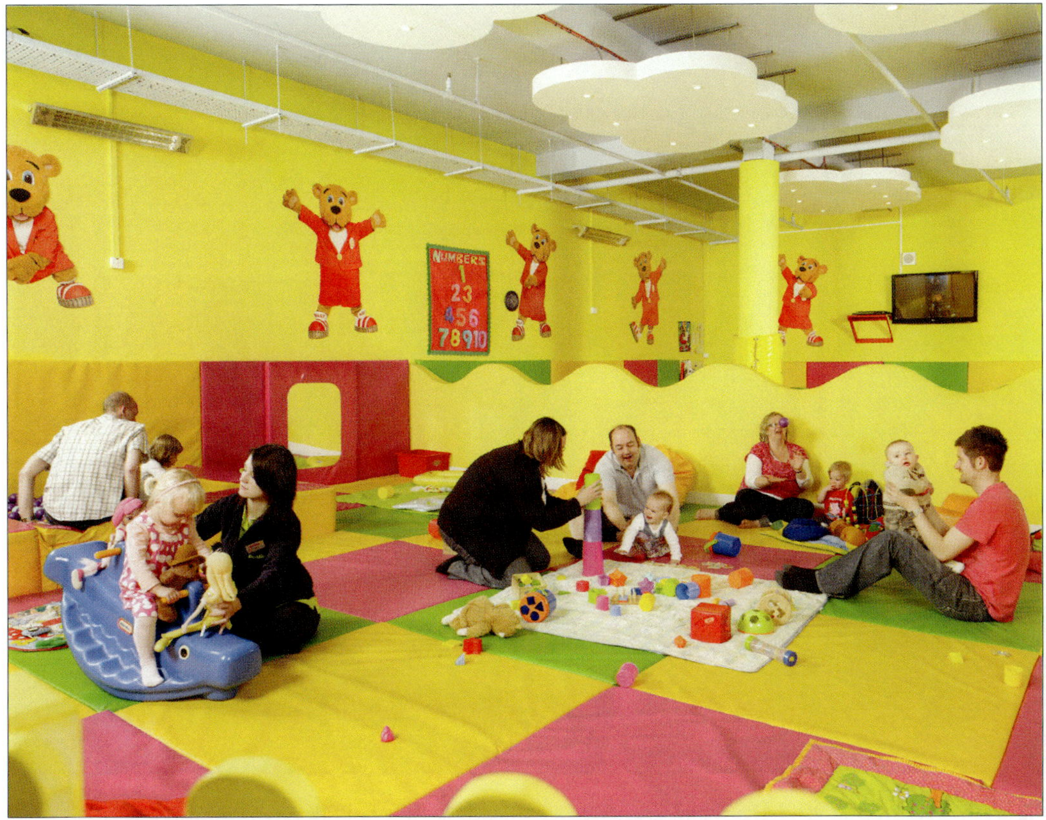

Fig 3 Anna Fox, *Billy's Buddies*, 2011. Play area for toddlers and their parents. From the series "Resort 1," photographs of Butlin's at Bognor Regis. Courtesy of James Hyman Gallery, London.

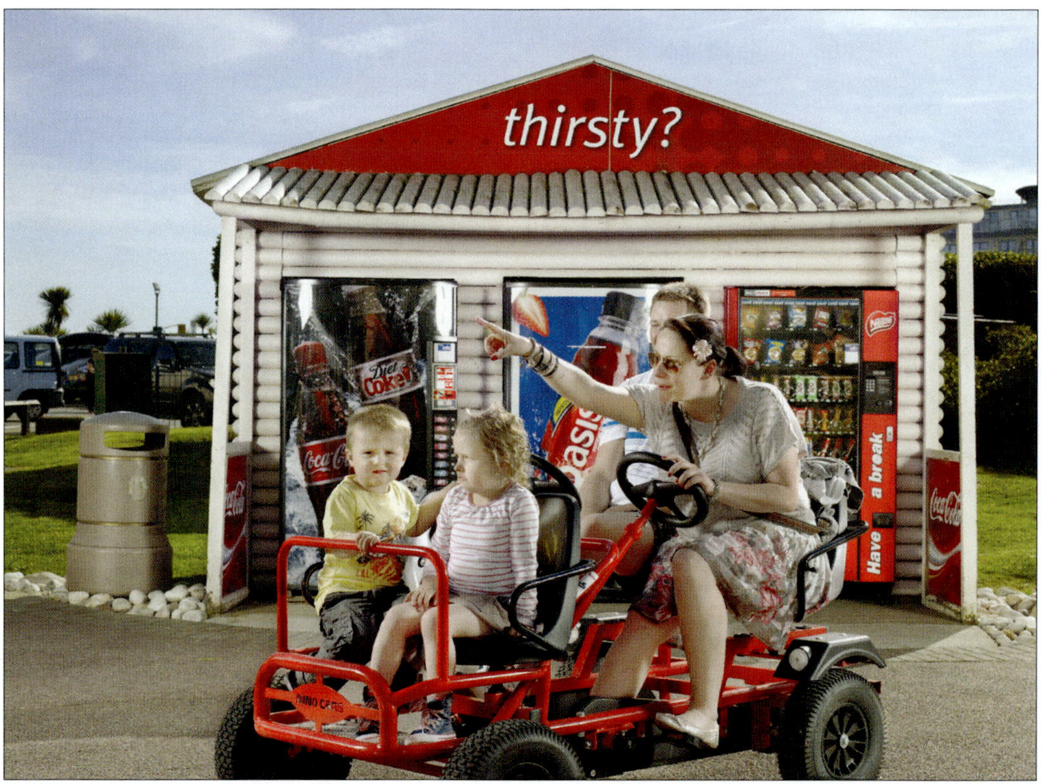

Fig 4 Anna Fox, *Family*, 2011. From the series "Resort I," photographs of Butlin's at Bognor Regis. Courtesy of James Hyman Gallery, London.

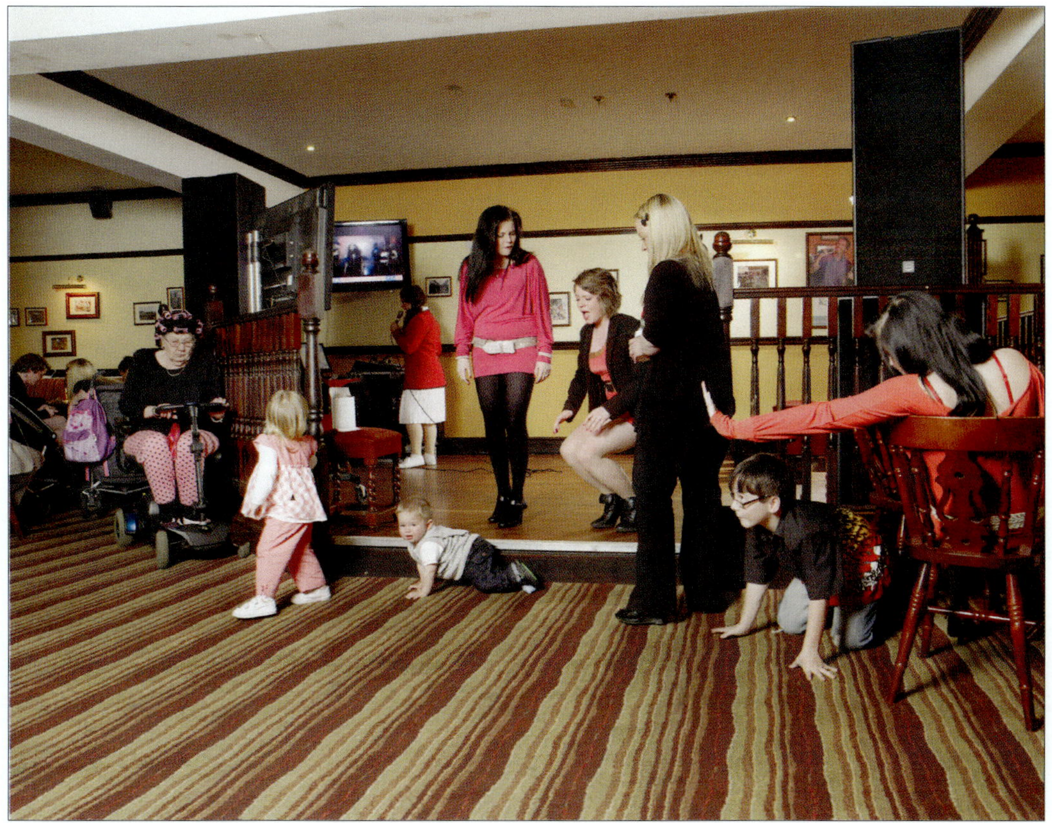

Fig 5 Anna Fox, *Karaoke Night*, 2011. From the series "Resort I," photographs of Butlin's at Bognor Regis. Courtesy of James Hyman Gallery, London.

Photography & Culture   Volume 5   Issue I   March 2012, pp. 81–88

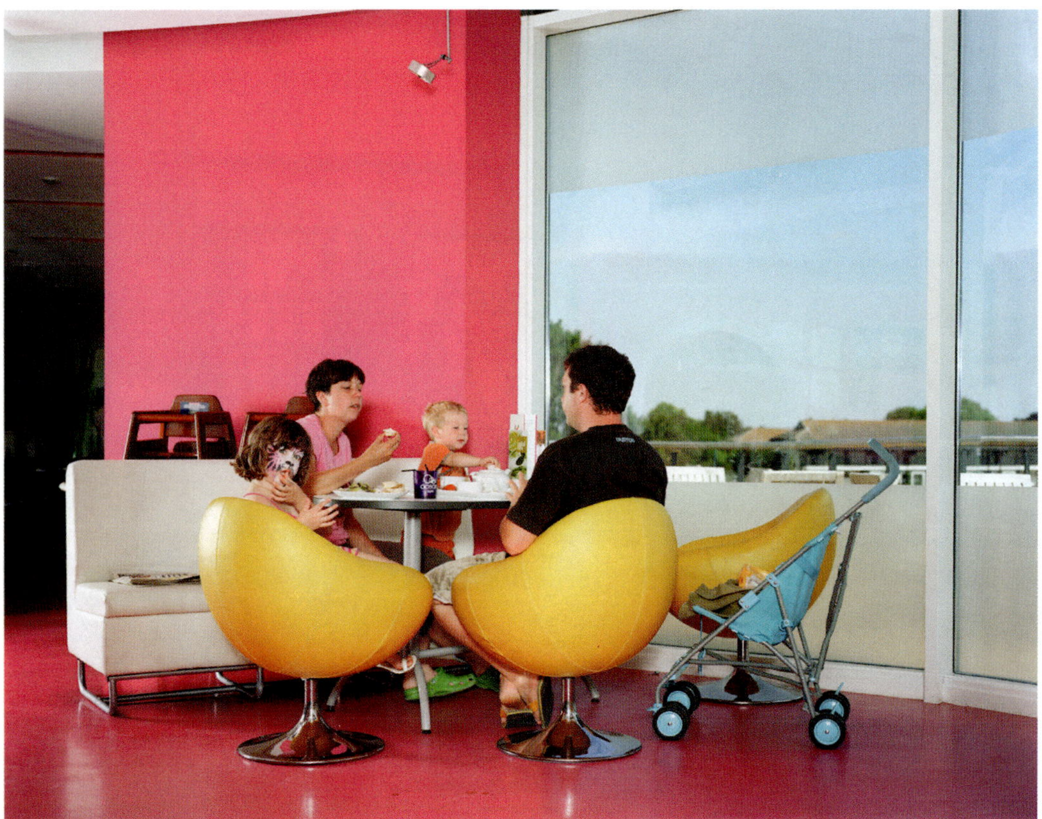

Fig 6 Anna Fox, *Ocean Hotel Restaurant*, 2011. From the series "Resort 1," photographs of Butlin's at Bognor Regis. Courtesy of James Hyman Gallery, London.

**Photography &
Culture**

Volume 5—Issue 1
March 2012
pp. 89–98

DOI:
10.2752/175145212X13233396185152

Reprints available directly from
the publishers

Photocopying permitted by
licence only

Blutsport: An Archive on the Pain of Being Proud

Brad Feuerhelm

German fencing or *Fechten* is a sport very much like any other. The principal characters remain stoically bound to the development of their skill and the fraternal admission it represents. Traditionally, the *Mensur* or duel can be found reaching its zenith in the period of roughly 1870–1945. It is mostly ascribed to being of pan-Germanic origin with a few exceptions to the east, such as Poland and Latvia. The participants in this action are predominantly male, almost without exception. It is well reported that nineteenth-century and early twentieth-century collegiate affiliations and university sports systems were relegated to the fraternal male admissions policies.

The anxiety of the sport is neither easy to interpret nor easy to reason with. The promotion of sport between males of competing positions is not one of university adversary, but rather an internal practice within each individual university. Duels were held just as often outside of the sporting arena as a way of communal male bonding through the letting of blood ritual. The young male participants in the sport were not bound to strike for the sake of physical harm or destruction, but were in effect cast as enablers of a rite of passage into German manhood through the act of drawing blood. The scars produced were gauged as a lifelong totem of the pain of exchange. To completely understand the basis of these associations, one cannot look past the Teutonic overtones of nationhood and the perceived importance of German mythos and the conjecture into spiritual advance of the Blood and Soil mentality present at the time. A prerequisite to budding neo-Aryan thought and Ariosophist engagement with the divination of racial thought and root ancestry of the Germanic people as outlined by Guido Von List, however tragic, it would blossom in the end. In this statement, I do not purport to advance the concrete terms which completed notions of the Germanic Ariosophic thought and how the sport was collectively assembled. I do, however, purport to query the ties between German blood sport, nationalism, and the esoteric tendencies found in the ritual of male pride in fraternal university sport.

The album and images within date to 1932–1933 and take place at the height of oncoming cultural anxieties personified by the coming waves of nostalgia and what would become the prewar focus on the German reevaluation of its national identity at the end of the Weimar period. The album contains roughly 120 photographs that detail the *Studentenkorp* from Kleefeld, just outside Hanover. The first words printed in the album, on typed script, read: "Mensurtag (Scar Day) April 23, '32." There are other titles throughout the album that make some conclusive thoughts about the sport itself and perhaps even the mood of the time, such as "Wie Stolz," which translates as "As Proud." This particular image depicts Herr A. B. Grun with blood streaming down the side of his neck and onto his pure white training garb. "Paukate aus" is a technical term, which I can only guess alludes to a position of the winner or perhaps a wild man in the duel. Mr. Grun stands proudly with hands on hips, full of pride and blood, if a bit camp.

The album continues through the high times of 1932 into 1934 (a very few) with much more blood and many scars, the legitimate successors. Of particular note is the joy and sense of stoic pride one can perceive in many of the post-duel snapshots, with opposing individuals linked cuff to cuff for the camera, their collective regalia and leather suits stained in viscous crimson allure, even if declared in black and white.

There are a number of non-dueling events within the album, such as weddings and social gatherings where the *Mensur* men seem to spend a healthy amount of time camping (the other camp) outdoors alongside simple interactions with the camera on the main street of the university towns. Throughout the album there are images of the young men in their student military hats and jackets, with barely a metallic accolade or button to declare their official military status; that is, until the end of the album, indicated as June 18, 1933. The following month would see Hitler destroy political opposition and separate parties within Germany, declaring them an offense to the

state. This move would coalesce all parties. The pages that follow make it clear that the saccharine days of bittersweet student dueling have ended. Their *Studentenkorp* uniforms disappear and a new uniform emerges, and the brotherhood of the saber dissolves into military columns of nationalist fervor. There is a selection of three images of the young cadets, fresh out of university, being saluted by a new commandant with a new salute (*Heil!*), wearing a red, black, and white armband. The march toward oblivion had begun. From blood-drenched affinities of male pride into the ceaseless black sun of a new and disturbing ideology which praised scars and pride, though on different bodies and for a different sense of purpose.

It would be a futile gesture to ascribe complete credence to this rendering of a handful of moments between 1932 and 1934, as it would seem too obvious for what was to be forthcoming. The gesture would also be perhaps too easy, and full of the inevitable fallacy of truth in the document. That being said, there is a semi-coherent record of not only dueling life and student fraternity, but also the lurid rise of a nationalist pride fully indoctrinated in the bloodshed of the dueling *Mensch*. Another example of history's uneven paradoxes brimming with urgeful insight into a posthumous and seemingly unhealing scar on twentieth-century social discourse and nefarious counter-beginnings in an era exemplified by blood culture and upheaval.

Brad Feuerhelm is the director of ORDINARY-LIGHT, a photographic company based in London. Although located in England, it deals globally and collaborates with individual collectors, artists, scholars, institutions, and other aficionados of photography throughout the world. It aims to present a general history of the medium while always keeping one eye on emerging talent, and exhibits at a number of art fairs. As of 2011, Brad Feuerhelm has also taken on a directorial position at Daniel Blau Ltd. in Hoxton Square, London.

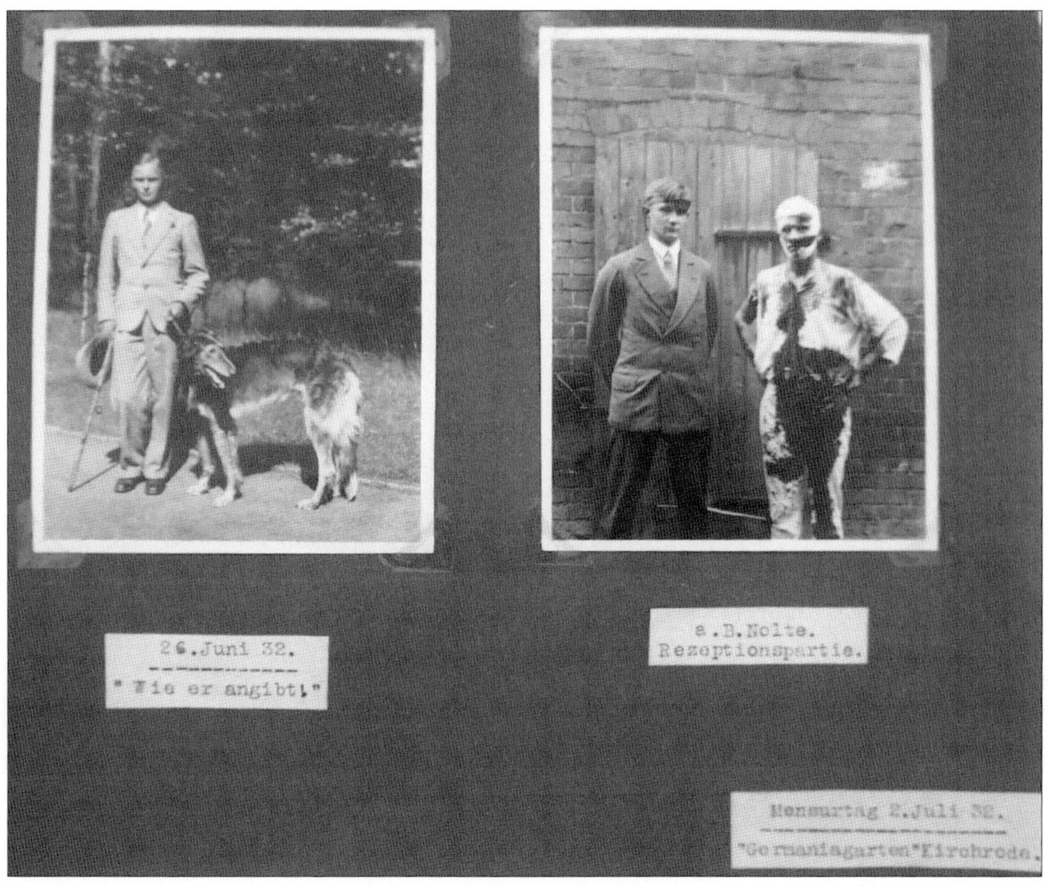
26.Juni 32.
" Wie er angibt!"
a.B.Nolte.
Rezeptionspartie.
Mensurtag 2.Juli 32.
"Germaniagarten"Kirchrode.

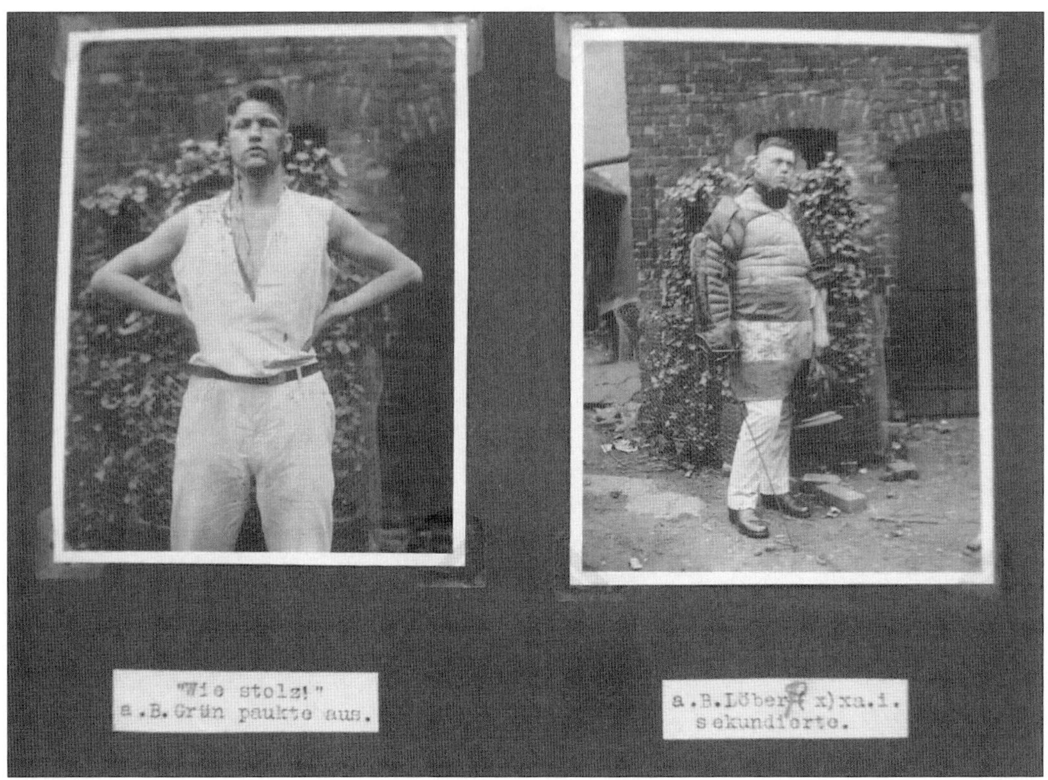
"Wie stolz!"
e.B.Grün paukte aus.
a.B.Löber x)xa.i.
sekundierte.

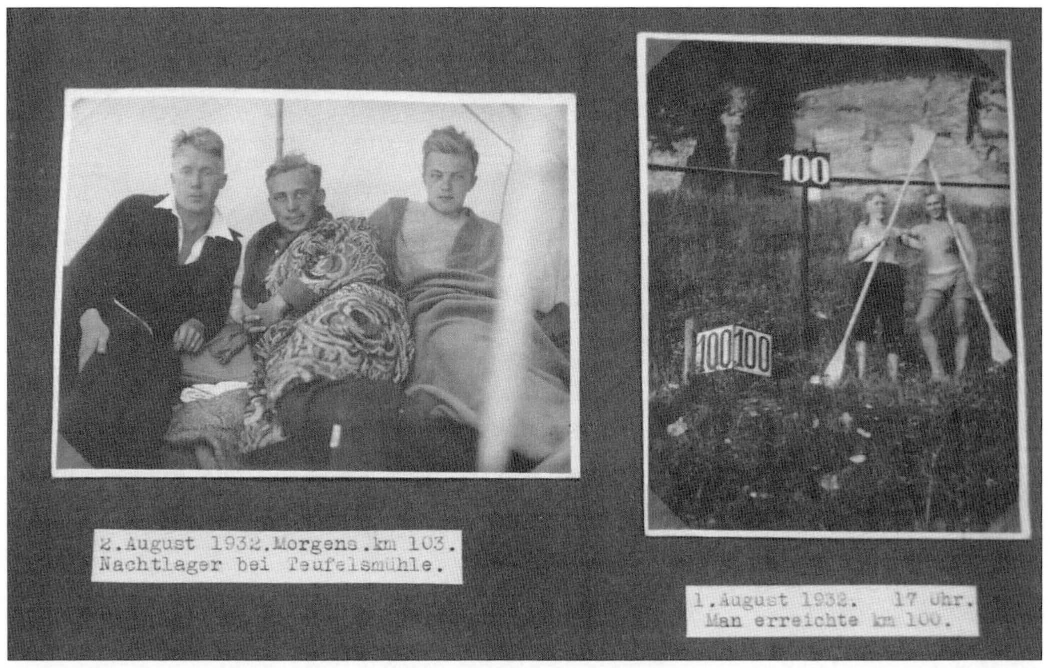

2.August 1932.Morgens.km 103.
Nachtlager bei Teufelsmühle.

1.August 1932.   17 Uhr.
Man erreichte km 100.

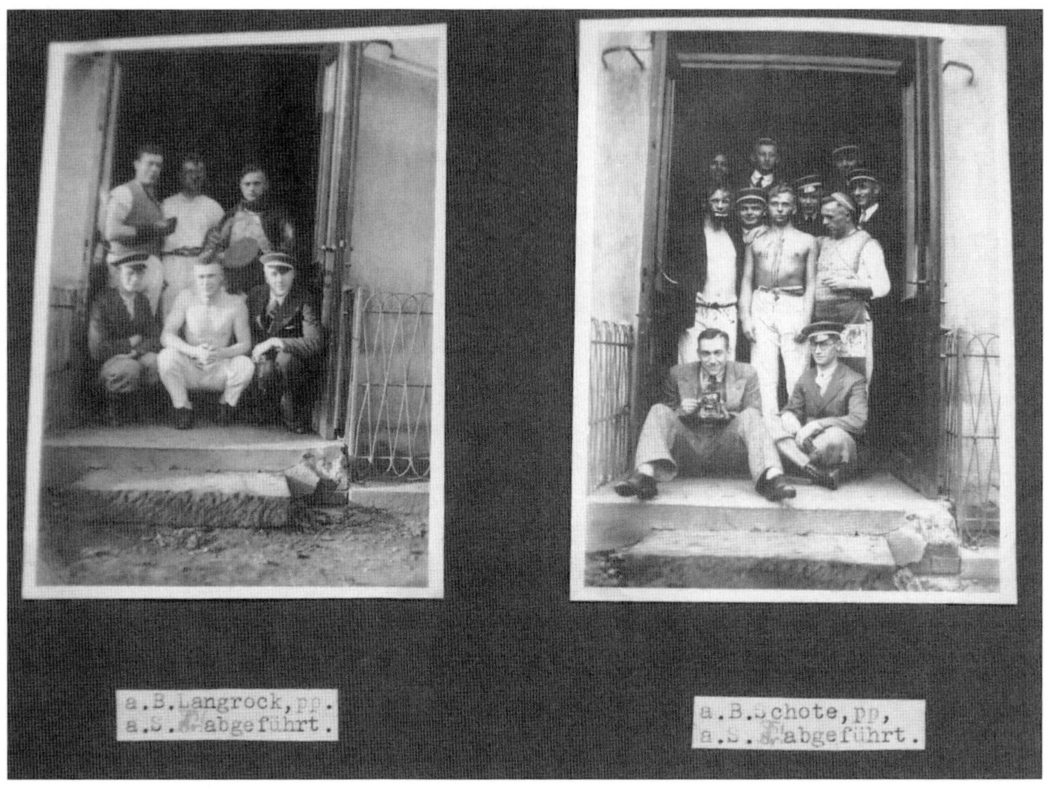
a.B.Langrock,pp.
a.S. abgeführt.

a.B.Schote,pp,
a.S. abgeführt.

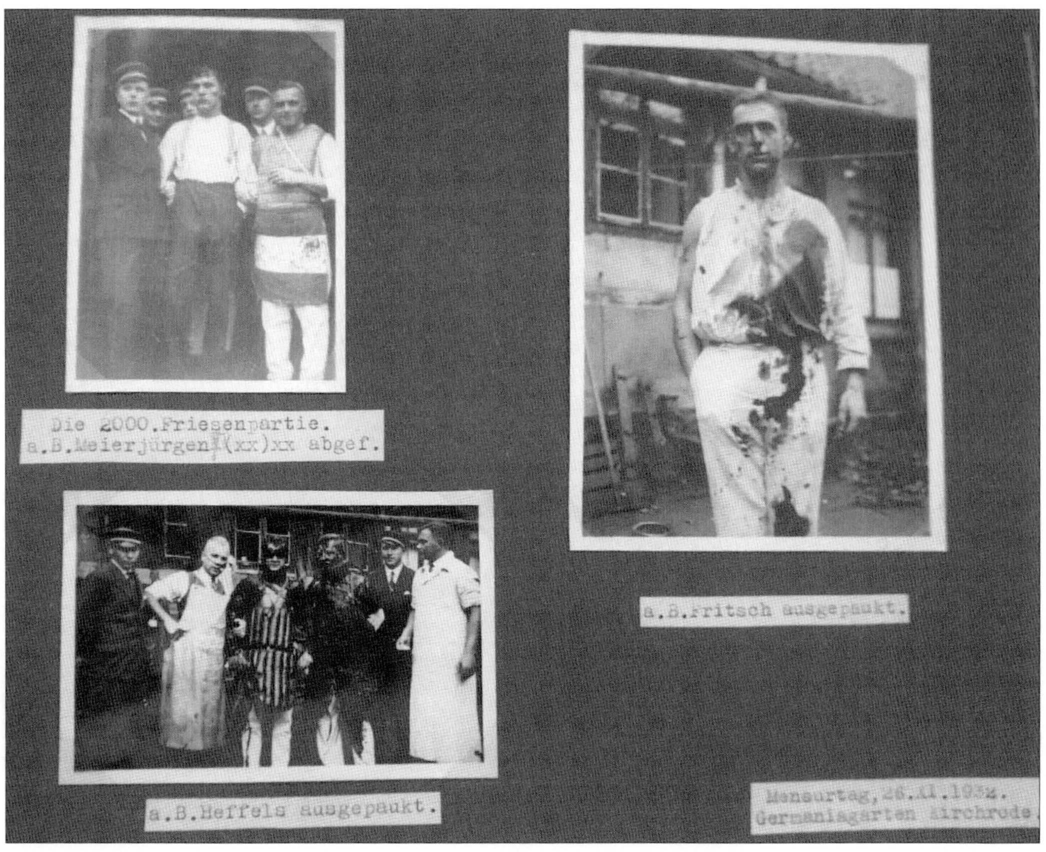
Die 2000.Friesenpartie.
a.B.Meierjürgen (xx)xx abgef.
a.B.Heffels ausgepaukt.
a.B.Fritsch ausgepaukt.
Mensurtag,26.XI.1932.
Germaniagarten Kirchrode.

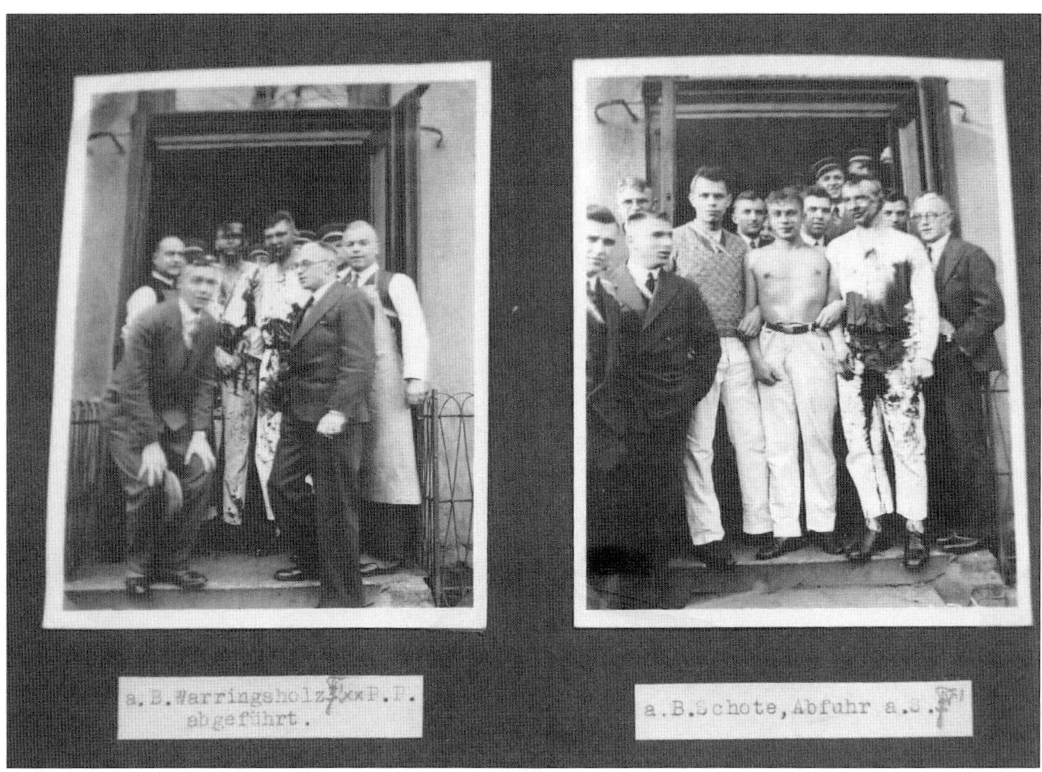
a.B.Warringsholz xx P.P.
abgeführt.

a.B.Schote,Abfuhr a.d.

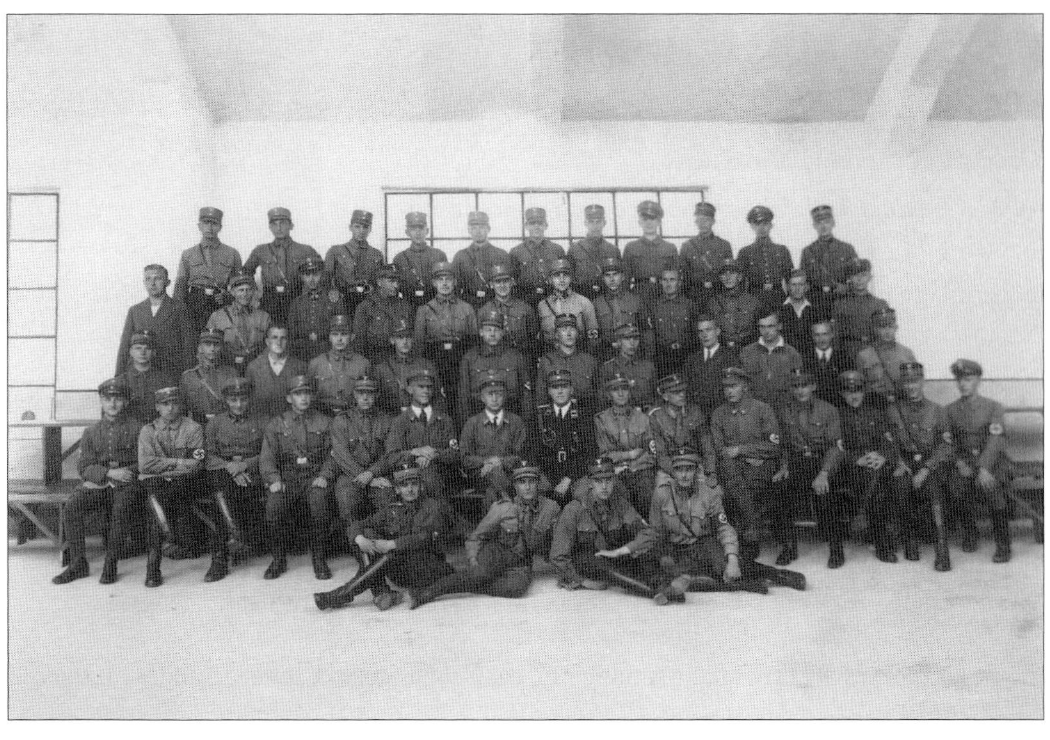
Photography & Culture   Volume 5   Issue 1   March 2012, pp. 89–98

IMAGES
Critical and Primary Sources

Edited by Sunil Manghani

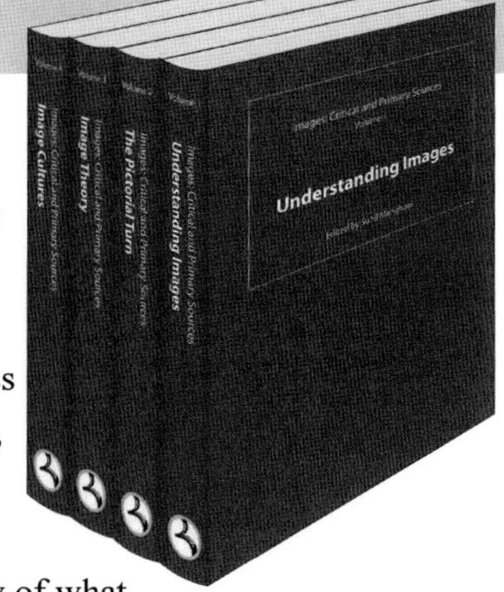

Images: Critical and Primary Sources is a major multi-volume work of reference that brings together seminal writings on the image.

Taking an interdisciplinary approach, the essays range across the domains of philosophy, history, art, aesthetics, literature, science, anthropology, critical theory and cultural studies. The essays reveal a wide set of perspectives, problematics and approaches, helping to frame a rich, encompassing view of what we can broadly term 'image studies'.

The four volumes are arranged thematically, each separately introduced and with the essays structured into specific sections for easy reference.

Volume 1: Understanding Images establishes conceptual, historical, ideological and philosophical framings for understanding and defining the image

Volume 2: The Pictorial Turn with a focus on the most enduring and constitutive question of the image: its relationship to, with and against text and textuality

Volume 3: Image Theory offers representative materials covering key theoretical approaches for analyzing, interpreting and critiquing the image

Volume 4: Image Cultures examines a wide range of social and cultural contexts of the image, which covers aspects of visual evidence, image and memory, visual methodologies, scientific imaging and the practical engagement of image-makers.

Images: Critical and Primary Sources offers a major scholarly resource for any researchers involved in the study of the image and visual culture.

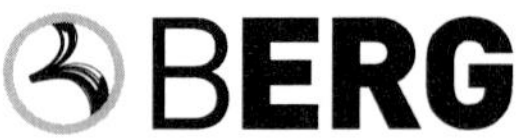

Order online at www.bergpublishers.com

**Photography &
Culture**

Volume 5—Issue 1
March 2012
pp. 99–104
DOI:
10.2752/175145212X13233396185314

Reprints available directly from
the publishers

Exhibition Review

Art and Antiquities

Sarah Pickering (2010), for *Locate*, Jerwood Space,
August 11–September 12, 2010

Reviewed by Leah Lovett

Sarah Pickering's *Art and Antiquities*, an ambitious installation
comprising photographs and objects, saw her sustained negotiation
with slippery notions of authenticity take center stage. The project
was commissioned for *Locate*, an exhibition of works developed in
response to real or imaginary sites, and was presented alongside
an immersive soundscape by Aura Satz and Mel Brimfield's video,
Four Characters in Search of a Performance (2010). The site that
Pickering took as her starting point was, in fact, another exhibition:
The Metropolitan Police's Investigation of Fakes and Forgeries (January
23–February 7, 2010). Held at the Victoria and Albert Museum,
this unusual event showcased the Art and Antiques Unit's own
investigative prowess in a presentation of faked artworks and
information detailing the means of their detection. The unlikely star
of that show, and already the subject of two separate BBC television
broadcasts, was the notorious and then incarcerated art and antique
forger, Shaun Greenhalgh.

In appropriating Greenhalgh's most infamous forgeries from
their museum context, Pickering engaged a curious (and variously
reconstructed) narrative; that of a man who, together with
his inspired elderly parents, deceived scores of specialists with
sculptures and paintings created in his garden shed-cum-studio on
a council estate in Bolton. The images and objects she presented
in the gallery resulted in part from research conducted at and
facilitated by Scotland Yard's fakes and forgeries archive, where the
fakes presented in the V&A show are permanently stored. This
source was particularly visible in a grid of nineteen scanned mini-lab
prints of amateurish photographs of a forgery, its masterly rendering
shown from all different angles propped in a brown living room.
The pictures were apparently used by the Greenhalghs in the first
instance for valuations, but in this context their copies were framed
and displayed on the far wall of the gallery. With their casually
staged subjects and curled corners (a result of the scanning process)
contradicting the uniform white frames and meticulous hang, these
prints also retained something of their status as evidence. In this
respect, they set the tone for the installation as a whole, indicating

Pickering's appeal to her viewers' sleuth-like curiosity.

Turning on conventions of appropriation advanced by artists such as Sherrie Levine and Louise Lawler, this sleuthing was directed toward the criminal but also art historical veracity of the objects represented in the gallery. As well as invoking the crime scene, Pickering's installation as a whole aped the formal language of the museum display. For instance, two sculptural versions of the *Amarna Princess*, which Greenhalgh sold to the Bolton Museum as an Egyptian antique for £440,000, were shown side by side on white plinths under perspex. If the improbable doubling of the bust shown in differing states of completion sabotaged its (singular) reality, then a glance at the labels confirmed any suspicions. Indicating as their likely provenance the BBC props department, this text at once undercut their presentation as sculptures and brought television and the BBC itself into the picture, as yet another popular, but nonetheless authoritative, site of representation.

A portentous velvet curtain hung on the wall directly opposite these two figures

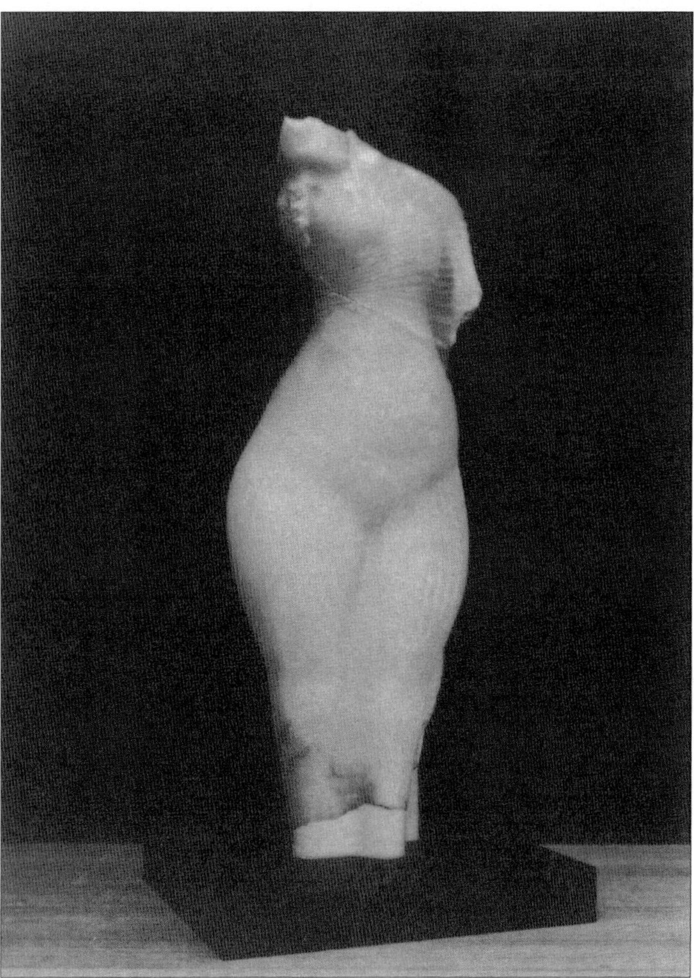

Fig 1 Egyptian Princess, Museum Collection. Salted paper print circa 1852–60. Unknown photographer. Image courtesy of the Victoria and Albert Museum, London.

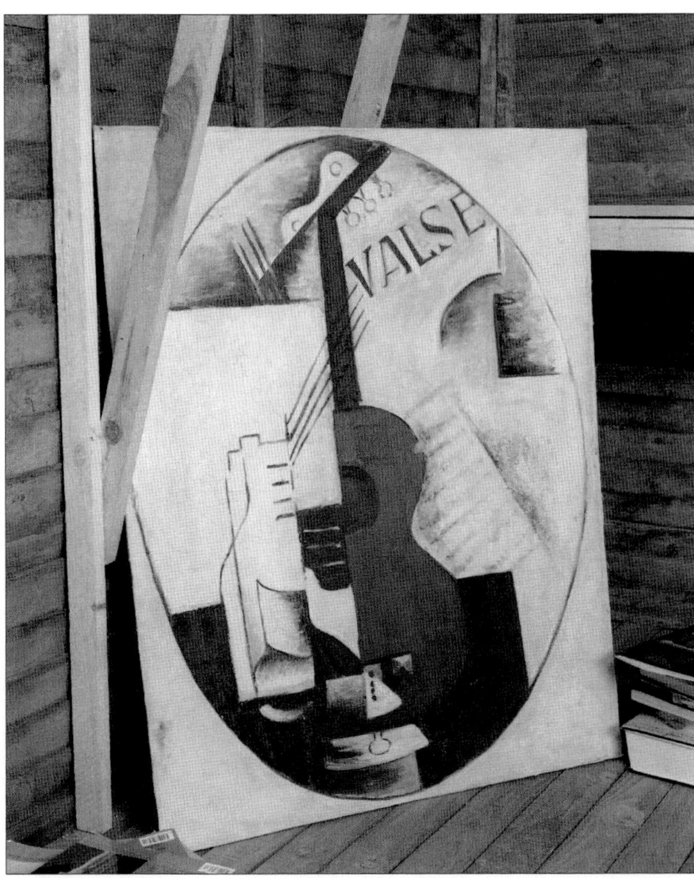

Fig 2 Cubist still life with Popova (version 2). Image courtesy of the artist and Meessen De Clercq Gallery, Brussels.

shielded a salt print, a further representation of Greenhalgh's original fake. Attributed to an "Unknown Photographer," this photograph of the *Egyptian Princess* was Pickering's most fitting homage to the forger. With its fragile materiality emphatically staged, the calotype process—the earliest positive printing technique, developed in the mid-nineteenth century by William Henry Fox Talbot—gave credence to the print's alleged date of 1852–60. An astute viewer might also have recognized the correlation here with Roger Fenton's brief but prolific photographic career, those being the precise dates during which he documented (among other things) the British Museum's collection of antiques. The

gallery caption, meanwhile, informed us that this particular photograph was on loan from the V&A. As well as further insisting upon the work's antique status, this detail recalled the Greenhalgh family's ruse of smuggling documentation into library archives to verify their forgeries. A fake enmeshed with another, Pickering's salt print augmented the Greenhalghs' historicization of their *Amarna Princess*, not to mention the mythification of the family itself, all the while depending on our doubt to achieve its cogency.

Pickering's work often turns on photography's ambiguous relationship to the real. On the one hand, the indexical veracity of her photographs insist that what we see (now) was really there (then); on the other hand, her uncanny subjects urge us to question the conditions of their framing. Her decision for this work to present *The Faun*, falsely attributed to Gauguin, via its reproduction in six separate fine art catalogs did more than convey the reach of Greenhalgh's trickery; it also undermined the very processes and structures by which authenticity is established and maintained. Almost a century ago, Walter Benjamin observed that, with mechanical reproduction, the aura associated with the "original" art object is radically superseded by the political. By showing art as already corrupted by its transmission via reproducible media, *Art and Antiquities* reinvigorated Benjamin's suggestion, and intimated the reach but also the fallibility of authority more broadly.

This understanding of the arts as socially and politically inscribed has surfaced in earlier works, not least *Public Order* (2002–5). The first of Pickering's projects to engage the authorities, this series of photographs witnesses sites of police riot training. In their description of eerily vacant streets, lined only with buildings' façades, the images simultaneously expose and destabilize the state apparatuses for maintaining civil order by lifting the curtain on the scene of rehearsal. In *Art and Antiquities*, Pickering employed reenactment, rather than the rehearsal, to defamiliarize and so reveal usually imperceptible mechanisms of power. This shift in emphasis is apt given the photograph's always past tense (albeit a past deferred to unknowable, future viewers), and as such permitted greater reflexivity, not least in enabling Pickering to implicate and problematize her own working processes and status as a fine art photographer.

Both the BBC's dramatization, which reconstructed the making of the *Amarna Princess*, and the subsequent reframing of (we assume) their copy of that sculpture within the salt print, can be understood as attempts to resurrect the forger's imitative processes. Further efforts to access Greenhalgh's experience through

reenactment were subtly dramatized by Pickering in a series of silver gelatin and C-type digital prints. Among these were two photographs of a Cubist still life painting artfully propped in a wooden shed, the black and white image more sympathetic to the historical claims of its subject than the image in color, but otherwise at first glance the same. On closer inspection, however, several clues—a stack of books that was not there before, the knots in the wood varying from one picture to the next—disclosed the distinct and therefore the sequential relationship of one setup to the other.

In fact, Pickering's reconstruction was indebted to the Metropolitan Police's decision to display Greenhalgh's work in a cleaned-up version of his studio, and thus authenticate the experience of visitors to their *Fakes and Forgeries* display. In supplementing this decision, her photographs pointed up its absurdity. Not only did their reconstruction imbue the scene of the crime with the aura of originality (I was reminded of Paolozzi's "studio" installed in the Dean Gallery, Edinburgh) but it also implied that some deeper truth, or perhaps the past itself, might be accessed through reenactment. What, then, of Greenhalgh's own attempts to reactivate the past?

If his sculptures and paintings were illegitimate, this evidently had little to do with their appearance: after all, the family's meticulously researched and executed activities remained undetected for seventeen years. Nor could it simply have been because of the works' ultimately dubious authenticity (the Greenhalghs' careful deceptions were finally undone by a spelling mistake in an "Assyrian relief"). Indeed, Pickering's installation demonstrated the extent to which reenactment—whether police reconstruction, TV dramatization, literary citation, or (recognizing herself as involved) photographic representation—is legitimated within social and cultural relations. The problems arose, she quietly insisted, with the transgression of market forces. While her own acts of appropriation were presented courtesy of her gallerist, Meessen De Clercq, Greenhalgh's activity was never sanctioned, and as a result he was eventually sentenced to four and a half years' imprisonment.

Of course, the Greenhalgh family was undeniably guilty of fraud, of knowingly committing acts of deception for financial gain. Nonetheless, situated in relation to various institutions—police, media, museum, gallery, art markets—for regulating visual culture, *Art and Antiquities* prompted us to reflect on art and its structures as active and involved in broader distributions of power. After puzzling out the "actual" status of Pickering's appropriations as reproductions of former art objects since denounced as forgeries, two thoughts persist. Firstly, what is really at stake—for artist, audience, wider society—in making and, crucially, viewing objects that have been designated as art? (To be sure, my role as writer, here, is also implicated in this question.) And secondly, with his release from prison just a fortnight before the opening of *Locate*, it will be interesting to see whether Shaun Greenhalgh's notoriety has afforded him that elusive mark of authenticity: a market value all his own.

Leah Lovett is a London-based writer and artist currently researching performance as urban activism at the Slade School of Fine Art.

Journal of the Social History Society

An invaluable source for the original study of cultural and social history

Cultural & Social History

Editors
Padma Anagol, Cardiff University, UK
John H. Arnold, University of London, UK
David Hopkin, University of Oxford, UK

"Cultural & Social History is essential for anyone who wants to follow the most recent debates on the sharpest of the cutting edges of history writing."

Lynn Hunt, University of California, Los Angeles, USA

Cultural & Social History seeks to move the traditional discipline beyond the limits of both cultural and social history by emphasizing the ways in which the social and the cultural are inextricable. It makes connections across chronological and geographical boundaries within the discipline and links across neighbouring subjects which concern themselves with the history of culture.

Cultural & Social History is the official publication of the *Social History Society (SHS)*. Join *SHS* and benefit from a wide range of membership offers.

For complete details on membership, visit the SHS website www.socialhistory.org.uk.

Expand your knowledge, widen your research!
Sign up to RSS feeds and new issue alerts at IngentaConnect.com!

Free trials available at www.ingentaconnect.com/content/berg

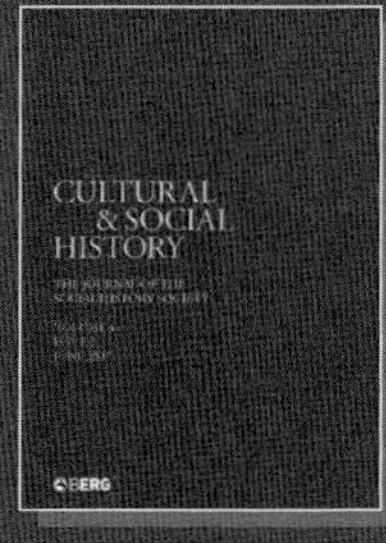
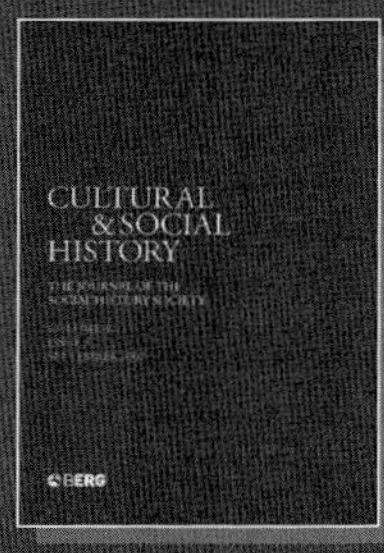
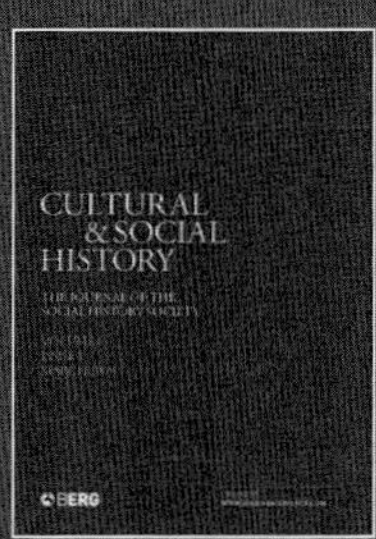

Print ISSN: 1478-0038
E-ISSN: 1478-0046

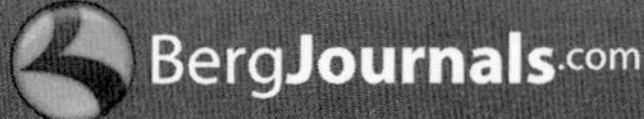

**Photography &
Culture**

Volume 5—Issue 1
March 2012
pp. 105–108

DOI:
10.2752/175145212X13233396185233

Reprints available directly from
the publishers

Delia's Tears: Race, Science, and Photography in Nineteenth-Century America

Molly Rogers

New Haven: Yale University Press, 2010

Reviewed by Shawn Michelle Smith

Molly Rogers's *Delia's Tears: Race, Science, and Photography in Nineteenth-Century America* is not a book about photography. Rather, it is a book inspired by a collection of infamous daguerreotypes—Joseph Zealy's images of South Carolina slaves, in various states of undress, made for the naturalist Louis Agassiz in 1850. Beginning with these disturbing images, Rogers sets out to determine how they came into existence in the largest sense. It is as if she has taken Pat Ward Williams's passionate cry in the face of a lynching photograph—"How can this photograph exist?"—and used it as the impetus for a wide-ranging cultural and intellectual inquiry.

To begin to answer the question of how these daguerreotypes exist, Rogers goes back to the founding of Columbia as the capital of South Carolina, where the images were made, and to the birth of Louis Agassiz, on whose behalf they were made. If one expects the book to be about the images per se, this seems a rather long and curious wind-up. But if one approaches the book as a vast social, cultural, and intellectual history, one is likely to be intrigued by the wide framing.

Delia's Tears is most successful, and indeed it is fascinating, as an introduction to nineteenth-century natural history, and as a biography of Louis Agassiz, one of the most famous natural historians of the early nineteenth century. Agassiz, born in Switzerland, was educated mostly in Germany, but was also, briefly, a student of Georges Cuvier in Paris, and eventually became a professor of natural history in the Prussian city of Neuchâtel. His first successes as a natural scientist were in studying and describing different varieties of fish. He came to the United States in 1846 in the hopes of conducting a grand expedition, but found himself caught up in a more lucrative, if less exciting, lecture circuit. American scientists were eager to consult with Agassiz on the problem of racial difference, as this was both a great scientific question and a great political concern in the 1840s. The legitimacy of slavery seemed to reside on the natural relation of the races to one another, and Americans North and South wanted to know how Agassiz would weigh in on the matter.

The broad outlines of the race and science debates of the early to mid-nineteenth century are well known. Most scholars who have written about the Agassiz/Zealy daguerreotypes have noted that they were procured as evidence to support Agassiz's theory of polygenesis, which maintained that the different races were created separately and unequally. What most do not elaborate, and what Rogers makes clear, is the degree to which Agassiz's thoughts about polygenesis were in flux over time, and actually seemed to contradict his most famous and extensive work on the "Plan of Creation," which was more consistent with his religious beliefs.

Rogers details Agassiz in all his complexity as a scientist. She situates him at the center of natural history debates, and describes his intellectual interlocutors. She discusses the American School of Ethnology, and Frederick Douglass's challenge to its claims about Negro inferiority. Moving beyond the realm of scientific discourses, she also locates the question of race politically, in the context of slave rebellions and finally the Civil War.

The book also provides an illuminating history of Columbia, South Carolina and its white male cultural, political, and intellectual elite. Seemingly peripheral figures to the study of race and natural history, such as the politician James Henry Hammond, come alive in intriguing, and

sometimes disturbing ways. Rogers situates them in a larger political landscape of racial thinking in the South, and shows how they participated in pro-slavery debates that drew upon science to argue for the natural order of slavery.

Rogers's study proposes that photographs and photographic conventions serve a wide range of cultural discourses that in turn determine much of their meaning. Because she is committed to establishing the intellectual and political milieu in which the images were made, her book implicitly argues that photographic meaning is determined by cultural context. Her explicit statements about photographic meaning, however, are more narrowly focused on individual viewers. She argues that "Meaning is contingent on the experience, knowledge, and beliefs a viewer brings to the act of looking" (246), and although she avers that "Meaning is also derived from how the images are put to use," she concludes rather too simply, "It all depends on who is looking, and why" (247). Such statements would seem to contain photographic meaning to the whims and experiences of individual viewers, but the implicit argument of Rogers's book proposes that one cannot understand photographs without understanding the cultural contexts in which they are made and circulated in considerable detail. The book suggests that larger cultural institutions and discourses, such as science and religion, powerfully shape the experience, knowledge, and beliefs of individual viewers as well as the contours of photographic meaning.

In the preface, Rogers describes her book as a "hybrid," "a blending of fiction with nonfiction writing." The fictional portions of the book are clearly delimited interludes, set off in italics between chapters, in which Rogers reproduces one of the Zealy daguerreotypes, names its subject, and imagines a scene from his or her life. These brief vignettes are beautifully written and compelling. Rogers is somewhat tentative in making her case for this imaginative work, however, for as she notes, there are important political decisions to consider in such an endeavor, especially when one is trying to imagine the experiences and thoughts and feelings of individuals who have been silenced and made largely invisible in the historical record, even as their bodies and images have been made overly visible in the service of other histories. Rogers is right to address these potential dangers directly; nevertheless, I found myself wishing she might have been bolder, taking greater risks with her imaginative experimentation, testing further the limits of historical and photographic scholarship. In the acknowledgements she notes that her first work on the daguerreotypes resulted in a play, *Natural History*, which depicts "the meeting of a daguerreotypist and an enslaved African-American woman" (341). I am curious now to read that version of this story, and to see how the narrative shifts when presented as a fully fictional account.

This is an ambitious book. Whether or not it accomplishes everything it sets forth, it does accomplish a good deal. *Delia's Tears* elaborates the intellectual and political milieu in which Joseph Zealy made a series of enigmatic daguerreotypes for the naturalist Louis Agassiz, and in which the images came to have, as they continue to have, an uncertain meaning.

Shawn Michelle Smith is Associate Professor of Visual and Critical Studies at the School of the Art Institute of Chicago. She is the author of *American Archives: Gender, Race, and Class in Visual Culture* (Princeton University Press, 1999), *Photography on the Color Line: W. E. B. Du Bois, Race, and Visual Culture* (Duke University Press, 2004), coauthor with Dora Apel of *Lynching Photographs* (University of California Press, 2007), and coeditor with Maurice Wallace of *Pictures and Progress: Early Photography and the Making of African American Identity* (Duke University Press, forthcoming 2012). She is also a visual artist and has exhibited her photo-based artwork in venues across the United States.

Photography & Culture

Volume 5—Issue 1
March 2012
pp. 109–112
DOI:
10.2752/175145212X13233396185279

Reprints available directly from
the publishers

Photocopying permitted by
licence only

Book Review

About to Die: How News Images Move the Public

Barbie Zelizer

New York: Oxford University Press, 2010

Reviewed by Kate Palmer Albers

I read Barbie Zelizer's book, *About to Die: How News Images Move the Public*, in the period following the January 8, 2011 shootings in Tucson, Arizona, where I live. I was frequently struck, in the aftermath of that terrible event, that there was not a single photograph of the shooting itself in the Safeway parking lot where nineteen people were shot, six of whom were killed. In this very public place, no witness made a record, even with a cell phone camera, of the "Congress on Your Corner" event that US Representative Gabrielle Giffords was hosting, or recorded the seconds and minutes immediately following the gunfire. Indeed, news photographers were allowed on the scene only after the paramedics had arrived, well after the shooter was tackled and stopped.

This is not to conclude that no such photographs exist, as several surveillance cameras captured video of the shootings (described verbally by law enforcement officials and, subsequently, repeated by journalists) that has not been made public. Rather, I found it surprising that in this age of ubiquitous and pervasive amateur documentation, with such ease of access to cameras, especially through the cell phones we carry everywhere, that not a single such photograph appeared in the press or was circulated through a blog or social media outlet. This void was filled by a more generalized kind of disaster photograph in the press, those of ambulances and helicopters at the scene with first-response personnel as well as "everyday" people who stepped in to help. But, by a day or so later, photographs of the victims that had been made months or years prior to the shooting, showing them smiling, healthy, and happy, began to flesh out the human face of this tragedy.

About to Die assesses and explains this phenomenon. Most of Zelizer's book is actually not devoted to photographs of people literally about to die, but to the photographs that circulate in news publications and stand as visual proxy for human death without graphically depicting dead bodies. Zelizer seeks to understand not why viewers would or would not want to confront gory and graphic images of death (though she often tracks notable moments of extreme compulsion one way or another), but why news organizations choose to print images that, far more often than not, convey open-ended ambiguity and uncertainty over their more factually certain counterparts. Ultimately Zelizer concludes that the more ambiguous and uncertain images serve a powerful function: in visually suspending what is often the already-known conclusion, these photographs get the viewer invested and involved. Rather than sealing the story's conclusion with visual certainty, the images serve an anticipatory moment, leaving the story's resolution open to question and encouraging the viewer's engagement.

Zelizer began her career as a journalist herself, and is now a professor in the Annenberg School for Communication at the University of Pennsylvania. The book covers a tremendous range of journalistic imagery, including photographs of and around genocide, famine, disease, natural disaster, shuttle explosions, suicide jumps, capital punishment, atomic bombs, terrorist attacks, and war, among other subjects. To manage this array, Zelizer breaks down the "about-to-die" photographs into three broad categories: "Presumed Death," "Possible Death," and "Certain Death." The breadth of these categories all but assures that Zelizer will have a hard time squarely dividing up particular images into one category or another, and this quickly proves to be the case. Her descriptions of the three types of images make more sense than the broad names for the categories, however. For instance, in Zelizer's definition, an image of "presumed death" will

"signal impending death through inanimate landscapes—fallen buildings, devastated physical settings, and crushed structures—but no people about to die" (76).

To this end, Zelizer analyzes illustrations of the Great Chicago Fire of 1871, photographs of the atomic clouds over Hiroshima and Nagasaki in 1945, the 1906 San Francisco earthquake, the 1937 Hindenburg explosion, the 1986 and 2003 space shuttle disasters, and the 2001 terrorist attacks in the United States. Of these last four, the Hindenburg and space shuttle disasters are subcategorized under "Presumed Death" into "Accidental Death" while the events of September 11 are subcategorized as "Intentional Death." Despite the overall strength of Zelizer's thesis—that illustrations and photographs around death are ultimately more effective in compelling viewers to engage in a news story than those photographs that bluntly describe dead bodies—the extent of this parsing becomes distracting and counter-productive. Why, a reader is left wondering, is Zelizer critical of the journalistic absence of photographs of Hiroshima's Ground Zero, when the only photographs that exist, made by Japanese military photographer Yosuke Yamahata with grievous consequences for his own health due to the extraordinary levels of radiation he encountered, were not made available to Western journalists for seven years? And what television viewer did not understand—even if we wished it otherwise—that the catastrophic 1986 Challenger explosion resulted in certain death for all aboard? Photographs of dead bodies are not always necessary to convey a result of "certain death" rather than "presumed death." And, in the case of the Challenger, the bodies were so terribly atomized upon the explosion that no such photographs exist as a viewing option. But despite the quibbling that these categorical divisions inevitably invite, Zelizer is right that photographs of inanimate structures and devastated landscapes pervade the news, as they have in the aftermath of the horrific earthquake, tsunami, and ongoing nuclear disaster that has unfolded in Japan since March 11, 2011. As Zelizer effectively argues, these photographs may ignite the imaginations and emotions of an international audience, and allow viewers to more slowly come to grips with an overwhelming event.

Zelizer's second category, "Possible Death," includes photographs of people who *may* die, whether from famine, disease, or genocide, but whose death remains unconfirmed in the text that accompanies the photograph. Here, Zelizer closely tracks the journalistic and ongoing appearance in the press and other venues of such iconic images as the young man facing a military tank in Tiananmen Square in 1989; a boy in the Warsaw Ghetto in 1943, with a gun pointed at him; the now infamous portraits of prisoners held by the Khmer Rouge; and Keith Carter's harrowing photograph of a vulture waiting for a starving Sudanese child to perish. Zelizer treats these photographs in some detail, opening up the moral and ethical complexity of their initial making and tracking their ongoing and unfolding reception as the images continued to compel viewers over a period of decades. Zelizer is at her strongest when she engages in this kind of close historical tracking, which reveals not only how the images were (or were not) first seen in the press, but how they have changed over time, have been used by differing constituents, and have conveyed shifting messages. Notably, Zelizer is much more precise in her dating and tracking of specific photographs than she is in her introductory theoretical material where the arguments of scholars and writers are often presented in only the loosest historical framework, in contrast to the details of certain historic and otherwise newsworthy events for which she includes specific dates when photographs were taken, attention to the publications that printed them, and precise sequencing of the images' reappearance in other venues.

The third section of *About to Die* focuses on photographs that convey "Certain Death"

which, counter to a reader's expectation that these images will show dead bodies, in fact, for Zelizer, still present as much visual ambiguity as photographs in other sections but are now clearly anchored by textual descriptions that clarify for the reader that death has definitively occurred. And, yet, Zelizer breaks down this category even as she constructs it. Through her examination of several photographs, such as Robert Capa's iconic 1936 photograph from the Spanish Civil War, *Death of a Loyalist Soldier*, or video footage from 2000 of a young Palestinian boy being ineffectively shielded by his father against Israeli gunfire, Zelizer shows how rather than conveying the certainty they first seemed to, both ultimately convey controversial and as yet unsettled conclusions regarding whether the images were staged and what the final outcome was for the subjects in question.

Zelizer's own conclusions from these terribly ambiguous documents finally bring us to the heart of her analysis: that these photographs, which with their accompanying text seem to convey the most certainty of all, are, in fact, as uncertain as any other image in the book, and perhaps more so. In fact, it is these most seemingly certain photographs—anchored as they are by certain textual outcomes—that best demonstrate, as Zelizer writes, "how paradoxical is the relationship between what viewers see and what they understand from news images … rather than anchoring meaning, as words have been thought to do for images, they create openings for an image's uneven interpretation, its vigorous debate, and its strategic employment" (216).

The central theoretical hinge in Zelizer's analysis, which she returns to consistently throughout, is between a visual depiction of an event "as is" and of the event "as if." Drawing from linguistics, Zelizer explains that the "as if" signals the subjunctive voice: words like "could," "should," "would have," and "if" allow room for uncertainty and ambiguity as well as emotion, possibility, and contingency. Journalism is not conventionally associated with this "subjunctive" voice, as Zelizer terms it: its job, after all, is to tell us the news with clarity, factuality, and efficiency. Photographs, as seemingly objective documents, seem to underscore journalism's aim, but, Zelizer argues, "The voice of the visual is subjunctive in character" (14). Ultimately this suggestion has far-reaching implications for the field of photojournalism, suggesting that "Images work by their own logic, even in a milieu like journalism, which strives to make them more like words than not" (217). Rather than photographs as providers of certainty, again and again Zelizer points out how photographs work in the news to offer uncertainty instead and thus to prolong a viewer's state of affective engagement.

Upending our assumptions about journalistic practice, Zelizer concludes that "The more informational detail—either verbal or visual—that is provided, the greater may be the potential for provoking debate, conversation, interpretation, and contestation" (315). And while it may be professionally strategic on the part of journalists to keep us engaged in news stories that seem to have concluded, or on the part of fundraising organizations to appeal to our charitable impulses in helping fund disaster relief, Zelizer also makes an argument that the viewer's or reader's engagement "becomes an end in itself" (315). In terms of understanding the text-image relationship we encounter in journalism, then, Zelizer argues that the "as if" voice that prevails so consistently in "about to die" photographs "offers an opportunity to clarify what is singular about journalism's visual relays and to position those attributes squarely on the table as a choice equal to but different from words" (322). Zelizer ends her book with an assessment that the "as if" subjunctive voice of the visual "still awaits widespread appreciation" (326) and calls on her readers to accept its invitation of "possibility, chance, experimentation, hypothesis, play, elaboration, involvement, supposal, denial, liminality, impossibility, and speculation" (326) as we consume, analyze, and engage with news images.

Kate Palmer Albers is Assistant Professor in the Art History Division at the University of Arizona School of Art. Her current book project is *Uncertain Histories: Accumulation, Inaccessibility, and Doubt in Contemporary Photography*.

**Photography &
Culture**

Volume 5—Issue 1
March 2012
pp. 113–116
DOI:
10.2752/175145212X13233396185350

Reprints available directly from
the publishers

Photocopying permitted by
licence only

The Urban Spectator: American Concept-Cities from Kodak to Google

Eric Gordon

Lebanon, CT: University Press of New England for
Dartmouth College Press, 2010

Reviewed by Erin Leary

In Erich Mendelsohn's *Amerika* (1926), New York skyscrapers
ominously rise above the camera, their spires barely recognizable
above the hulking, monolithic masses that block out the sun
and surrounds. These emblems of modernism, and American
modernism in particular, become oppressive bodies, machines
of industry that blot out humanity. Indeed, there are few humans
featured in these photographs, and by foregrounding the building
over the people, these overwhelming volumes ultimately crush
the masses, the people who generally inhabit the space of the city.
This mode of the oppressive city, the disaffected populace, and
the capitalist complicity of the modern skyscraper—and modern
architecture more generally—became the dominant theoretical
framework for urban studies throughout the twentieth century, from
Georg Simmel to Mike Davis and David Harvey. This model of the
city renders city dwellers as capitalism's victims.

Eric Gordon intervenes in this narrative with *The Urban
Spectator: American Concept-Cities from Kodak to Google*, arguing for
a different model of American urban spectatorship that ultimately
foregrounds the consumption and use of American cities through
imaging technologies. Within this argument, Mendelsohn's images
represent a distinctly European view of American cities, opposite
the "possessive spectatorship" that defines American views of
American cities. Because of the emphasis on technologies, the text
is structured chronologically rather than geographically, beginning
with the camera and progressing through early cinema and the
electronic billboard, moving to radio and television, computers and
operating systems, television reruns and syndication, and finally
databases and handheld imaging technologies across the major

US cities of Chicago, New York, Boston, and Los Angeles. As Gordon aptly argues, these emblems of modernity—technology and the city—developed alongside one another, and the relationship deserves interrogation. Thus, possessive spectatorship—"a way of looking that incorporates immediate experience with the desire for subsequent possession" (3), a desirous, consuming form of looking, is integral to Americans' views and experiences of the city. In America, democratized imaging technologies democratized the modern city.

Gordon's text begins in 1893 in Chicago during the World's Columbian Exposition, which presented a gleaming white city to audiences both national and international, a utopian vision of city planning designed under the leadership of Daniel Burnham, an important figure in the City Beautiful movement. Today the Columbian Exposition is remembered for both the city and its photographs, and this remains so because of the deliberate actions of amateur photographers, hobbyists who photographed the fair. These city plans were not only accepted but beloved in part because of the imaging technology of the camera, which allowed visitors to the fair to not only dictate their relationship to the fair, but

also to its administrators. Despite efforts to limit photography to that of Buffalo photographer Charles Dudley Arnold, the official photographer, and his apprentice, H. D. Higinbotham, amateurs and hobbyists alike consumed the concept-city by not only walking and living it, but capturing it like prey with the camera, a trophy of modernism in the duplicated and restaged photographs taken during a day at the fair. Indeed, these rabid photographers' actions pushed fair officials to sell day permits for amateurs and hobbyists, and to rent Kodak "C" cameras.

Here, Gordon's argument hinges on the consumptive possibilities of the camera. Turning to period advertisements for Kodak, he ably argues that the technology of the camera allowed photographers and the fair's visitors to capture these vistas and to make the White City their own. Gordon culls the parallel relationship of cameras and capture in hunting and safari for comparison. In the advertisements and even on today's safaris, the camera allows viewers to capture the animals—to own them as prizes. As the period Kodak advertisement suggests, "There are no game laws for those who hunt with a Kodak" (cited 48), and the camera allows the photographer to own everything caught

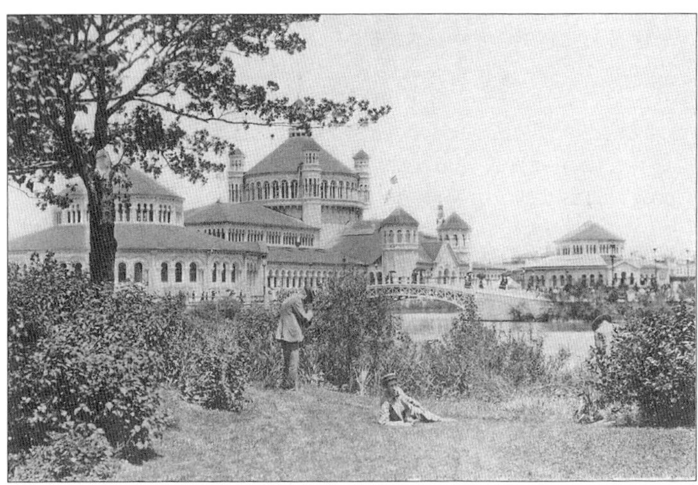

Fig 1 From *Official Views of the World's Columbian Exposition* issued by the Department of Photography, C. D. Arnold and H. D. Higinbotham, official photographers.

by the lens. This possession becomes the crux of Gordon's argument in *The Urban Spectator:* consumptive imaging technologies created and assisted an American form of possessive urban spectatorship, one in which the viewing subject is in control. Technologies shaped and mirrored the development of modern subjectivity in America and the imaginative potentials of the modern city. This parallel becomes, in Gordon's view, more inclusive, or incorporative for Americans because of the newness and optimism of all involved. Americans embraced modernity in urbanism.

This optimism is pervasive in *The Urban Spectator*, and technologies remain largely enabling and empowering rather than cast as technologies of oppression or despair. Unlike theorists from the Frankfurt school, Gordon remains optimistic about technology and sees its democratic potentials. Like early cinema, electric billboards provoke awe and excitement, and bring objects to life through movement. They cast the city as an exhilarating space of modernity. Rockefeller Center in New York is viewed alongside the power of communication technologies, and the fantasies of modernism expressed in renderings like those of Hugh Ferriss, and stands as an icon of democratic possibility. The view of the postmodern city, or "rerun city," is also friendlier to the practitioners than other histories or critiques of postmodernism by Frederic Jameson and David Harvey. The historicism of postmodern architecture and urban planning is frequently derided as pastiche, but also bad history, and a whitewashing of the urban space, a falsity in both hope and prosperity. And it was, at least in terms of prosperity. As Gordon notes, the historically inspired shopping enclaves such as Quincy Market in Boston were found to cost three times as much per square foot to build as a typical mall and returned one-third of the profit (165). The comfort of these postmodern reincarnations was not too different, Gordon notes, from the comfort that comes in watching reruns of old television shows. Though these acts of nostalgia

are often voided of the progressivism that has shaped modern cities, the interest in New Urbanism was marked not only by consumption, but a desire for a (historicized) home.

There is a shift in the middle of the text, as media and imaging technologies are used less for the consumption of the city and serve more as an imaginative framework, allowing Gordon to continue a chronological narrative. Though still productive, the technology becomes less a tool for the consumption of the city as a tool for its manipulation. This is, at least in part, due to the shift from specific objects—as in photographs of the fair, period advertisements, and speculative architecture of renderings—to theoretical constructs. This shift feels somewhat forced, as Gordon moves through computers, syndicated television and databases, and the analysis comes less from the images than from the discourse. A key case in point is the "operative city." Relating suburbia and white flight to emerging computer technologies, the relationship between the urban center and suburbia becomes much like the relationship between the operator and the computer; the city becomes the "functional city," one in which programmers in the suburbs and city halls calculate data. Robert Moses's plans for New York and urban renewal in Los Angeles, namely the project at Bunker Hill, are seen as "operative image" in the terms of Norbert Wiener, and spectators are outside the city rather than in it. The operative image, however, can be imaginary, and therefore does not always leave a document or artefact for study, and so when Gordon turns to Heidegger, the theoretical discussion becomes the basis for the argument, as opposed to an argument based on the images and objects. There are, however, images and objects that can support this notion of control, including video games, which directly engage this outsider or suburban perspective through computing. Though a compelling argument, there is a marked shift in tone and position that continues throughout the rest of the text.

Importantly, Gordon offers a view of American spectatorship that is contrasted to a European model without specific reference to European subjects in American cities, Europeans in European cities, or Americans in European cities. Returning then to the juxtaposition between Mendelsohn's photographs, the absence of people as objects in the frame can distract from the existence of the human subject behind the camera. But this subject remains a European artist, and one invested in critique, as indicated by his subject headings, which include "Typically American," "Exaggerated Civilization," "Center of Money—Center of the World," "The Gigantic," and "The Grotesque." Gordon's subjects are not critical of American urbanism because they are not particularly critical of capitalism, as are Mendelsohn and his cohort.

Gordon's examples all include viewing subjects, and though they may be small, people are always included in these images, presumably as more than mere markers of scale; they are the city's users, the city's consumers. These users implicate a relationship between us—the viewers—and them. We too are awed and engaged, consuming a city that was made for us. This engagement enacts "possessive spectatorship." But how does this notion of a specifically American form of spectatorship change if Gordon's examples are juxtaposed to these other relationships between viewers and cities (European–American, European–European, or American–European)? The accepted narratives of the modern city are already complicated by photographs made by figures such as Laszlo Moholy-Nagy, whose photographs from the Funkturm, or Berlin Radio Tower (1926–28), are marked by a controlled enthusiasm for the modern city, and so the question becomes: Is this a uniquely American form of spectatorship and urban subjectivity, or is it a larger, even global, counter-narrative? Such voids are characteristic of texts focused wholly on the American context. Given *The Urban Spectator*'s position as a counterargument to broad Marxist arguments on urbanism, such lingering questions indicate a myopia verging on American exceptionalism.

Despite these concerns for American urban studies more broadly, *The Urban Spectator* is a fun text to read, as creative, empowering, and imaginative as the technologies that shape its arguments, and will prove beneficial to scholars invested in the empowering potential of imaging technologies and to those seeking counter-narratives to the common history of the city as an oppressive industrial enterprise. Gordon's juxtaposition of modern technology and the modern city is fruitful, and moves beyond a comparative history to create a valuable narrative for American modernization and urbanism.

Erin Leary is a Ph.D. candidate in Visual and Cultural Studies at the University of Rochester and adjunct faculty at Parsons, The New School for Design, and the Sotheby's Institute of Art in New York. She holds an MA in the History of Decorative Arts and Design from Cooper-Hewitt, National Design Museum and Parsons, The New School for Design.

**Photography &
Culture**

Volume 5—Issue 1
March 2012
pp. 117–120
DOI:
10.2752/175145212X13233396185431

Reprints available directly from
the publishers

Photocopying permitted by
licence only

Book Review

Doing Family Photography: The Domestic, the Public and the Politics of Sentiment

Gillian Rose

Farnham, UK: Ashgate Press, 2010

Reviewed by Jane Simon

Gillian Rose's *Doing Family Photography* highlights the under-theorized and under-examined practice of family photography. What is compelling about Rose's approach is that she highlights the mobility of family snaps—indeed the *global* mobility of family snaps—that is often elided from critical discussions of the movement of media across international borders. While attention is readily given to the role of news media, film, television, and websites, family photographs tend to escape notice in debates about contemporary global visual culture. Rose's book makes a case for the need to critically attend to how family photographs move and circulate in contexts beyond the domestic sphere, as well as pay attention to their functional role within the family home. *Doing Family Photography* covers this dual territory by focusing, in the initial chapter, on the results of a series of interviews with middle-class mothers in South East England with young children. This section of the book clearly makes the case for conceptualizing family photography as a social practice that is less about what is represented within the images and more about what is done with the images: how they are shared and circulated as material objects. The latter chapters focus on how family photographs are distributed in the mass media, with a specific case study of how family photographs were utilized after the London bombings in 2005.

As Rose highlights in chapter two, "How to Look at Family Photographs," the small amount of critical work done on family photographs has tended to critique the shared banality and celebration of nuclear familial bliss. What family photographs share

are the content of birthday parties, weddings, baby photos, and barbeques while the realm of temper tantrums, sickness, dishwashing, or ironing remain unrepresented. Alongside this selective representation of family life is a shared lack of innovation and an "unpolished style" that causes theorists such as Geoffrey Batchen to claim that the content of family albums are "cloyingly sentimental in content and repetitively uncreative as pictures" (cited 11). Responding to Batchen and others who have dismissed the realm of family photography as a naïve repetition of nuclear stereotypes, Rose asks, "Perhaps if what is ordinarily done to and with photos was given more attention, their sentimentality and repetition might become rather interesting, instead of a reason for dismissing them?" (12).

This attention to family photographs as "objects embedded in practice" is what makes *Doing Family Photography* persuasive. The mothers that Rose interviewed all shared a similar understanding of the—deeply gendered—work of "doing things" with family photographs. The domestic labor of dating images, printing images, sorting photographs into digital files or material storage boxes, compiling family albums, and the sending and sharing of family photographs with other family members and friends is work done largely by women. As well as providing a framework for considering why family photography practices are so enmeshed with mothering and the maintenance of domestic space, Rose's discussion also highlights that digital technology has not dramatically changed how family photography works. Instead, the practices of Rose's interviewees suggest that if new technologies are used, they are used in a way which builds upon, rather than replaces, existing practices.

Chapter four, "What Happens With this Doing? Family, Domestic Space and Mothering," extends upon the previous chapters by asking about how family snaps produce complex geographies of domestic space. Family

photographs on display in the home work to effectively "gather" family members together. Photographs of absent members or photographs from the distant past operate to produce a temporal and spatial mixing of absence and presence. The daily "caught in the present" temporality of domestic routines and mothering of young children also means that family photographs can play a particular role in the way mothers negotiate their relationship with their children and are able to assert their own subjectivity "against (the trace of) that of their child" (55).

The latter chapters in the book shift focus to the circulation of family photographs in the public sphere. Here Rose knits together family photography with questions around the construction of racial and gendered difference and our everyday negotiation of what Lauren Berlant calls the "intimate public sphere." The publishing of family photographs of missing persons after the 2005 London bombings produces a range of ethical questions about how we look at, identify with, and differentiate ourselves from those represented. For Rose, the answer lies partly in looking back at what we already know about family photographs and their material presence in our everyday lives. When Rose asks, "What is there about family photos that is not part of their public display, and that might help me to see them in the intimate public differently?" (121), she ties together her emphasis on what we *do* with family snaps as objects, with a tunneling beyond "crude empathy." Turning back to the "life" of the photograph means that when we look at the familiar yet unknown family photographs of the dead or missing in a newspaper or other mass media form, we are also asking ourselves about who else has looked at the photograph, whose living room wall carries a framed version, or whose wallet contains a creased and well-loved print. Such questions halt a too easy identification and assimilation of somebody else's loss.

Rose's background as a cultural geographer means that she brings the interpretation of the visual together with an emphasis on material culture, subjectivity and the politics of everyday life. Domestic photography is rich territory here for an exploration of both politics and sentiment and this book clearly demonstrates their entanglement.

Jane Simon is Associate Lecturer in the Department of Media, Music, Communication and Cultural Studies at Macquarie University, New South Wales, Australia.

Photography & Culture

Volume 5—Issue 1
March 2012
pp. 121–124

DOI:
10.2752/175145212X13233396185477

Reprints available directly from
the publishers

Photocopying permitted by
licence only

Book Review

Galleries of Friendship and Fame: A History of Nineteenth-Century American Photograph Albums

Elizabeth Siegel

New Haven: Yale University Press, 2010

Reviewed by Lauren Lessing

In his seminal 1938 social history of American photography, Robert Taft mused, "It is curious that no one has described the origin of the ubiquitous family album." He continued:

> How many a bashful beau has had his pangs of embarrassment eased by the relieving words, "Let's look at the pictures in the album!" How many an unsuspecting swain has had his likeness examined by ardent eyes that to him were forever unknown! How many a tear-stained mother has leafed through an album until she reached a well-worn page and there gazed on the one whose presence was still insured by the blessed bit of cardboard! How many a tottering warrior has renewed the spirit of his youth, and relived his vigorous past by still other bits of cardboard and paper! How many a grandchild of such a warrior has been seized with sudden and uncontrollable mirth when carelessly thumbing its thick pages![1]

Taft wrote at a time when heavy, leather or velvet-covered albums of *carte de visite* and cabinet card photographs occupied the memories (and attics) of most adults. More than seventy years later, with these once ubiquitous objects largely forgotten, Elizabeth Siegel has taken up Taft's challenge by exploring the origin as well as the original uses and understandings of American photograph albums.

The French photographer André Adolphe Eugène Disdéri patented *carte de visite* photographs—albumen prints mounted on small rectangles of cardboard—in 1854. By 1861, they had become wildly fashionable in the United States. Siegel describes the reasons for this. Taken in photographers' studios, where sitters were carefully posed before elaborate backdrops and surrounded by appropriate props, these photographs allowed socially ambitious Americans to present themselves as genteel and affluent. Unlike the daguerreotypes that had preceded them, they were relatively inexpensive and endlessly reproducible, and they could be carried in pockets or sent through the mail in order to be exchanged with family members and friends. Both during and after the Civil War, *cartes de visite* served as vital links to distant loved ones and treasured memorials of the dead. To supplement portraits of their families and friends, buyers could also choose from among thousands of mass-produced photographs depicting celebrities, notable views, works of art, and staged genre scenes. Not surprisingly, albums that allowed people to store, organize, and display their overflowing *carte de visite* collections quickly became household necessities. American manufacturers patented such albums by the score and marketed them with sentimental rhetoric that emphasized the bonds of family and home. When the larger format albumen prints known as cabinet cards emerged on the market in the 1870s, a new wave of albums followed. By 1880, a family photograph album sat weightily on nearly every American parlor table.

In four well-researched, engaging chapters, Siegel discusses the manufacture, distribution, assembly, and various social uses of American *carte de visite* and cabinet card albums from their inception in the early 1860s to their displacement by less formal snapshot albums at the end of the nineteenth century. Hers is one of a number of recent studies that, taken together, constitute a movement away from the canon-building agenda of much previous scholarship on the history of American photography. Indeed, Siegel makes it clear in her introduction that she is interested in nineteenth-century family albums precisely because they were ordinary household objects. Approaching albums as examples of both visual and material culture, she explores

how they reflected and shaped the affinities, viewing practices, domestic rituals, systems of representation, and commercial behaviors shared by a broad middle-class American audience. In addition to albums themselves, Siegel draws upon a wide range of historical sources that includes trade literature, household account books, magazine articles, popular illustrations, poems, and songs.

Siegel makes three principal assertions. The first is that card photographs and the albums that contained them represent an intrusion of commerce into the supposed "separate sphere" of the home. She is not alone in examining the relationship between commerce and nineteenth-century American domestic culture. Lori Merish, for one, has argued that Victorian housekeepers created sentimental visions of home and family (and of themselves) by filling their parlors with consumer goods. Siegel joins Merish and others in pointing out how dependent the nineteenth-century domestic sphere was on the busy world of trade, and in exploring how mass-produced goods construct identity.[2] In her second argument, Siegel contends that photograph albums created a new understanding of family by allowing ordinary men and women to assemble the kinds of visual genealogies that were previously available only to those with ancestral wealth and status. This is a compelling claim that she convincingly supports. She describes, for example, the ritual of narration that typically accompanied album viewing—a practice that helps us understand how nineteenth-century card portrait albums (which often seem standardized to the point of being impersonal) were filled with meaning by family members who identified and described each photograph to visitors and one another. Lastly, Siegel broadens an argument already made by Andrea Volpe in regard to albums of Civil War photographs: that *carte de visite* albums created "imagined communities," as that concept has been defined by Benedict Anderson.[3] Specifically, Siegel argues that—through their standardization and their frequent inclusion of mass-produced celebrity photographs—nineteenth-century albums allowed viewers to imagine themselves as part of a shared American culture. To support her argument, she reprints an 1867 comic song titled "The Carte de Visite Album" that describes the nation metaphorically as a motley collection of celebrity portraits gathered together in "Uncle Sam's Big Album."

Siegel rightly points out that by associating themselves with the prominent clergymen, war heroes, and politicians whose portraits frequently appeared in their family albums, viewers could define themselves as American, as well as devout, courageous, and moral. Throughout her study, she stresses nineteenth-century Americans' desire to affiliate with the praiseworthy and the normative; but she avoids the dark shadow cast by this desire—their fascination with the disturbing and the foreign. For instance, she does not discuss the fact that mass-produced *carte de visite* photographs of circus freaks sold very well, or that one could also buy photographs of white slaves, murderers, denizens of Eastern harems, and "primitive" tribesmen. Genre scenes featuring grossly stereotyped Irish and African Americans also circulated widely in card photograph form and found their way into family albums. James Brust has discovered one such image—a staged recreation of a Currier & Ives print depicting a down-at-the-heels Irishman smoking alone in the disheveled interior of a rude hut—in the *carte de visite* album carried by a Union officer during the Civil War.[4] Placed side-by-side with his family portraits, this photograph must have allowed its owner to reflect humorously on his own distance from the comforts of home, while also serving as a Constitutive Other, defining who he was by articulating who he was not. Siegel herself reproduces a page from a family album showing three portraits of children beside a photograph of the "fairy wedding" of two of P. T. Barnum's living exhibits—the dwarf Charles Sherwood Stratton (whose stage name was General Tom Thumb) and

the equally diminutive Lavinia Warren (billed as the most-photographed woman of the century). By displaying their *cartes de visite* as they did, I would argue that this album's owners not only participated in an imagined community, but also created a visual joke that defined their family against the foil of Barnum's human oddities.

In her discussion of how photograph albums were successfully marketed to a broad American audience, Siegel writes that they "supplanted all other forms of picturing and recording the family" (85), and became "*the* mode of representing the family and the nation in the Civil War and Reconstruction eras" (95). These are unfortunate overstatements in an otherwise thoughtful and rigorous book. In fact, family albums coexisted with a rich array of domestic and nationalist imagery that included paintings; prints; sculptures in marble, bronze, ceramic, and plaster; stereographs; illustrated magazines, books, and sheet music; ornaments made from hair; and needlepoint.[5] The Victorian home (and the parlor in particular) can usefully be viewed as a rich spatial text where such objects came together and informed one another. Perhaps because of her eagerness to emphasize the significance of early photograph albums, Siegel overlooks their relationship to (and possible influence on) these other contemporaneous depictions of families and the nation. But these criticisms should not undermine the importance of what she has accomplished. Card portrait albums have been largely overlooked by historians of photography and American culture. Siegel's long-overdue study illuminates how these objects engendered new understandings of family and nation among a broad audience of Americans in the second half of the nineteenth century. Now that she has uncovered their importance, scholars will be able to build upon the foundation she has provided and more fully explore how card portrait albums and their associated viewing practices fit within the complex visual and material cultures of the nineteenth-century American home.

Notes

1 Robert Taft, *Photography and the American Scene, A Social History, 1839–1889* (New York: Macmillan Co., 1942, c.1938), 138.

2 Lori Merish, *Sentimental Materialism: Gender, Commodity Culture, and Nineteenth-Century American Literature* (Durham: Duke University Press, 2000). See also Cathy N. Davidson and Jessamyn Hatcher, eds., *No More Separate Spheres!* (Durham and London: Duke University Press, 2002).

3 Andrea L. Volpe, "Collecting the Nation: Visions of Nationalism in Two Civil War-Era Photograph Albums," in Leah Dilworth, ed., *Acts of Possession: Collecting in America* (New Brunswick, NJ: Rutgers University Press, 2003), 89–111; Benedict Anderson, *Imagined Communities*, rev. ed. (London: Verso Books, 1991).

4 James Brust, "Learning about Currier & Ives from Nineteenth-Century Carte-de-Visite Photographs," *Imprint* 28 (November 2003), 36–7.

5 See for instance the chapter "Around the Parlor Table" in Louise L. Stevenson, *The Victorian Homefront: American Thought & Culture, 1860–1880* (Ithaca and London: Cornell University Press, 1991), Kenneth Ames's discussion of needlepoint in *Death in the Dining Room & Other Tales of Victorian Culture* (Philadelphia: Temple University Press, 1992), 97–149, and Thad Logan's study of the Victorian parlor in Britain—much of which is also relevant to the study of American parlors—*The Victorian Parlour* (Cambridge and New York: Cambridge University Press, 2001).

Lauren Lessing is a historian of American art who received her Ph.D. from Indiana University in 2006. She is currently the Mirken Curator of Education at the Colby College Museum of Art. Her most recent article "Ties that Bind: Hiram Powers's *Greek Slave* and Nineteenth-Century Marriage" appeared in the Spring 2010 issue of *American Art*.

**Photography &
Culture**

Volume 5—Issue 1
March 2012
pp. 125–126

DOI:
10.2752/175145212X13230986022736

Reprints available directly from
the publishers

Photocopying permitted by
licence only

© Berg 2012

Books Received

Feuerhelm, Brad and Campbell Blight, Daniel. *Haunting the Chapel,
Photography & Dissolution.* Daniel Blau Gallery, 2011.

Hariman, Robert and Lucaites, John Louis. *No Caption Needed: Iconic
Photographs, Public Culture, and Liberal Democracy.* The University
of Chicago Press, 2011.

Meadows, Daniel. *Edited Photographs from the 70s and 80s.*
Photoworks, 2011.

Well, Liz. *Land Matters.* I.B. Tauris, 2011.

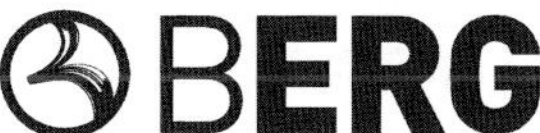

PHOTOGRAPHY & CULTURE
Notes for Contributors

Call for Papers

The editors welcome submissions to Photography & Culture that explore the social and cultural aspects of photography, for example in Art History, Anthropology, Cultural and Media Studies, History and Practice of Science, Contemporary Art and Documentary Practice, Sociology and Popular Culture. The only requirement is that aspects of both photography and its practices form the core of the submission.

Manuscript Submissions

Submissions aimed at being major articles should be approximately 3,000–10,000 words in length and must include a brief (two- or three-sentence) biography of the author(s), an abstract (up to about 200 words) and up to five keywords. Shorter papers ("Notes") should range between 500 and 2,500 words in length. Interviews should not exceed 15 pages (about 4,000 words) and do not require an author biography. Exhibition and book reviews are normally 500–2,000 words in length. It is requested that plain language be aspired to, with the use of jargon or specialized terminology kept to the absolute minimum. (Where specialized terms are unavoidable, please supply a glossary.) All submissions considered for publication will be subject to peer review.

Electronic submissions (preferred, certainly in the first instance) should be sent to photographyandculture@ bergpublishers.com. Microsoft Word is the preferred word-processing program, where possible. Scanned illustrations will suffice, though originals may possibly be requested in certain circumstances if the submission is successful. (Originals will be returned.) Please scan to letter or A4 size at 300 dpi for photographs/halftone, or 600 dpi for maps or illustrations containing text. Illustrations embedded in Word documents cannot be used. Similarly, graphics downloaded from webpages are not of sufficient quality for print reproduction.

A disk as well as a hardcopy of any finally accepted contributions may occasionally be requested. (Please mark clearly on the disk what word-processing program has been used. Berg accepts most programs with the exception of Clarisworks.) Manuscripts or disks should be submitted to the current *Photography & Culture* postal address: Photography & Culture, PO Box 11, Moreton-in-Marsh GL56 0ZF, UK.

Submissions will be acknowledged by the managing editors, and those accepted for further consideration will be entered into the review process. Electronic manuscripts and scanned illustrations will not be returned. Submission to the journal will be taken to imply that the article is not being considered elsewhere for publication, and that if accepted for publication it will not be published elsewhere, in the same form, in any language, without the consent of the editors and publisher. It is a condition of acceptance by the editors of a submission for publication that the publishers, Berg, automatically acquire the copyright of the published article throughout the world. *Photography & Culture* does not pay authors for their submissions nor does it provide retyping, drawing, or mounting of illustrations.

Style

The journal's text will use US spelling and mechanicals. *The Chicago Manual of Style* (15th Edition) is our style guideline, and *Webster's Dictionary* is our arbiter of spelling. While it would be preferred if contributors used US English, submissions in British English will be acceptable (though such submissions will be transliterated into US spelling and mechanicals). We encourage the use of major subheadings and, where appropriate, second-level subheadings. Manuscripts (whether electronic or hardcopy) submitted for consideration as articles must contain: a title page with the full title of the article, the author name(s), address and affiliation where relevant (do not place the author name(s) on any other page of the manuscript), a two- or three-sentence biography for each author, and a 200-word abstract. Up to five keywords are requested to aid in any future library searches. Please present the keywords after the abstract.

Electronic manuscripts can be either single- or double-spaced. If hardcopy manuscripts are involved, then they must be typed double-spaced (including quotations, notes, and references cited), one side only, with at least one-inch margins on standard paper using a typeface no smaller than 12-point. Authors should retain a copy for their records.

It would be preferred that submissions be presented with paragraph breaks involving a line space (double line space if presenting a double-spaced text, of course) between paragraphs and without first-line indentation, as in this set of guidelines.

Notes and References

References to *notes* are to be by means of consecutive numbers inserted in-text throughout the paper and are to be written up at the end of the text. (Do not use any footnoting or end-noting programs that your software may offer as this text becomes irretrievably lost at the typesetting stage.)

For *references*, the "Harvard system" is to be used in-text, thus:

> Centuries ago in Europe, country people were terrified of the walking dead, of "revenants" (Smith 1989). They developed all kinds of protective procedures (Jones 1957; Morris 1972, 1984), and though these may seem bizarre to us now they were deemed absolutely necessary at the time.

The cited references should be presented at the end of the paper, after any notes, in this manner:

References

Dewdney, S. 1962. *Indian Rock Paintings of the Great Lakes*. Toronto: University of Toronto Press.

Dowson, T. 1992. *Rock Engravings of Southern Africa*. Johannesburg: Witwatersrand University Press.

Fagg, B. 1957. Rock Gongs and Slides. *Man* 57: 30–2.

Goldhahn, J. 2002. Roaring Rocks: An Audio-Visual Perspective on Hunter-Gatherer Engravings in Northern Sweden and Scandinavia. *Norwegian Archaeological Review* 35(1): 29–61.

Hedges, K. 1990. Petroglyphs in Menifee Valley. *Rock Art Papers* 7: 75–82.

Lawson, G., Scarre, C., Cross, I. and Hills, C. 1998. Mounds, Megaliths, Music and Mind: Some Thoughts on the Acoustical Properties and Purposes of Archaeological Spaces. *Archaeological Review from Cambridge* 15(1): 11–34.

Palmer, D. and Pettitt, P. 2001. In Search of our Musical Roots. *Focus* 105: 80–4.

Rajnovich, G. 1994. *Reading Rock Art: Interpreting the Indian Rock Paintings of the Canadian Shield*. Toronto: Natural Heritage/Natural History Inc.

Reznikoff, I. 1995. On the Sound Dimension of Prehistoric Painted Caves and Rocks, in E. Taratsi (ed.), *Musical Signification*. Berlin: Mouton de Gruyter.

Rowland, I. and Howe, T.N. (eds.) 1999. *Vitruvius: Ten Books on Architecture*. Cambridge: Cambridge University Press.

Offprints

On publication, first-named authors will be sent a PDF eprint (with nonprinting watermark) of the final, published version of their article for personal use, and will be able to order a free copy of the issue in which their article appears.